D1569517

Don't Let the Fire Go Out!

Also by Jean Carnahan

If Walls Could Talk:
The Story of Missouri's First Families

Christmas at the Mansion:
Its Memories and Menus

"Will You Say a Few Words?"

Don't Let the Fire Go Out!

Jean Carnahan

UNIVERSITY OF MISSOURI PRESS
COLUMBIA AND LONDON

University of Missouri Press, Columbia, Missouri 65201
Printed and bound in the United States of America
All rights reserved
5 4 3 2 1   08 07 06 05 04

Library of Congress Cataloging-in-Publication Information
    Carnahan, Jean.
Don't let the fire go out! / Jean Carnahan.
    p. cm.
ISBN 0-8262-1513-0 (alk. paper)
1. Carnahan, Jean. 2. Legislators—United States—Biography.
3. Women legislators—United States—Biography.
4. United States. Congress. Senate—Biography. I. Title.
E840.8.C365A3 2004
328.73'092—dc22

                                        2003023683

∞™ This paper meets the requirements of the
American National Standard for Permanence of Paper
for Printed Library Materials, Z39.48, 1984.

DESIGN AND COMPOSITION: KRISTIE LEE
PRINTER AND BINDER: THOMSON-SHORE, INC.
TYPEFACE: ADOBE CASLON

To the memory of Mel, Randy, and Chris,
whose lives warmed our hearts and fired our spirits.

Contents

Introduction 1

One In the Blink of an Eye 5

Two Moving Forward 17

Three Mrs. Carnahan Goes to Washington 39

Four Root Causes 53

Five Magnificent Dreams and Noble Plans 89

Six Mansion on the Hill 113

Seven One in a Hundred 151

Eight Be Not Overcome 189

Nine An Ember in the Soul 215

Farewell to the U.S. Senate 239

Epilogue 245

Acknowledgments 247

Dressed for the school May Day program.

My love of horses began early.

Posing with my Shirley Temple banana curls.

Mel and I were high school sweethearts.

High school graduation, 1951.

With my parents on my wedding day, 1954.

The family campaigning in 1966.

Mel ends his Walk Across Missouri.

My favorite photo of Mel.

An inaugural hug. WIDE-WORLD PHOTO

Our first grandson, Austin

The inaugural ball, 1997.

The family on election night, 1996.

At the farm in Rolla.

A photo session for our Christmas card.

Relaxing at the farm.

Getting ready for a bike ride.

Easter at the Governor's Mansion.

Touching up the official portrait.

The Missouri Governor's Mansion.

The family dressed for the mansion "Spooktacular."

Preparing for a helicopter view of the 1993 floods. MISSOURI NATIONAL GUARD

Pope John Paul II visits St. Louis. WHITE HOUSE PHOTO

The 2000 whistle stop campaign stops in Independence.

WENDY L. WERNER PHOTO

Chris Sifford
with Mel.

Randy and Mel.

My grandsons, Andrew and Austin.

WE LOST OUR
LEADER
BUT GAINED
A
LEGEND

The funeral of Governor Mel Carnahan, October 20, 2000.

Announcing for the U. S.
Senate. KANSAS CITY STAR

Questioning Enron CEO Ken Lay during his
appearance before the Commerce Committee.
DICK BERKLEY

Casting my last vote for
Mel, November 2000.
KANSAS CITY STAR

A warm welcome by St. Louis supporters. ST. LOUIS POST-DISPATCH

Speaking at a Democratic rally.

Working at a Habitat for Humanity site.

Freshman Democrats with Senate leaders Reid, Daschle, and Mikulski.

Staffers Ryan Rhodes and John Beakley.

Women of the Senate at an evening get-together.

Don't Let the Fire Go Out!

Introduction

What is the use of living if it be not to strive for noble causes and to make this muddled world a better place for those who will have it after we are gone.

— Winston Churchill

This is not a sad book.

If you're looking for a good cry, put this book back on the shelf and look elsewhere. This book is only sad like Good Friday is sad. Like Easter Sunday morning, it is packed with hope and joy. The theme within these pages is as ancient as the prophet's words and as recent as the poetry of Maya Angelou.

"If I fall, I shall rise!"

It's an assurance I see reaffirmed each morning as the sun comes streaming through my bedroom window.

But how do we cope with "the thousand natural shocks that the flesh is heir to"—some that pierce the heart and cripple the will? How do we respond to the unexplainable, the unpredictable, and the unplanned events that shake the foundation of our being?

I was spared having to deal with any major trauma for more than a half century. Not many people can say that. The "Big D" words had never been a part of my life: Death, Disease, Divorce, Debt, Disappointment, Depression, Disaster, Disillusionment, and Doubt. But, as I found out, that can change in a moment and without notice.

I was reeling and groping for answers following the loss of my husband, Mel, my oldest son, Randy, and our longtime staffer, Chris Sifford. Nine months after the plane crash that took their lives, a fire destroyed my home. Later, an anthrax-laced envelope was unleashed in my Wash-

1

ington office building, and the following year I lost my election bid for the U.S. Senate. I found many reasons to wallow in self-pity, remorse, and second-guessing. (I could write another book on that alone.)

My frenzied search for answers was not unlike that of the proverbial dog chasing his tail. There was no end to be found, no victory, only frustration and failure. "What might have been" tantalized my imagination but served no purpose.

In time, I made a wonderful discovery!

If the happenings of the last several years have taught me anything, it is that the human spirit, as well as our national purpose, can be rekindled by small acts of courage performed by ordinary people. We need not be cowed by weighty events, feeling we are unequipped to handle what comes our way. There's a God's plenty of courage within each of us, ready to be activated on a moment's notice.

One of my favorite heroines understood the strength of bold deeds. Harriet Tubman, the former slave, ushered hundreds of slaves to a new life in Canada. No one who started the journey under her guidance was allowed to turn back. All along the treacherous path, she buoyed their flagging spirits with words of inspiration.

"Children, if you're tired, keep going. If you're hungry, keep going. If you're scared, keep going. If you want to taste freedom, keep going."

I think this hearty woman was on to something!

Ignore what you feel or fear.

Act! Act decisively! Act now!

By definition, courage is doing what we're afraid to do. The key word is *doing*. When we act in the face of fear or uncertainty, our smallest deeds are amplified beyond measure.

I recall Mel or Randy, bending over the fireplace on wintry mornings, stoking the languishing embers that nearly went out during the night. By blowing on the coals and adding more wood, they rekindled a warm blaze that I had thought would be impossible to recover. The breath from their bodies brought the fire back to life.

To me the fire is a splendid metaphor for life. Sometimes raging and fervent, sometimes glowing softly and evenly, other times reduced to struggling embers. In her funeral oration, my daughter, Robin, told of her Dad starting a warm blaze in the fireplace on a cold morning. In his last words before leaving the house, he would admonish those remaining at home, "Don't let the fire go out."

During the 2000 election, the phrase became the rallying cry for supporters wanting to revive what appeared to be a lost cause. Within days, a political campaign halted during a disastrous hour was transformed into a hopeful movement. We were warmed by the "helper's high" that comes to those who pitch in and give themselves wholeheartedly to a cause.

During those few weeks in October, our lives touched in common purpose, enabling us to do extraordinary things never thought possible. We discovered that like the loaves and fish in the biblical story, courage could be passed around, shared, and multiplied to great benefit.

On Election Day, a majority of Missouri voters did something that had never been done before. With my husband's name still on the ballot, they gave him a final vote of confidence, the last and greatest honor they could bestow on their beloved governor. For the first and only time in our nation's history, a candidate was elected to the U.S. Senate posthumously. The faith and trust of Missouri voters empowered me for the task that was then mine. I took Mel's place in the U.S. Senate.

By not accepting defeat, we reframed reality—like the elderly man, looking into the mirror, who dismissed his image, saying, "Mirrors just aren't what they used to be."

Life is not what we see in a mirror. Within each of us, regardless of age or circumstance, is an indomitable spirit waiting to be tapped, wanting to shape a new reality that enables us in remarkable and unprecedented ways. Each decision I made, each determined step I took, fueled my strength. I still marvel at the "unintended courage" that bubbles up from within when it is needed. There are still times when I think: "Did I do that? Did I say that? How was I able?"

Fortunately, we are not alone in our efforts to bestir courage. Never underestimate the strength that comes from a hug, a smile, or an encouraging word from those around us.

Albert Schweitzer was right. He observed, "In everyone's life, at some time, our inner fire goes out. It is then burst into flame by an encounter with another human being. We should all be thankful for those people who rekindle the inner spirit."

Indeed, I am.

Had it not been for the heartening advice of a friend and writer, Inda Schaenen, I would never have written this book. After the 2002 election, I had abandoned the idea. A publisher had earlier assured me that if I won reelection, my book would sell "like hotcakes." We admire winners; we ignore losers.

But Inda would not let me give up, though I was convinced that there was no interest in a story without a Cinderella ending.

I was wrong.

After all, for most of us, life is more conquest than victory. More story than glory. Life is about squandering ourselves for a good and godly purpose.

Mostly it's about stoking the fire.

One

In the Blink of an Eye

Life is not the way it's supposed to be. It's the way it is.
The way you cope with it is what makes the difference.

—Virginia Satir

For most of us, life is built on certain assumptions;

. . . that our loved ones will come home for dinner;

. . . that we will share the day's events together;

. . . that we will wake up the next morning to our usual routine;

. . . that we will grow old together and enjoy grandchildren and retirement.

But all that can change in the blink of an eye.

It did for me.

The moment was Monday, October 16, 2000, at 7:33 p.m.

Monday had started much like any other at the Missouri Governor's Mansion. Mel and I had been in the old, Victorian home for nearly eight years. In just three weeks we would know whether he would move on to the U.S. Senate as the past two governors of Missouri had done. But running against John Ashcroft, the current senator, was no easy task. Still, Mel had performed well at the debate the previous night, and the latest polls showed him pulling ahead.

He had been to the gym that morning for the hour of exercise, stretching, and weight lifting that had become a regular part of his routine, even though it meant getting up before 6:00 a.m. I was already in my office in the family quarters on the second floor, preparing to fly to northeast Missouri. During the day, I would visit several schools and libraries and do a few press interviews about education. It was a topic dear to both our hearts. During Mel's first year as governor, he had fought successfully for the largest funding increase in history for Missouri's public schools.

Both of us were running behind. As I shuffled papers on my desk, I caught a glimpse of Mel, briefcase in hand, moving at full stride toward the elevator that would take him to the basement exit, where a car waited. We blew each other a goodbye kiss from across the hallway.

"See you tonight," he said, just as he had so many times before. "Hope your day goes well," he added, knowing that I did not adjust as easily as he did to a tight travel and speaking schedule.

It was not a physically strenuous day for me, yet I was bone-tired when I arrived back at the Governor's Mansion late that afternoon. Meeting so many people, listening, responding to questions, catching names, making speeches, and giving interviews can be wearing.

I worked my way through the mail on my desk and turned to the final chore of the day, writing my speech to deliver to a group of senior citizens the next morning. I was so completely absorbed that the sound of the telephone startled me.

It was Mel.

Randy was preparing to fly his father and Chris to New Madrid for a meeting with African American leaders. The roar of the engines in the background made it difficult for us to speak very long.

"You can tell me all about your school visits when I get back," he said. "I'll be home earlier than I thought. Save me some dinner," he added, as we unknowingly shared our last words with each other.

I hung up and returned to the computer screen, trying to dredge up some words of inspiration for my next day's audience. Less than an hour later, the phone rang again. This time it was Alan Walton, one of the governor's security guards who staffed the mansion from a command post in the basement.

"Can I come up to see you?" he asked.

It was an unusual request, I thought. Perhaps he needed to discuss a travel or security matter with me. Within minutes he entered the room, approached the desk, and, without saying a word, dropped to one knee so that we were eye to eye. As he reached out to take my hand, I knew . . . I knew what had happened before he ever spoke.

"The plane is missing," he said haltingly. "The governor and Randy and Chris were onboard."

Stunned with disbelief, I stood up from my desk. Dazed. How can this be? I had just talked to Mel minutes ago from the plane.

"Do the children know?" I asked.

"No, we are trying to get hold of them now."

When he returned to his post, I was all alone, as alone as I have ever been.

"This isn't happening," I thought. "Not to Mel, not to Randy . . . Chris. They were all so cautious. This happens to other people, not to them . . . not our family."

For a moment, I was stirred by hope. Maybe they survived. But in my heart, I knew it was unlikely.

My eyes scanned the room, unable to focus on anything. Familiar objects appeared meaningless, distant. The items on my desk all seemed strangely hollow and insignificant, as though there was no longer any context in which they fit. The computer, where I had earlier been working on a speech, was now frozen in time, leaving a half-finished sentence dangling on the screen. The painstakingly assembled schedule for the final three weeks of the campaign lay on the desk. Now it was just wastepaper to be swept into the trash basket.

Everything seemed pointless . . . irrelevant.

My eye paused on the wall of family pictures. Pictures of Mel and me . . . of Randy . . . of our other three children, daughter-in-law, and grandsons . . . of happy, precious moments captured and forever preserved. All were reminders of how our lives were linked so tightly . . . so lovingly over the years. Mel and Jean . . . It had always been that way, ever since we were high school sweethearts.

It would be hours before our three children and two grandsons arrived in Jefferson City. A retired Methodist minister, whom I barely knew, decided on his own that he might be of help. The Reverend Gene

Rooney had heard the news and felt compelled to be there with me until my family arrived. His presence, his prayers, his assuring manner convinced me that there are, indeed, times when we are served by "angels unaware."

John Beakley, a staffer from the governor's office and family friend, arrived to join me for the long night vigil.

About 1:00 a.m. the phone rang.

"The president is on the line," John said. "Do you want to take the call?"

"Of course," I said, knowing from experience how difficult it was to make such calls, but how meaningful they are to hurting people.

"Mr. President, it is so kind of you to call."

"I just heard the news. I'm here in Cairo now. We're having an emergency summit with Israeli and Palestinian leaders, but I'll be back this week. Is there anything I can do to help?

I assured him that I was being cared for well. We talked about Mel.

"I will never forget that he supported me when I was lower than a snake's belly in the polls. You remember that?" he asked.

I certainly did. In 1992, Mel went out on a limb and against the advice of his staff announced his support of Bill Clinton. The president never forgot that.

My children arrived between 1:00 and 3:00 a.m., some of them having been brought by a highway patrol car from their homes in St. Louis, two hours away. By then reality had begun to take hold in different ways for each of us. But we all knew that from that moment on, nothing in our lives would ever be the same.

We grappled to put together the pieces of the day. Where we had been. When we last spoke. No matter how hard I tried, I couldn't reconstruct much of that last telephone conversation. It had been so . . . ordinary. Much like the hundreds we had over the last year. We stayed in contact, trying to keep some order to our lives in the frenzied political campaign that his race for the U.S. Senate had imposed on his already demanding duties as governor.

Tom recalled having been with his Dad, brother, and Chris at a fundraiser in St. Louis. The weather in the immediate area was dreary, but other instrument-equipped planes were coming and going that evening. Before leaving, Tom had turned to Randy and said, "Be careful, the weather doesn't look too good."

To which Randy replied, in a statement that now seemed prophetic, "Yeah, but it's better where we're going."

Perhaps the most haunting recollection was of an incident that happened on Sunday evening, prior to the senatorial television debate. In retrospect, it seemed like an eerie scene from a bad film. Mel, the family, and the staff were all crowded into a small anteroom at an auditorium in Kansas City, waiting for the debate with John Ashcroft. I suggested that everyone leave and let Mel lie down on a raised, padded table in the middle of the room that looked much like a solid-based massage table. Mel took the few moments to stretch out, close his eyes, and relax before going onstage.

As staff and family passed the table to leave the room, everyone gave Mel some final words of encouragement. But Chris Sifford, whose father was an undertaker, turned to me as he left.

"I can't watch this," he said with feigned humor. "I've been around funeral homes too long."

I dismissed the strange feeling we all had at the scene before us. There were more urgent things to consider. I reached over and gave Mel a brief kiss, and we all left him alone for some final moments of solitude. Exactly twenty-four hours later, three who were in that room would be dead.

It was a strange and perplexing moment to recall.

For the next four days, I was cloistered within the mansion, planning the details of a state funeral. But before I could focus on that, I was asked to make a statement concerning the presidential debate scheduled for the next evening in St. Louis. A statement from me would alleviate concerns that the television stations and the candidates had in continuing with the event. I found it helpful, personally, to put my feelings into words.

The sadness that now engulfs our family would be unbearable except for the support of friends and our firm and abiding faith in a loving God. My husband sincerely believed that government could be honest, good, and noble, just as the founders of our nation meant for it to be. He devoted his life to fighting for the principles of justice, freedom, and opportunity wherever it was needed. Because my husband cherished our democracy and its expression, he would very much want the debate scheduled for tonight to go on. We are honored that it is being held in the state that Mel, Randy, and Chris loved so much.

I returned to the more ponderous decisions involved in preparing for three funeral services on successive days. Precedent is both a comfort and a guide in such times. Only one other Missouri governor, John Marmaduke, had died while living in the old Victorian mansion.

Back in 1887, the fifty-four-year-old governor lay in state in the mansion's Great Hall as the townspeople filed through to pay their respects to the beloved statesman and general. The next day, in his honor, thousands of mourners walked the quarter mile to the cemetery in the rain for the final rites. I would follow that precedent, except that the walk would be to the outdoor service at the Capitol, two blocks away.

I could not believe it when the marble catafalque upon which Marmaduke's casket had rested was uncovered somewhere in the Capitol.

"Do you want to use it?" asked the national guardsman overseeing the arrangements.

"Yes, by all means."

I was less decisive when asked if I wanted a horse-drawn carriage from the local funeral home.

"Wouldn't a caisson with a military escort be more appropriate for a state funeral?" my daughter, Robin, inquired.

"There's none to be found in the Midwest," the officer replied.

"Can we get one from Arlington Cemetery?" she pressed.

"Possibly. But let's not count on it. The time is so short."

I have no idea how the National Guard was able to acquire a caisson within a few days, but one arrived from Indiana in time for the funeral.

Of even more concern was the weather. As it turned out, the day was mild enough for the mass processional of walkers who followed the caisson over the two-block route from the Governor's Mansion to the State Capitol.

The solemn assemblage included President and Mrs. Clinton, Vice President and Mrs. Gore, and a score of senators, congressmen, and governors, along with thousands of friends, children, and state workers who came to pay their respects.

The music was heart lifting. I was especially touched by the choir of nearly one hundred children singing the simple but assuring words of the old hymn, "Jesus Loves Me, This I Know." It was an uncomplicated theology, but one on which I had always relied.

Each speaker rose to the occasion.

Former senator Thomas Eagleton evoked the memory of Missouri's favorite son. "There was much of Harry Truman in Mel Carnahan.... No slick package, no phony spin ... a decent, honorable, forthright, quiet, courageous man."

Roger Wilson, the state's lieutenant governor who had taken office as governor following the plane crash, said, "Mel Carnahan loved children.... His legacy lives in every schoolhouse and in every child."

My son Russ spoke in similar fashion. "His life was about education. He was a teacher at heart.... As governor he carried the hopes and dreams of so many Missourians. Dad we love you. We will remember your example ... we will honor your legacy."

My daughter was also among those who spoke. She told what it was like sitting at the dinner table of a family committed to public service.

"We learned about the promise of our democracy ... and just a little bit about the Democratic Party," she said, masking a tear with a soft smile.

"But more important, we learned that government can make a difference in people's lives and that one individual can make a difference in government."

Yes! That was exactly what Mel wanted his family and staff to know. He believed that with all his heart.

She continued.

"To me, he was always Dad. His jobs and his title never changed him. He was shy, really. At home, just as in public, he was quiet and kind and gentle. During the forty-six years he and my mother spent together, they inspired anyone who saw them. The most striking thing is that he never preached and he never lectured. Instead, he taught by example...."

Robin had struggled to find a closing for the eulogy until I reminded her of what Mel often said to the family before leaving the house on a chilly morning. She recalled that memory at the close of her remarks.

> One of my fondest memories growing up was coming downstairs on a winter morning and seeing a warm, glowing, bright fire in the fireplace.
>
> Dad would get up early and light the fire and, without fail, before he walked out the door in the morning to go to work he'd say, "Don't let the fire go out."
>
> So, I'm here today to say, "Dad, I promise: We won't let the fire go out."

Little did I know that in the weeks ahead that simple phrase would become a rallying cry to be displayed on hand-drawn posters and hastily printed onto bumper stickers and buttons.

Secluded within the confines of the mansion, I was cut off from the reaction of people all over the state and nation. I could not bring myself to watch television or read the newspaper then, or for the next few weeks. Still, I sensed that something was happening from the number of cards, gifts, and notes that poured into the mansion. Thousands and thousands of letters! I couldn't read them all, but I insisted that they be recorded and stored so they could be acknowledged.

The funeral ended with the mournful sound of a single bagpipe playing *Amazing Grace*. The earlier flyover by the F-15 "Missing Man" squadron from Whiteman Air Force Base called for one plane to break from formation, making a sharp upward zoom into the atmosphere. It was spectacular! I couldn't help but think of what Sojourner Truth said, "I'm not going to die. I'm going home like a shooting star!"

Still, I was later told the air display was less dramatic than it should have been. The extended flying time caused by the length of the service used the extra fuel required for the planned finale.

Back at the mansion following the funeral, I looked from the window to see hundreds of men, women, and children standing along the black wrought-iron fence that surrounds the yard. Visitors had turned the area into a wall of remembrance, posting pictures, flowers, flags, and candles along the full length of the fence.

One drawing of a flag was done by a child and included such tender, consoling words: "I believe in you Mrs. Carnahan. I know you miss them and so do I. You can make it through the rest of your life. Love, Elise."

A photo of the drawing still hangs on my wall.

Later another youngster would give me a small purple frog, his favorite toy. He said it would make me "feel better." And he was right. The purple "Feel Better" frog would travel with me from then on as a reminder that love makes all things better.

We were to leave soon after the funeral, driving in a procession along the country roads that led to our hometown of Rolla, more than an hour away.

"Hurry," I was told repeatedly. "We need to be leaving. People are waiting."

For some reason, I interpreted that to mean people were waiting outside to see me, as were many others inside the mansion. So I lingered to visit.

It was dusk by the time we got on the road. Only then did I realize what was happening. In each of the small towns through which we passed—Westphalia, Freeburg, Vienna, Vichy—people were standing along the road, on their porches, in the fields, waiting to pay their respects.

"They've been here for hours. The communities have been in contact with the mansion wanting to know when to expect the procession to pass through their town," a security officer informed me.

As I looked from the tinted windows of the limousine that carried our family, I couldn't believe what I was seeing! People standing somberly, holding candles, signs, flags, forming a human corridor through each town we passed. Between towns, cars pulled off the road, their occupants often standing alongside, hat or hand over the heart. I had never felt, or seen, a more tender and sincere outpouring of sympathy.

"Don't let the fire go out," the words Robin had spoken earlier that day, were already appearing on signs. But one poster in particular caught my eye.

"You Can Do It, Jean," it read in large bold letters.

"What do they mean by that?" I asked.

"They want you to carry on this race for Dad," one of the kids said gently, almost as though the subject was too difficult to broach at the time.

I dismissed the idea, as I had an earlier reference that day when the St. Louis Black Clergy Coalition had visited with me. We had met in the family quarters on the second floor for a time of prayer just before the funeral.

In the group was Pastor B. T. Rice, a dear friend and supporter of my husband. I later learned that, within hours of the crash, he had experienced an epiphany of sorts. He felt an urgency in suggesting that I take Mel's Senate seat. Counseled against broaching the subject too soon, he had first cleared the way with my children.

"It would be a great honor to the governor's memory if the mantle of his leadership fell upon your shoulders," he told me. I was touched by his confidence.

"But whatever you do, we're behind you," the group had indicated. At the time, I was intent on making it physically and emotionally through the next three days.

Our journey home took several hours. Randy's funeral would be the next day at the local Baptist church surrounded by old friends and fond memories. We had raised our family in that church. Mel had sung in the choir, served as deacon, and chaired the building committee. Both Randy and I had taught Sunday school there for many years. I found comfort in the familiar faces and the memories within those church walls.

There was yet another funeral the next day, some two hours away in the Bootheel area of southeast Missouri. For that, I needed to muster all the strength I could in order to speak at the memorial service for thirty-seven-year-old Chris Sifford, Mel's loyal and talented campaign aide.

I had initially declined to be an active participant, feeling there was no way I could handle it emotionally. But I soon realized that it was important for me to speak what was in my heart. I wanted to express our family's love and gratitude for this wonderful young man as his grieving father laid his son to rest. My being there meant a lot to the Siffords, but it also had meaning for me.

At such times, it is difficult to use humor in a speech, but I felt that I had to tell a story about Chris that so typified his good nature. One day when Randy was flying Chris and me to Branson for an event, the two of us spent the time sitting knee-to-knee in the back of the small aircraft, talking and laughing. When I arrived at the event and stopped in the ladies' room to freshen up, I noticed I had inadvertently put on unmatched earrings. When I rejoined Chris, I jokingly chided him for his failure to mention it.

"I can't believe that you sat across from me during the entire plane trip and never noticed that I had on earrings that didn't match."

A smile lit up his face as he hugged me and said, "Jean, I have never noticed anything wrong with you. You always look good to me." Chris knew the right thing to say whether he was dealing with the press corps or reassuring the First Lady.

It was a week of incomparable sadness for both our families and our state.

The journey ended for Randy, forty-four, and Mel, sixty-six, in a remote cemetery in Wayne County, where they were buried alongside relatives who had settled in the Ozark hills a century and a half earlier.

In the twilight, as the fading sunlight etched the horizon, the minister lifted our hearts in prayer. A bird chirped pleasantly in the nearby pasture. A gentle breeze rippled through the autumn leaves. A child who had climbed onto a tree branch watched the solemn ritual from a different perspective.

Nearby the little clapboard church looked out over the old graveyard, a guardian of many memories and a storehouse of countless sorrows.

At the conclusion, my son Tom asked each person there to pick up a small stone and place it upon the grave marker as a sign of our presence. It's an ancient custom that we saw observed in Israel. One colorful adornment to the site was a Tibetan prayer flag sent by Randy's fellow mountain climbers as a memento of an earlier Mount Everest adventure.

It would be a year before I had permanent markers affixed upon the graves, but I knew what I wanted. For Randy—the rock climber, pilot, runner, and outdoorsman—a rough-hewn piece of Missouri red granite with one smooth area for the inscription from Isaiah: "I will bear you up on eagles' wings and bring you unto Myself." For Mel, an obelisk with a simple inscription: "Mel Carnahan, a servant of God and the people."

I left the cemetery uncertain of what would happen next. Tragedy and heartache churn up such raw feelings: loneliness, despair, confusion, a search for meaning. As when lost in a forest, it is not always apparent in which direction to turn.

I wrote a brief statement reflecting my feelings and released it to the media.

It seems that I have lived a lifetime in a span of days . . . discovered a multitude of things about myself, my family, and others that are revealed only in times of great sorrow.

Never let anyone tell you that prayers can't be felt or that hugs don't help. I have been encircled by thousands, and they are the only thing that makes the hours bearable.

And I have seen the goodness of God in the faces of countless mourners who lined the roads and towns along the way.

While I still ponder the mysteries of God, I do not for a moment doubt His purpose or His love for us.

My family and I thank the people of Missouri for every expression of that love.

Two

Moving Forward

*Sometimes you don't really decide. You just move forward
and that is what I did—moved forward blindly and
mindlessly into a new and unknown life.*

— Katharine Graham on taking over the
Washington Post upon her husband's death

During those days before the funeral, it seemed as if everything Mel stood for . . . fought for . . . had perished on that wooded hillside along with our dreams and hopes. At the St. Louis campaign office, the wonderful, loyal young people on his staff were packing boxes, consoling each other through tears.

An uptick in the polls just days before had given them—had given all of us—good reason to believe that victory was within reach. According to a Hickman-Brown Research poll taken October 10–12, Mel had 45 percent and Ashcroft 42 percent of the vote. *A three-point lead!* And, by all accounts, Mel had bested Ashcroft the night before in their only televised debate. Polling also showed that our television ads were working. Ashcroft was on the defensive. We were headed down the homestretch with everyone excited about a close but potential victory.

Now it was all over . . .

Or was it?

Behind the scenes a number of people were unwilling to give up. Among them were former lieutenant governor Harriett Woods, who twice ran for the U.S. Senate, and her political coworker Sally Barker.

Their group, called Win with Women, had grown into a real power-house in Democratic politics. Within days of the crash, they churned out a brief fax message to their members and supporters, calling on them to vote for Mel despite the tragic accident.

About the same time, Bob Kelley, a staunch supporter and president of the Greater St. Louis Labor Council, called Roy Temple, a former staffer and executive director of the Missouri Democratic Party.

"The fight has to go on," Kelley concluded, not fully knowing what that might involve. He, Harriett, and Sally all understood what was at stake—issues important to children, workers, women, and seniors. They were not about to call it quits.

Nor was our campaign manager, Marc Farinella. In the end, he would be the driving force that pulled together labor, women, staff, and volunteers, forging a team and giving everyone a sense of mission. He would later explain, "We all began to understand that this election was not just about Mel Carnahan. It was about the things he stood for, and we still had the responsibility to carry those ideas forward." "We didn't come this far to stop now," he had said bravely to a state senator inquiring about the seemingly lost cause.

When Marc called and asked to see me, I had returned to the mansion, preparing to move back to our farm within the next few weeks. There was urgency in his voice. Marc is by nature intense, cerebral, and focused. At times, he is seemingly burdened by all the angst and introspection of a character in a Woody Allen film. When he arrived at the mansion, he was clearly a man on a mission. Not given to small talk, Marc got to the question of the hour.

"As you know, Mel's name will be on the ballot, because according to law it can't be removed at this late date," he said by way of review.

"But no one will vote for him," I said.

"But what if they do? Just, what if? What if Mel *is* elected anyhow?" Marc asked.

"That can't possibly happen," I replied.

"Don't be so sure. If you were to indicate your willingness to serve, should he be elected, well . . . that would be all that people want to hear. They'd understand what a vote for him would mean. What do you think?"

I was perplexed.

I couldn't help but recall a recent comment made by the new governor, Roger Wilson. Officially, he would be the one to designate who would fill the term should Mel be elected.

"Jean Carnahan can will herself to do whatever needs to be done to help people," he had told a reporter. It was a wonderful affirmation from a kind and caring friend, and I prayed that it was true.

"I don't know," I sighed. "I've never thought of being a candidate for office—unless you count the time I was elected committeewoman of South Dillon Township twenty years ago. I was always behind the scenes. I'll have to think about this some more."

"There's not much time," he replied. "You need to give some signal if you're willing. There are a lot of people ready to go to work to make this happen, but they need to hear from you."

"Isn't there anyone else to do this?" I protested. "One of the kids, maybe?"

"But you're the one who could most likely win. People don't want to give up on this race. They want to believe that something can come out of tragedy. For you to pick up the banner, so to speak, and go on with the battle at this point in your life . . . well, bluntly, . . . that would take real *guts*. It's that simple."

Feeling, perhaps, that he had overstated his case, he added, "But if you don't feel like you can do it, well, people would certainly understand that as well. But we definitely have to say something by the weekend."

We both felt uneasy in the protracted silence that followed.

Marc spoke first, referring to our media consultant, Saul Shorr.

"I tell you what let's do. Let's get Saul here on Sunday. We'll shoot two statements. In one, you'll accept; in the other, you'll say no. That way you'll have more time to decide, and we'll be ready in either event."

I agreed.

My next conversation was with the family: Robin, Tom, Russ, and his wife, Debra. They were 100 percent behind the idea of my agreeing to serve.

"Remember those lines we used to read from *Winnie-the-Pooh*?" Tom injected. "'You're braver than you believe, and stronger than you seem, and smarter than you think.'"

I laughed. I realized I hadn't laughed in more than a week. It felt good. It was not like me to be gloomy. I am a cheerful person whose good humor had been shrouded by the intense sorrow I now felt.

"But what if we were to win?" I said, testing their capacity to deal with all my questioning.

What followed was another round of affirmation.

"You can do anything you set your mind to," Russ said. "Isn't that what you always told us?" (Mothers hate to have their own words thrown back at them by their children.)

I listened.

"There's no question but that you are smart enough and capable enough to learn whatever you need to do the job," he added.

At that point there was a moment of levity when they all agreed that if "smart" were a requirement for being elected, then so-and-so would never had made it. I discouraged them from broadening the list any further. They seemed to be enjoying it too much.

"Mom, you would be a refreshing breeze in Washington compared to all those professional politicians," Tom and Robin chimed in. "It's what you are . . . what you stand for. We need people who make decisions and cast votes for the right reasons, not because of some special interest group."

"That's right," Debra joined in. "People want someone who is real . . . someone who understands their own feelings and hurts. You do that. You connect with people."

"Everyone should have a group of cheerleaders like you 'guys,'" I said. "You really know how to make me feel good. But when it comes down to it, I'm the one who has to do the job everyday, take the heat, leave home . . ."

I knew that last protest was less valid than the others were, but I threw it in nonetheless. I had grown up in Washington and graduated from Anacostia High School and George Washington University. I once did some temporary secretarial work for a congressman. The nation's capital was not strange to me. Still, the thought of packing off to the East Coast alone did not have much appeal at this stage of my life.

Although we talked openly and aggressively, as we always had with each other, I felt no pressure. I knew they would accept whatever decision I ultimately made.

I had no trouble with the thought of becoming a politician. That term did not have a bad connotation in our family. Rather, it defined one who served the interests of others in the public arena, even to his own detriment.

For Mel to be able to run for office nineteen times required a sizable commitment on the part of our family. We each stepped up and did our part, so that he could have that opportunity. While Mel campaigned, I taught the kids to ride a horse, throw a baseball, and kick a football. I worked with our boys on their scouting requirements until each earned his Eagle award. Fortunately, I was a "tomboy" in my youth and acquired some athletic and outdoor skills that the more proper young ladies of my era did not.

Early photos of our children show them decked out in political buttons and caps, handing out campaign literature. In school, all of them ran for class office, conducted vigorous campaigns, and, in most instances, were successful.

Still, we knew that in many ways we were not like other families. Not every father in a household is consumed with a passion to build a progressive community, state, and nation. Ours was.

Despite my forbearance, Mel occasionally pushed my tolerance to the limits. I never let him forget that we spent our twenty-fifth wedding anniversary at the Ninth District Women's Democratic Club banquet because an overzealous staffer had scheduled him to speak that night.

We all saw the humor in such nonsense. Had we not, our lives would have been ruinous. We accepted his political "aberration" as part of a high and noble calling—though at times I jokingly referred to it as a "genetic defect," evidenced earlier in his father and grandfather, and now in our own children. Like television's weird Addams family, we had to be there for each other. No one else understood our peculiarities.

Nonetheless, being part of a political family was not always easy for our kids. They were subject to much greater scrutiny, held to a higher standard, expected to be a "funnel" to their parents for whoever bent their ear, and often thought to have more "inside" information than they actually did.

I'm sure that each of the kids could elaborate further on this list of expectations. The perks were few—occasional tickets to a ball game or the chance to meet some celebrities. Most often, however, Mel took great pains to see that no one in the family achieved an advantage because of his position, whether it involved a traffic violation or some schoolyard fracas.

Now, without the leadership of their father and older brother, the remaining children were stepping up to bat, assuming new duties, doing all the things you hope your kids will do when the time comes. I was glad for their counsel and support. But in the end, I was the one who had to make the decision.

In my heart, I knew what Mel would expect me to do. He was one to carry on in spite of any difficulty. I remember when he was severely burned on one thigh by hot drippings spilled from a roasting pan. Caring for the wound required that he get up an hour early each morning to treat and bandage his leg. He limped for weeks and grew weary before the day was out, but it never altered his campaign schedule.

A bone infection acquired from an injury that happened while playing with our dog, and was later aggravated by handshaking, left Mel with a crooked finger that sometimes made it painful for him to greet voters. He also fought bouts of lower back pain brought on by long stretches of riding in cars and small planes. During those times, he fortified himself with a couple of aspirins and kept on going.

If there was a theme that underscored his life it was "never give up." Chart a course and stick with it. There were bumps along the political road, but he expected them and took them in stride. His loss for the state senate at a critical juncture in his political career put him on the sidelines for fourteen years. In retrospect, those setbacks gave us a chance to take part in community and church activities that might not otherwise have been possible.

In the days following the funeral, I pondered the wonderful moments we had shared and the many campaigns we had been through together. Just that summer we had made a whistle-stop train tour of the state—a four-day journey, visiting about two dozen cities. The trip was inspired by the one Harry Truman made during the final days of his 1948 presidential campaign. I had pushed for the train ride because of the symbolism it had for Mel, seeking the U.S. Senate seat once held by Truman. At first, the campaign staff members were reluctant to take on a task requiring such an enormous amount of time, money, and effort. But when they saw the potential for energizing supporters, they agreed and literally "got the train rolling" for one of the most ambitious political events ever attempted in the state.

Besides having our family and staff onboard, in each city we were joined by supporters who rode with us to the next stop. The authentically restored train with its Pullman, dining, and dome-topped viewing cars was reminiscent of the leisure travel of a bygone era. At each stop, Mel spoke from the rear platform of the train much as Truman had done. Adding to the nostalgia, Mel was introduced in Springfield by the same man who had introduced the president when the train stopped there fifty-two years before.

All across the state, we encountered enthusiastic crowds fascinated by the old-fashioned, grassroots campaign style. But, of all the cities we visited, I will never forget how I felt when the train rolled into Independence—Harry Truman's hometown. There was not a dry eye on the back platform of that train. Before us was a sea of friendly faces, a lively band, and a train station decked with flags, banners, and posters. It could have been a movie set.

Marc Farinella, standing in the crowd, described it this way: "The stop in Independence was magical! All you could see was people, filling the train station, sitting on top of roofs and buses. Mel delivered one of the best speeches of his life. It was a flawless, remarkable delivery. After the first four minutes, I knew something extraordinary was happening, so I called Saul right then and there. I held the cell phone in the air so he could hear what was happening. All he could say was, 'Wow, that's incredible! That's incredible.'"

The train trip was the high point of our many campaigns. Four months later, the *St. Louis Post-Dispatch* would commemorate the whistle-stop journey once again. Following the crash, they ran an editorial sketch showing Mel, Randy, and Chris waving farewell from the back platform as the train departed the station.

Saul arrived on Sunday with a camera crew and two sets of television statements for me to choose between. In one, I agreed to serve if Mel was elected; in the other, I bowed out.

I was not used to reading a statement from a teleprompter or even one that I had not written myself. My being a writer was always a frustration to others who wrote for the campaign. So Saul was not surprised when I started rewriting the script.

"Just remember it can't be more than sixty seconds," he cautioned.

My face had already been "revised" by a professional makeup artist, who assured me that she was there to prevent me from looking washed-out on camera.

"I don't want to look like Tammy Faye Baker," I said, hoping she would get the point.

"My dear, television has a flattening effect. We just want to bring out your features," she said authoritatively, adding more eye makeup.

"Let's roll," Saul called out impatiently. "Which script do you want to do first?"

Without waiting for me to answer, he said, "Let's do the 'Yes' script. Okay? Don't worry about making mistakes. We'll do as many takes as we need."

The room that had moments earlier been a hubbub of activity and sound fell silent. Saul pointed his finger at me as a signal to begin.

The teleprompter began to roll.

For the first time in my life, I was the one on camera, not the spectator on the sidelines. From my years as a viewer of this process, I remembered the instructions given to Mel for television interviews. "Look into the eye of the camera as though it's the eye of the viewer . . . because it is."

We did several takes. The final version went like this:

As you know, this has been a very difficult time for me and my family. For forty-six years, my husband and I shared a life—a life dedicated to faith, family, and public service.

We also shared a commitment to provide opportunity for families, to give children a good start in life, and to treat the elderly with dignity and respect.

Our common values guided us in our everyday lives, and they are the values and beliefs that Mel Carnahan wanted to take to the United States Senate.

Soon Missourians will reaffirm their belief in self-government by casting their votes.

Mel Carnahan's name will still be on that ballot, and his vision for Missouri can still prevail, if we want it to.

With the support of my family, I've decided to do what I think Mel would want me to do.

What he wants all of us to do.

To keep fighting with all the strength we can muster for the values and ideals that he lived for.

Now the choice is up to you.

Saul was pleased with what he got.

I had learned to read his expressions over the length of our decade-long friendship.

"You're better at this than Mel was," he said, trying to make me feel comfortable.

Saul later told Robin, "Your mother is really dynamite looking into the camera. She really gets it. Not all politicians do."

Mel disliked making campaign commercials, and it showed. They seemed phony to him. He preferred talking directly to people, one-on-one, rather than through some slick thirty-second sound bite requiring rehearsed lines, a cast and crew, and, of course, the dreaded makeup artist. With that in mind, Saul tried to make the shoot as pleasant as possible.

Still, Mel had a general disdain for the "hired guns" and their know-it-all approach.

"I hired you because you're the only media consultant I could stand to be in the same room with," he often reminded Saul.

Mel's comment denoted more respect for Saul than criticism. Political consultants have notoriously big egos and warped personalities. Saul seemed less encumbered. In fact, our families had become friends over the years.

We took a break and nibbled on some chips before resuming our places for the next script.

"Are you ready to do the other version?" he asked.

I stood up.

"No," I said. "Let's go with the first one."

Everyone in the room applauded, from cameraman to makeup artist to family members. The die was cast. I had no idea what the next two weeks would bring. I remember that the words of some ancient catechism gave me confidence. "Do the thing at hand, the thing that seems to be a duty . . . and the next step will be shown to you."

The boxes at the campaign office were pulled from storage and re-opened. Computers began to whir once again. Phone lines backed up with callers.

Hundreds of volunteers from off the street—retirees, teachers, children, whole families—came to see how they could help. Chris Sifford's aunt, Martha Ware, still in mourning for the loss of her nephew, drove to St. Louis from the Bootheel, bringing with her a group of women to join the effort.

The plan devised by Shorr and Farinella was to get out a seven-hundred-thousand-piece mailing along with a button that read, "I'm Still with Mel"—the same words that Win with Women had faxed to its membership just a few days earlier.

The problem, of course, was timing and space. With little more than a week before the election, such a mailing would be a mammoth undertaking. We needed more space than could be found in our cramped headquarters in an old medical office with cubicle-sized rooms. But it was too late to relocate now. With nowhere else to go, tables and chairs were hauled into an adjacent hallway and set up to form an assembly line for stuffing and stamping.

Infused with hope, and apparently undaunted by the immensity of the task, workers sat elbow to elbow, subsisting on colas, chips, and donuts during those long days. Those without a space to sit worked from the floor or the stairs. For a few nights, shifts of volunteers worked around the clock.

"The place looked like a sweatshop," Roy Temple would later recall. Part of the project was parceled out to labor halls and homes, wherever there were willing bodies and available space.

I was not there to see all that went into this effort, but I heard the stories. I saw the photographs. Workers felt as if they had fought on some historic battlefield. People still tell me with a gleam in their eye, "I was there! I worked The Mailing in the 2000 election!"

It was a proud time for all when the final mail pieces left the office and those buttons started popping up on lapels at malls and grocery stores all over the state. The limited number of bumper stickers were gone upon arrival. New yard signs were all handmade. It was a ragtag operation, but it had spirit. And, in the end, that's what makes the difference in a campaign.

Eight days before the election, I made my first public statement about the upcoming election. It was not from a studio or at a public event, but outdoors from the deck of our farmhouse in Rolla.

On the morning of the news conference, before I was even out of bed, trucks with satellite uplinks began pulling into the driveway. A bevy of camera crews from all over the state and nation stomped through my flowerbeds. The backyard was a jumble of equipment, lights, and wiring along with reporters jockeying for position, eager to film my first words—or my first mistakes.

Encircled by family, I made the statement that I had written the night before, expressing my gratitude for the many kindnesses shown to me. I ended with my declaration to carry on the battle. It was a heartfelt statement that summed up the situation and my mental processes in reaching a decision.

Last week a number of children came to visit me at the mansion. Many brought cards, flowers, teddy bears.

One brought me his favorite comfort toy—a small purple frog—because he knew it would make me feel better.

It sits on my desk as a reminder that some day I will feel better.

My husband and I shared more than forty-six years together.

Not only did we share a lifetime, we shared dreams.

Those who worked with him know that his ideals and vision were contagious.

He sincerely believed that every person could make a difference, if they took the risk of trying.

He took that risk for Missouri's children time and time again.

He knew that next to love, education is the most powerful and lasting gift we can give one another.

He also took the risk of standing up for the weakest among us by working to lessen the fears and insecurities of the elderly, sick, and disabled.

He worked to reinvent government, to elevate the tone and manner of public discourse, and to rekindle civility in the public arena.

He believed that government could be good, and noble, and worthy of our lives.

He believed, as I do, that what makes the difference in the United States Senate—or anyplace else—is the direction of the heart.

While we grieve at the loss of the man whose life and vision inspired us all, this campaign was never about just one person.

It was about giving a voice in the United States Senate to the everyday working families of Missouri—especially to children.

Eight days from now Missourians will reaffirm their belief in self-government by going to the polls to vote.

My husband's name will still be on that ballot.

His memory still lives in our hearts.

His vision for Missouri families can still prevail, if we want it to.

In recent days, I have spent a great many hours reading notes and expressions of sympathy from people all over the country.

They warmed my heart—especially those from the children.

I have learned so much from you . . . so much about the incredible triumph of the human spirit.

And now, with the support of my family and an abiding faith in a loving God, I've decided to do what I think Mel would want us to do.

To keep the cause alive.

To continue the fight for the values and ideals for which he lived.

Should the people elect my husband, I pledge to take our common dreams to the United States Senate.

Now the choice is up to the people of Missouri.

Mel always trusted them.

And I do too.

. . .

I took a few questions that dealt mostly with my feelings at the moment. But I knew that in the days that followed the questions would get tougher . . . and so must I.

By now, interview requests were pouring in from around the country. All the national talk shows wanted to "sit down with me for a few minutes." It would be difficult to do them all. I finally came up with a rationale for doing only one—an interview with ABC's Cokie Roberts.

Cokie's father, Louisiana congressman Hale Boggs, died when his plane disappeared in Alaska on October 16, 1972. Ironically, it was the same month and day on which my husband died, and the aircraft was similar as well. Lindy Boggs took her husband's place in the Congress and remained there for seventeen years.

It made sense to me to speak with Hale and Lindy's daughter. Cokie came to the farm on the Friday before the election. At my request, we did the interview outdoors. I felt that the brisk autumn air would help fortify me as I laid bare my feelings. I think Cokie would have preferred the indoors, but she gamely went along with my suggestion.

We sat on the back deck of the farmhouse, just the two of us, talking on a topic that we both understood all too well. Cokie briefly mentioned the similarities in the plane crashes that our two families had experienced. Then she delved into the subjects that were on everyone's mind.

One of those was the possibility of a legal challenge should Mel be elected. There was already talk within the Ashcroft camp that a dead candidate is not legally a resident of the state. At the time, I had no idea whether that would become an issue.

> **Roberts:** Now, there've been lots of articles in the paper and discussions of legal wrangling . . . should that happen . . . a challenge to your seat, should you be appointed. Do you think this is just politics, or do you think this is real?
>
> **Carnahan:** I can't believe that anyone would attempt to thwart the will of the Missouri voters if they vote and say they want to continue the ideals and the things that my husband stood for, and they know that Governor Wilson will appoint me to carry that out.

Cokie broached yet another subject that was being discussed by opponents—the power of sympathy to affect the outcome of the election.

Roberts: I read a voter being quoted as saying, "I don't like the idea of a pity vote." Do you think that's what we're talking about here?

Carnahan: No, I don't like the idea of that either. I like the idea that my husband stood for something, and that the people believed in what he stood for, and they want that to continue.

Roberts: Now, the *Kansas City Star* also said, "Her views on most major issues confronting the country are unknown." So, let me give you a chance to say some of those views.

In looking at the differences between Mel Carnahan and John Ashcroft, it looked pretty similar to me to the differences between Al Gore and George Bush, on things like prescription drugs, a patients' bill of rights, taxes. Would you say that that's an accurate, first of all, assessment?

Carnahan: Yes, I think my husband and I agreed on most things. I think, like most couples, you have occasional things you don't agree on. But we agreed that the important things were to pay down the national debt. This was the best way we could invest in our future. To shore up Social Security, to have a real patients' bill of rights, and a prescription drug benefit under Medicare.

And that it was important to give targeted tax cuts to working families so they could send their child to school or they could care for an elderly parent or buy a home. And it was so important to do something on a national level, some new major commitment for education.

These are the things I believe in. I think, perhaps, being a woman, I would have an additional commitment to some things involving women. I'm very concerned about breast cancer research, pay equity, child care, those sorts of things. I would carry that additional commitment. . . .

Her conclusion brought some introspection on my part.

Roberts: You must feel like in some ways you're just in the twilight zone.

Carnahan: Yes, some things don't seem real. Occasionally, I feel like I'm sitting in a play . . . or that I'm part of the play. That it will end. And I'll get up and go out and life will be the way it was. But I know that's not the case.

Following our visit, Cokie sent me a copy of her mother's book, *Washington through a Purple Veil.* I would later meet the amazing Lindy Boggs who, at age eighty-five, had just finished a three-year tour as ambassador to the Vatican for President Clinton.

The amusing story that inspired her book title occurred when Mrs. Boggs first arrived in Washington as the wife of a congressman and wanted to attend one of the important, but crowded, hearings.

"I went up to the young clerk outside the hearing room door and said, 'My husband is a member of this committee and he asked me to come down to the hearings. May I please go in?'"

The clerk responded sarcastically, "Honey, tell me something else," and dismissed her request.

Remembering that a friend had told her the most sophisticated item for Washington women was a purple veil, Mrs. Boggs rushed to a department store and had a sales clerk drape a purple veil over a black velour hat. On her return to the Capitol, she marched to the head of the line and demanded a seat on the first row.

The clerk took one look at her and said, "Certainly, madam, step right this way." Lindy proved to be one spunky lady during her seventeen years in Congress and a model for other women who would follow her.

Her son-in-law, Steve Roberts, amuses audiences by saying if you see a little old woman standing next to the ailing pontiff as he shuffles along, it is probably the indomitable Lindy Boggs with her soothing southern accent whispering, "Com' on, darlin', you can make it."

Like Lindy Boggs, so many women have found the grit and courage in times of tragedy to do things they never dreamed of doing, surprising even themselves. Margaret Corbin was such a woman. When her husband was killed at the Battle of Fort Washington, she stepped up to fire the cannon in his place until she was wounded.

Another woman of the Revolution, Mary Ludwig Hays, earned the name "Molly Pitcher" for carrying water to the troops during the Battle of Monmouth. But when her husband fell on the battlefield, she put the pitcher aside, took his place at the cannon, and continued the fight.

For years, Marie Curie and her husband, Pierre, worked side by side in their research leading to the discovery of radium. When he died from long exposure to the radioactive element, she went on with their work and became the first woman professor in France.

Katharine Graham took on the task of running the *Washington Post* after her husband's suicide. In her autobiography, she wrote, "I didn't understand the immensity of what lay before me, how frightened I would be by much of it, how tough it was going to be, and how many anxious hours and days I would spend for a long, long time. Nor did I realize how much I was eventually going to enjoy it all."

Katharine proved to be a superb journalist and a business visionary, winning a Pulitzer Prize for her newspaper's role in exposing the Watergate scandal. Walter Cronkite said of her: "Kay was a bereaved widow who surprised everyone with her strength and took over the *Washington Post* to make it one of the world's great newspapers."

But the names of countless other women do not appear in print. They are the wives of farmers, bankers, storekeepers, and realtors who pick up the pieces after the loss of a spouse and move forward on their own.

Katharine Graham told how those decisions are made.

"Sometimes you don't really decide," she said. "You just move forward and that is what I did—moved forward blindly and mindlessly into a new and unknown life."

Overcoming tragedy, or anything else, is a matter of putting one foot in front of the other every day. Not giving up . . . not giving in . . . not giving out. As Theodore Roosevelt reminded himself repeatedly, "Joy comes in not shirking life's burden."

On page eleven of the *St. Louis Post-Dispatch* for Wednesday, November 8, 2000—the day after Election Day—you'll see a picture of me standing in American Legion Post 270 in Rolla, Missouri.

I'm waiting my turn to vote. The fingers of my hands are curled around a blank ballot. My daughter, Robin, is hunched into the voting booth, her back toward the camera as she completes her own ballot.

In the blurry newspaper image, my eyes are downcast, my lips compressed in deep resolve.

What should have been a moment of sublime celebration, the moment I could finally cast my vote for my husband, Mel Carnahan, whose race for the U.S. Senate was a culmination of a lifelong devotion to public duty, was instead a moment of solitary reckoning and grave public import.

In that picture I see in my face every bit of the sadness I felt, but also every bit of the determination that I needed to see me through the coming months, whatever the outcome.

That evening the family gathered at our farmhouse on the outskirts of Rolla. It's a quiet retreat. A place where we can be recharged by the power of familiar things.

Back in 1973, we had cleared the land ourselves, planned and built a two-story frame farmhouse, dug a pond, planted fields, and added cattle and horses and more acreage. Each summer, when it was time for the hard work of making a hay crop, we gathered back home as if for some festive reunion. But Randy saw to the daily farm operation. I often joked that he practiced law so he could afford to farm. He would hitch up our team of Belgian horses to haul hay or skid logs. When we wanted to go for a ride in the backwoods with friends there were always the quarter horses or, for the less equestrian, a couple of four-wheelers. A blanket of new-fallen snow was an invitation to hitch up the one-horse open sleigh for a ride across the quiet, moonlit fields.

Randy, "the renaissance man," as I often referred to him, could fix anything, shoe horses, climb mountains, operate farm equipment, and give fine legal and political counsel.

He found a soul mate in his grandfather, who came to live with us after my mother died. We became a three-generational family with all the adjustments in living patterns that such arrangements require. Still, I would not trade those seven years for anything.

"Grandpa," as everyone called him, loved to tell stories to anyone who would listen. He was quite good at it, knowing when to pause for effect and how to add animation or colorful southern expressions from his Virginia childhood. My bent for using stories in my speeches probably comes from having heard so many—often the same ones repeatedly.

Grandpa kept his good humor despite having to live with diabetes, asthma, and a family of politicians. We, in turn, learned to understand the health and nutritional needs of older people.

When I campaigned on the road for Mel, I'd tuck away enough meals in the refrigerator to see him through the day. We all learned to spot the early signs of an insulin reaction and how to respond. Grandpa found pleasure in watering plants and shrubs, feeding the dog, tending the garden, sweeping the kitchen, and seeing to other chores important in a household.

He even made a campaign commercial with Mel. Oh, what a pleasant scene it was, the two of them walking through our fields. Grandpa was using his hands to tell a story (no coaching needed there), and Mel was listening intently.

During the campaign, a number of seniors told me how much they liked the ad. "It shows that Mel listens to an older person," was the general comment. Grandpa loved making that commercial and scanned the television channels to see it as often as possible.

He lived to see Mel win the primary for governor in 1992 but died two months before the general election. I still have a picture of him on-stage with the family at the primary victory rally, waving broadly to the crowd.

We always laughed at that picture because only those of us standing next to him heard what he said as the crowd cheered wildly at the news of Mel's victory. Grandpa, never having been on a stage before and overcome by the jubilation of the moment, blurted forth the only political slogan that came to mind.

"TWO CHICKENS IN EVERY POT!" he yelled, recalling the ill-fated campaign rhetoric of Herbert Hoover in 1932.

Yes, there were many wonderful memories of our past campaigns and family gatherings at the farm. It felt right being there. But there was more than the good feeling of memories replayed; there was the strength that springs from the earth itself. Scarlett O'Hara's father was right: "The land is the only thing that lasts."

Still, it seemed strange that Grandpa, Mel, and Randy were no longer among us. The kitchen table that once was crowded when we all came home was now uncomfortably roomy.

My grandsons, Austin and Andrew, felt the emptiness, too. Earlier in the week, Andrew was standing with me on the back porch. It was one of those beautiful fall days that even an eight-year-old noticed. Looking up at the sky he said, "This is such a pretty day. I bet Grandpa and Randy are out flying somewhere."

His confidence buoyed my own. I smiled and replied, "Yes, I'm sure they are."

After dinner on election evening, we gathered in the family room where a warm fire blazed in the brick fireplace that Mel and I had designed many years earlier. It was the same fireplace that held the fires he had tended so lovingly and admonished the kids to keep burning brightly. We warmed ourselves from the glowing logs that we all knew Randy had split and stacked earlier that fall. As the evening grew late and there were still no complete election returns, I decided to go to bed. I had started toward the stairs, when Tom called me back.

New returns were coming in, he said, enough for the broadcaster to call the race. I sat on the sofa next to Tom. We all grew silent, straining to hear the outcome of this cruel political marathon that had devastated our lives.

"This news just in . . . Mel Carnahan has been declared the winner in the Missouri race for the United States Senate."

Tom put his arm around me and said gently, "Mom, we won . . . ."

There were no cheers . . . only tears.

The Irish poet Seamus Heaney had captured the moment when he wrote, "Once in a lifetime the longed for tidal wave of justice can rise up, and hope and history rhyme."

I made a statement to those who had kept the long, hopeful vigil across the state:

Mel would be so proud of you tonight.
You have stayed the course . . .
You have kept the faith . . .
You have carried our hopes and dreams.
Our common cause has inspired people all across the nation.
And tonight, we all stand on higher ground.
There is so much in my heart this evening.

It is flooded with emotion . . .

Sadness, because Mel, and Randy, and Chris are not here to see the fulfillment of this day.

Joy and gratitude, because you stood with them even in death.

I am reminded that so many leaders did not live to see the fruits of their labor.

. . . Moses died on this side of the Jordan.

. . . Lincoln never saw his nation made whole again.

. . . Susan B. Anthony never cast a vote.

. . . Martin Luther King Jr. never finished his mountaintop journey.

My husband's journey was stopped short, too.

And, for reasons we don't understand, the mantle has now fallen upon us.

We remain.

Heirs of a legacy.

Bearers of the dream.

On this night, I pledge to you—rather, let us pledge to each other—

We will never let the fire go out.

God bless you always.

Opponents of the unprecedented vote in Missouri attributed the outcome to the "sympathy factor." But Marc Farinella and others refused to see it that way.

"This election was between two sets of values and priorities," he explained. "To say this was because of a sympathy vote would be a fundamental misinterpretation of what happened here. This was much more durable, much more important than pity."

For the time being, I left the analysis to others and focused on the new demands that were uniquely mine. My first press conference following the election was in Jefferson City at a local hotel.

It was a strange moment. I stood solid on my own two feet, no staff, no family. I also stood solid in my belief that I was doing what I should do, what Mel would have wanted me to do.

The members of the press were perhaps less sure of themselves. After all, I was officially a grieving widow. How should they speak to me? What tone should they strike? This was uncharted territory for all of us.

I opened with a thank-you statement to supporters and took questions from the press corps.

Tuesday evening we witnessed an unprecedented event in Missouri history.
We saw the impact of three men's lives on this state.
If history has taught us anything, it's that great causes do not die with people.
Instead, they unite us and ignite us in ways we never thought possible.
There are so many to thank for keeping their dreams alive: those on Mel's staff who labored long, tiring days.
And the thousands of supporters and volunteers, and even youngsters, who worked harder than they had ever worked before because they believed in what they were doing.
I know this may sound unusual coming from someone in public life, but I want also to thank the media for the respect and courtesy shown my family and me during these past several weeks.
And I would like to thank Senator Ashcroft for the gracious manner in which he acknowledged the will of the people.
Yesterday I began a new chapter in my life.
And though the pain and the tears still come unexpectedly at times, I now see a renewed purpose to my life, and an opportunity to affect the future of Missouri's working families and children.
As you may know, Mel's childhood was spent in the Ozark hills where education and opportunity were hard to come by.
I grew up in a row house in an urban area where my parents worked two and three jobs to make ends meet.
And I was the first in my family to graduate from high school and college.
There are families like these today who need to be heard.
They need a voice and a vote in the U.S. Senate . . . and that's what I want to be.
My husband stood with the everyday working families of this state throughout his public life.
It is his vision, and their dreams, that I will take with me to Washington.

• • •

As I finished my statement, I called for questions. At first, the questions were straightforward. And then some brave soul said, "Mrs. Carnahan, given your background . . . uhh, . . . do you think you are, uhh, . . . qualified to serve as a United States senator?"

I was angered by that suggestion, and my response surprised even me. To this day, my children chuckle at my reaction. I had not prepared an answer to this question, yet the words came as though I'd rehearsed all morning.

I snapped back, "There are those who spent a lifetime underestimating my husband, and I suggest they not make that same mistake with me."

Every eyebrow in the room shot up!

I had just learned the power of the "ten-second sound bite."

Three

Mrs. Carnahan Goes to Washington

While God gives me the strength and the people show me their goodwill, it is my duty to try, and try I will.

—Winston Churchill,
seeking election at age seventy-five

"I do solemnly swear that I will support and defend the Constitution of the United States against all enemies, foreign and domestic; . . . so help me God."

With those few words, I officially became a United States senator—the first woman from Missouri to serve.

My head swirled in a myriad of emotions.

Sadness

. . . because this is the time that should have been Mel's—the moment he had worked toward for a lifetime.

Satisfaction

. . . knowing I had done the right thing and that Mel, Randy, and Chris would be very proud that we had carried on the cause.

Gratitude

. . . for those who believed in me—all those young staffers who had stuck by me during the past weeks, many of whom had now joined me in Washington to make this venture work.

Wonder

. . . at being in the center of such historic and uncertain times.
And *Determination*

. . . to work every day as hard and as long as necessary to do the job.

Yes, Mel should have been here, hand uplifted, solemnly pledging to serve honorably and well.

And I . . . well, I was supposed to be in the gallery, smiling, glowing with pride at our common victory. I stiffened my lip and resolved not to be the tearful widow. Standing on the dais of the Senate chamber, I was toe to toe with the outgoing vice president, Al Gore, as he delivered the oath of office to the newly elected senators in one of his final acts of office.

I suspect his heart was heavy with thoughts of his own, thoughts of "what could have been . . . what *should* have been." Just weeks earlier, he and Tipper had comforted our family and walked with us in the funeral procession for my husband. Tipper had taken my children aside and said, "If you need someone to talk to, please call me—anytime." It was an extremely kind offer to a bereaved and bewildered family. But I never doubted for a moment that she was completely sincere.

At the time, the Gores were buoyant with hope and I was reeling in confusion and despair. Now the turn of election events had removed him from office and propelled me onto the Washington scene.

Yes, life is not the way it's supposed to be.

I'm sure he was having some of those feelings as we faced each other over my old Bible, whose words and promises had sustained me during the past weeks.

Even before I stepped from the podium, Sen. Joe Biden (D-Delaware), who had just been sworn in for another term, deliberately turned back, walked toward me, and took my hand.

"I want to be of help in any way I can," he said firmly.

He reminded me that he had lost a wife and child in a car accident just weeks before he began his first term in the Senate. Joe would later tell me of his struggle to accept a political victory in the wake of such personal loss.

During those early days on Capitol Hill, he was counseled by John McClellan of Arkansas, who looked the young senator in the eye and said, "Work . . . hard work."

Joe felt that those were harsh words of advice at a time when his heart was so tender with pain. He later discovered the old senator had suffered untold tragedy, first, with the loss of his wife to spinal meningitis. Then, in a relatively short period, McClellan had lost *all three of his sons,* one in World War II, another in a car accident, and the last in a plane crash.

Now, in a far gentler fashion, Joe was giving me the same counsel he had received as a freshman senator. Later, Sen. Conrad Burns (R-Montana) spoke in a similar vein as he told me of losing his teenage daughter.

During that first busy week of the legislative session, Ted Kennedy took time to invite me to his office, its rooms lined with family pictures from the Kennedy presidential era.

He pointed out some of the photos that had special meaning to him and, before I left, presented me with a copy of John Kennedy's book *Profiles in Courage.* The touching inscription from Ted read, "To Jean Carnahan, who has written some profiles in courage herself."

The more I learned about these one hundred senators and their wide range of experiences, the more I realized what a unique group I was among. I felt especially drawn to John McCain (R-Arizona), the former prisoner of war, and Max Cleland (D-Georgia), who left three limbs in Vietnam. Max calls himself "a survivor attempting to be a thriver." That he is. Both men have triumphed over tragedy and built lives that refuse to give in to heartache and loss.

I began to understand what Albert Schweitzer meant when he referred to those who "share the fellowship of pain." There is a bond. We seek each other out like one beggar telling another where to find bread.

I was not alone.

Later that day, each of the new senators had a chance to speak before the Democratic Caucus in the Old Senate Chamber. Entering the small room in the Capitol is to step back into a bygone era when there were only thirty-one states and, thus, only sixty-two senators. Anyone with a feel for history can sense the spirit of such figures as Clay, Calhoun, and Webster, the oratorical giants of the past who rallied our nation in times of need.

When it was my turn, I spoke only briefly.

I don't remember all of my remarks, but I concluded by saying to my newly elected colleagues:

I know I did not come to the U.S. Senate in the same way you did.
I did not have a long-term, personal commitment to a campaign.
My name has never been on a ballot
On election night there was no victory celebration.
You are here because of your win; I am here because of my loss.
But we are all here to do the work of this great nation.

I, indeed, felt very different from the rest. My path to the U.S. Senate did not parallel theirs.

They were winners with great expectations.

I was the widow, for whom there was a low expectation. Traditionally, women replacing their husbands in Congress are referred to as "seat warmers." I would exceed expectations, as the saying goes, if I could "walk and chew gum."

Women always have to work harder to make their mark. Every woman knows that from the get-go. There's always someone eager to write you off before you even get started. It's true not only of women but also of minorities, the handicapped, the poor, the undereducated. Professional politicians are the worst at claiming the public arena for themselves, as they fend off pretenders who don't match their self-designed requirements.

Fortunately, the founding fathers did not intend for the elected to be professionals. They expected them to be much like George Washington, a farmer called to public duty who, upon completing his work, returned to the private sector. Today far too many officeholders spend their entire lives at the public trough with few intervals to learn what it takes to meet a payroll each week, to run a home, or to serve as a volunteer or in the military.

Later that afternoon I was interviewed at a news conference—my first since arriving in Washington. So far, the press had been generous with me. As Missouri's First Lady, I had always been available and straight-

straight forward. If you ever get off on the wrong foot with the media or they sense you are being evasive or untruthful, it is hard to reestablish their trust. Mel followed a policy of always shooting straight with reporters. Sometimes it annoyed me when he understated his accomplishments or what he hoped to do. I can never remember him boosting or exaggerating a point. It just wasn't his nature to do so.

Too many First Ladies had horror stories to tell about their relationships with the media, though it often appeared that they brought much of it on themselves.

"Don't trust the press. Be careful what you say. They will twist your words. They are not your friends." These warnings were passed among First Ladies when they gathered to ponder their common concerns during meetings of the National Governors Association.

I kept all those cautions in mind but never found them especially helpful. I recalled what happened to Gov. Samuel W. Pennypacker of Pennsylvania. In 1902, he was depicted by a political cartoonist as an overweight parrot. The provoked governor had his staff draw up legislation that made it a crime to portray humans as animals. The cartoonists got the message and never again drew the governor as a fat parrot. After that, he was always drawn as an oversize zucchini.

There is no doubt that the press gets the last word.

With all that in mind, I was somewhat guarded in my remarks, especially since many of the questions had to do with the nomination of John Ashcroft for attorney general—a contentious issue taking shape both in Washington and back home.

> **Carnahan:** Good afternoon. Thank you for coming. I have just gone through a very bittersweet moment in the Senate chamber. I always felt that I would be an observer from the balcony. It didn't happen that way. Instead, I was a participant on the floor. But I felt very strongly that there were three people smiling down on us today.
>
> It was a historic moment. First, because I'm taking Harry Truman's seat in the Senate. And I'm the first woman to represent Missouri in the United States Senate. So I think this is going to be a particularly meaningful time for me. It can be a very meaningful time for the state of Missouri as well. I am going to do all I can to be a voice and a vote

for the things that Missourians believe in and hope for. And the things my husband stood for. That's going to be the challenge that I see for myself during the next two years.

If you have any questions, I'll be glad to take them at this time.

Question: [Microphone off, but the question involved the Ashcroft nomination.]

Carnahan: We're going to have to give [the nominees] a fair and full hearing in the committee process. That's what I suspect we will do with John Ashcroft and with all the other nominees as well. I think that's the fair thing. I think that's what the Senator [Ashcroft] would want me to do.

Question: Senator Carnahan, are there any sticky little issues that you're going to look at in evaluating whether or not to vote for confirmation of Mr. Ashcroft?

Carnahan: I would like to see how he intends to carry out the duties of the office. I think he will tell us that in the questions that come up, and have already come up in various groups. He should address these. We should listen to him and evaluate him based on that. I don't want to prejudge him or anyone else.

Question: [Microphone off, but the line of questioning is still related to the Ashcroft nomination.]

Carnahan: Well, the issues that you heard voiced come from different interest groups so far. [They want to know] whether or not he would be willing to enforce laws that might be contrary to his ideology. These are the things people are asking about. We need to find those answers directly from him.

Question: Senator, some of the institutes you mentioned suggested that Mr. Ashcroft is racially biased, based on his involvement in political nominations. Did you develop your own opinion about whether he was or was not?

Carnahan: I've never felt he was racially biased. I don't know what was in his heart that caused him to vote the way he did on the Ronnie White issue, but I'm not convinced that it was racial. [Missouri Supreme Court Justice Ronnie White, a St. Louis African American jurist, was a Clinton nominee for the federal bench whose appointment was blocked in the U.S. Senate following an effort orchestrated by Senator Ashcroft.]

Question: Senator, knowing what you've gone through over the past few months personally and because becoming a senator is usually very traumatic. Is this hard to deal with, Senator?

Carnahan: I think it is. There's not been too much joy in the past three months. I'm going to try to make this a new phase of my life. I'm going to try to put this behind me. But as one of the senators told me today who had lost a sixteen-year-old. He said it's like having a pebble in your shoe. You always know it's there. It never leaves you, but it just gets easier. You can still make one step at a time each day, but you're always aware of it.

Question: And today, in particular.

Carnahan: Yes, I think today in particular.

Question: What will be your priorities legislatively?

Carnahan: Well, I think the same things in which my husband was much interested. You know, we have this very wonderful situation where it is predicted that we will have a $5 trillion surplus. I think normally when any family gets a windfall of any sort, the first thing they do is pay off their debts. This is what our nation should do too. We should pay down the national debt. And we should shore up Social Security and Medicare, get a prescription drug benefit, get some targeted tax cuts, and certainly have a new national commitment to education.

These things are important to Americans. They are things that are important to Missourians and important to me. Things that I want to work on.

Question: Speaking of education, how do you feel about vouchers?

Carnahan: I'm not in favor of vouchers.

Question: What was going through your mind as you were sworn in today?

Carnahan: Well, I thought how much my husband would love to have done this. It was his dream. He worked so hard, and so did my son and Chris Sifford. I have just walked in and become the senator. It was really something they had worked for so hard. And I would love very much for them to have had the opportunity to be here. But life goes on and we deal with it the way it is.

I'm so satisfied that I have a wonderful team of people who are working with me, many of whom worked with my husband and us for years and years. Some of them are standing over there now [points], as are my children.

I feel like I have a strong nucleus for doing some worthwhile things. Everyone around me has been very supportive. With that kind of strength, I'm going to be able to fulfill this job. I have always felt that God does not give us any task without giving us the strength for the job.

Question: Do you feel like you're under a microscope because of the circumstances under which you got here?

Carnahan: I think I will be for a while, but after a while that will pass, and people will judge me on what I'm doing and the programs that I'm backing. They'll see me more as an individual rather than as someone standing in the shadow of my husband.

Question: Senator, if there weren't a program for that laundry list that you ticked off a moment ago, what will be the first item that you pursue?

Carnahan: It's going to be difficult in this situation where we have a 50–50 Senate to say, "Yes, this is what I'm going to do." I'll have to look for opportunities to do things. I will look for those opportunities in the areas I have mentioned. I'm especially interested in education and issues relating to children. But to come up here in this atmosphere and say "I'm definitely going to do this or that" would be hard. You're going to have to look for alliances and places where you can make a difference. That's going to be the secret of success.

Question: Do you think there are going to be workable solutions?

Carnahan: I hope so. I look for what I call the "sensible center." I hope we can find that. There are a lot of people of goodwill who want to find that. They're searching for ways. I have met with the Centrist Coalition. I have met with the New Democrats. There are people of goodwill and good faith who want to make things happen. I want to be a part of that. My husband always said that he never wanted to go into government just to warm a seat. I have those same feelings. I want to do something that's going to make a difference. I don't want to be part of a logjam and deadlock up here. We're going to have to look for ways to make things happen.

Question: Where are you staying in Washington?

Carnahan: I have a place over at the Lansburg right now that I'll be moving into in February. I'll have two bedrooms and a sofa bed, so my children can come when they feel like it.

Question: Senator, you talked about the Senate. And yet, coming back to Ashcroft, he's been appointed to this most crucial position within the administration. [Remainder of question is inaudible.]

Carnahan: The president-elect sought to reach across the political spectrum and get a variety of people into his Cabinet. I think that he [Ashcroft] has become a lightning rod, attracting people from throughout the country that found his appointment does not suit their political persuasion. We're going to want to know how he feels about things like civil rights and women's equality. They're going to be questioning him, and I think he will want to respond. That's what we're going to see in those hearings.

Question: Senator, would you like to hear from Ronnie White on these things?

Carnahan: I don't know whether Ronnie White would be willing to testify or not. That's up to him as to whether or not he wants to pursue that. I know he was deeply hurt at being rejected. He's a fine individual. It was inappropriate that he was turned down at the time. He would make a wonderful judge. Whether or not he would be willing to testify, I have no idea.

Question: Do you think it would be appropriate for him to testify, in your opinion.

Carnahan: Would it be appropriate? I'm not sure about that. I just don't have an opinion. It's probably largely up to him and how he feels about it. He's been relatively quiet about the whole thing, up till now. [Justice White did later testify at the Judiciary Committee confirmation hearing.]

Question: Is there any nominee that you have reservations about?

Carnahan: I think all of them have to answer certain questions. We just can't carte blanche say, "We're going to accept these people without any questions." They're going to have to go through the full and fair hearing process. I want to give every one of them that. I'd rather see what they have to say on their own behalf.

Question: Have you made any decisions about committees?

Carnahan: No, in fact, I understand they [Democrats and Republicans] have not reached agreement on whether or not there will be parity on the committees. They will determine how many openings there will be. Any number of committees would be suitable for Missouri because we are such a diverse state and have such a range of activity there. I could serve Missouri on any one of the committees, so I'll be anxiously awaiting the outcome.

Question: Can you tell us what Senator Biden said to you on the podium right after you were sworn in.

Carnahan: Yes, I can. He reminded me that he had lost his wife just a few days before he was sworn in. I responded that I remembered when that occurred.

Question: I asked President Clinton, as he went by, if he had any particular thoughts relating to your situation, and he said that he was very happy for you and then thought for a second and said he was sure that Mel was very happy for you as well. Any response to the president's remarks?

Carnahan: The president has been so kind, as has the vice president. They've been very thoughtful. They've each called at various times. I just felt very, very supported by them and by people throughout the United States.

I have received ten thousand letters from all over the United States. Many of them included original music, poetry, books, and gifts of all sorts. Some tell of personal loss and the wonderful triumphs of the human spirit. They've inspired me. Such stories make me feel that something good can come out of all this, because others have overcome tragedy and made something worthwhile of their lives.

Thank you for being here.

Well, the press conference was over, but not the day. There was the traditional Supreme Court reception that evening for senators and spouses. Since Robin and Tom were there, they were my escorts for the evening. Russ had not been able to come because he, too, was being sworn in that day for his seat in the Missouri legislature.

After the reception, Bill Clinton sought me out and commented that he had heard about my very "moving" remarks that afternoon in the Old Senate Chamber. I took the opportunity to thank him for his kindness at the time of the funeral.

"I loved the guy," the president had said during his eulogy. "Anybody who thinks Mel was dull never looked him straight in the eye, because he had steel and passion and fire. I think he rather enjoyed being underestimated by people who disagree with him. . . . In a time when it's fashionable for people in public life to complain about the difficulties of it, he was frank to say that he liked politics and public service. Indeed, he loved it. He didn't understand why some people thought it was a sacrifice and a pain. For him it was a calling, a calling to work with people, and I saw it personally."

President Clinton has such a wonderful ability to connect with people. I marvel at his capacity to make you feel that you're the only person in the world. As he converses, he engages in what I call an "eye lock"—drawing you in like a fish in a net. I am convinced that Clinton has an honest and unfeigned interest in everyone he meets.

By contrast, there's an amusing photograph of Richard Nixon visiting along a rope line. He has one hand outstretched to the waiting crowd while his other arm is bent very obviously toward his face as he reads his watch. Clinton, on the other hand, gives no sign but that a visit with another human being is pure pleasure, defying time.

The former president was in fine form that evening in his new role as Senate spouse and escort. Obviously, Hillary had told him about my speech that afternoon in the Old Senate Chamber. I was pleased that she had.

In the days that followed my swearing in, there was so much to learn, meetings to attend, people to see, places to be. In many ways, it was like that first day in a new school when everybody knows the way to the cafeteria or the library, but you. While others are enjoying themselves, you're struggling to remember your locker number and the route to the restroom.

The Senate is an institution where seniority rules. "The last primitive society in the world," Sen. Eugene McCarthy called it, a place where "we still worship the elders of the tribe and honor the territorial imperative." That is certainly true when it comes to the allocation of offices, furniture, committee assignments, seating, and even Senate license plate numbers.

My "start-up office," in the basement of the Russell Office Building, was a bleak reminder of my newcomer status. It was a small room with one computer, no windows, a shared secretary, and the promise of better provisions in a month or so.

My hopes were not too high. I ranked ninety-ninth of the one hundred senators, with the other freshmen who had served as a governor or representative ahead of me. Those who had not previously held any elective office wound up at the bottom of the stack. Within that group, those from the most populated states prevailed, placing New Jersey's Jon Corzine (D) ahead of me. That left Mark Dayton (D-Minnesota) with the number one hundred slot—a position he held with feigned honor and good humor.

Even the desk assignments in the Senate chamber follow a sequence that puts the newest members at the edges of the half-moon chart and the longer-serving ones at the front and center. Under the longevity rule, Strom Thurmond (R-South Carolina), approaching age one hundred, and with half a lifetime in the Senate, held the position of honor.

Those in our class were seated in the "hinterlands" of the Senate floor, but we knew that in time we would have the chance to work our way around to the more senior stations. As former senator George Murphy (R-California) said, "The Congress is the only legislative body in the world whose members rise to power by merely surviving."

Seniority is most evident in committee chairmanships, where longevity is rewarded with a gavel. As one senator pointed out, it's like having the king's oldest son succeed to the throne. It saves a lot of trouble.

I sat in freshman purgatory alongside Jon Corzine, the financier who spent more than $60 million of his own money to win a Senate seat. For some reason, I expected him to be arrogant and unapproachable. Was I ever surprised! He is one of the most unpretentious and principled guys I've run into in politics.

On the other side of me was Tom Carper (D-Delaware). I knew Tom and his wife, Martha, when he served as governor. With his wry sense of humor, he will sometimes confuse you as to whether or not he is serious. But when it comes to keeping in touch with people, expressing his gratitude, showing his appreciation, he is most serious. He commutes by Amtrak from Delaware each day, doing his work on his laptop computer on the train. I seldom saw him without note cards and a pen, getting off a few lines to brighten someone's day.

Mark Dayton sat in the desk behind me and was always ready with a good-natured wisecrack. While he didn't take himself seriously, he took the business of the Senate most earnestly and could be counted on for a refreshing viewpoint, fervently pressed, in either committee or caucus.

Just in front of me was Zell Miller (D-Georgia). The Millers are another couple I came to know and admire when he served as governor. He retired from public life but was subsequently propelled back into office after the death of Sen. Paul Coverdell.

I loved to hear Zell speak with his deep southern drawl and even deeper political conviction. He's a good, solid public servant, and I wish he felt more at home in the Democratic Party.

Of course, there were the other three Democratic women who came to the Senate at the same time I did, increasing the number of female senators from nine to thirteen and greatly enhancing their influence in Congress.

None of us was supposed to win! The year 2000 was a great year for underdogs—perhaps an indicator that people had faith in the future and their ability to effect change.

Take Debbie Stabenow of Michigan. She was fourteen points behind in the polls just a month before the election but managed to pull out a victory. Her broad and instant smile is a trademark of a caring personality and a great benefit in negotiating for her agenda.

In Washington State, Maria Cantwell's razor-thin victory took weeks of recounting to confirm. Incredibly bright and thoroughly versed in hi-tech issues, she is a great asset to the U.S. Senate.

And who would have wagered a dime on Hillary Clinton's chance to win in New York? She has overcome incredible personal and political difficulties to become a powerhouse in her own right. But she is also great fun to be around and was always responsive to every request that I made of her.

"Jean, I'll come to Missouri or stay away, which ever will help you most," she would later say good-heartedly as my election approached. Like her husband, she gives the feeling that she has time for you and your problem, although you know she is one of the busiest of senators.

And then, there was the Missouri race, where we literally snatched victory from the jaws of defeat. Because we all stuck it out, we changed the face of the Senate with four new Democratic women!

The freshmen Democratic members, both women and men, were impressive and displayed great energy and a level of participation unexpected in new senators. Although off to a fast start, they each had six years to master the issues and to make their mark in Congress before seeking voter approval again. I was a bit envious, because I had far less time to do the same thing. The circumstances under which I served required that an election be held within two years. I was immediately pitched into another election cycle. If I wanted to finish out the term, I had to begin raising money immediately in order to run a high-profile Senate race. So while my colleagues were easing into their new role, I was hurriedly learning the ropes and preparing for another campaign on the heels of the last one.

Sometimes I felt sorry for myself, because I had to do everything in double time. But I tried to push those thoughts from my mind as often as they came. The pace would surely slacken in two years when the press of campaigning and fund-raising had passed. Meanwhile, I did not have the luxury of being able to complain.

During those times when I was tempted to feel sorry for myself, I made a point of recounting the things for which I was most blessed—

My children and grandchildren.

My staff members, who were much like my own family in their devotion and loyalty.

My health, which was better than it had ever been (a fact I attributed to good self-care because of my disdain for doctor and dental visits).

The encouragement and support of friends, and even strangers, who continued to amaze me with their devotion.

The opportunity I had to do some constructive work that would impact the lives of everyday people.

And, I had memories—wonderful and precious. Enough to last a lifetime.

But I also had a task that was uniquely mine. The next two years would be the toughest of my life because I would have to work harder, and longer, and smarter than I ever had.

That was the challenge of my two years in the U.S. Senate.

I felt like the Chippewa Indian woman who said, "Sometimes I go about pitying myself and all the time I am being carried on great winds across the sky."

Four

Root Causes

On one of my few weekend excursions, I visited the old neighborhood in Anacostia where I had grown up. As I wound my way from Capitol Hill along Pennsylvania Avenue toward southeast Washington, I thought of the title of Thomas Wolfe's book, *You Can't Go Home Again.* Yes, it hurts to see changes in the people and the places we love.

I didn't want to feel like Snoopy did in that cartoon episode when he returns to the site of his "puppyhood" at the Daisy Hill Puppy Farm. His fond memories are shattered when he discovers that his old home is covered by a five-story parking garage. Charlie Brown says sympathetically, "How sad it is when someone parks on your memories."

Ironically, I landed an apartment at the Lansburg, a converted department store where I often went shopping with my mother. So when I drove into the parking garage, I guess you could say that I was parking on my memories.

More of those childhood memories came to mind as I crossed the Anacostia River Bridge. My old stomping grounds showed signs of urban decay, as well as other changes—all in the name of progress, I'm sure. For instance, the baseball diamond on the Flats had been paved for an overpass. I scored many a run from that field, often leaving behind a little skin and blood from a collision at home plate.

My grade school had been torn down and replaced, but the new building carried the same name. Mr. Meyer's Grocery was now a dry cleaner, and the Gothic-style church of my youth had changed denominations. Pop's Candy, next to the school, was flattened years ago to allow for more playground space. How sad. I remember Pop's creaky screen door, its spring set so tight that it would slap you across the backside and plumb through the doorway.

With my few pennies firmly in hand, I would press one finger against the glass candy case and say slowly and repeatedly, "I want a penny's worth of that one . . . and a penny's worth of those . . . and a penny's worth of . . . ," until I had spent an entire nickel on sweets. Pop didn't have a scale. How he determined a "penny's worth" was unclear, but it was enough for two or more kids to ruin their appetites for dinner.

By now, I was approaching S Street, the block on which I lived for fifteen years. Children were playing in the street. Nothing new there. Only their toys had changed—roller skates had been exchanged for skateboards and cap guns replaced by ray guns. But the wonderful exuberance of childhood was still there.

At first, my old street seemed narrower and more crowded then I remembered. Then I realized why. My memories were of an era when homeowners had only one car that fitted nicely in front of the house with room to spare. Today's working families have two cars, and it was apparent that parking had become a problem.

I was pleased to see that the present owner of my old home maintained the property well. One improvement made a dramatic change in the lawn. The front yard that had originally been a steep slope was leveled and walled. When I lived there, mowing the grass gave quite a workout with repeated downhill plunges of the push lawn mower. Although a beast to keep trimmed in the summer, the hill became a child's delight in the winter when it was snow-covered and slippery.

When my family moved to S Street I was no more than four or five years old. But I still recall the huge billboard on the vacant lot across the street. It read, "New FHA Homes for Sale—$5,990. No Money Down. Government Guaranteed Loans."

These easy-to-acquire homes were designed for the many families like my own—all first-time homeowners in search of the American Dream. Built in the wake of the Depression, this government housing project was part of President Roosevelt's economic recovery plan. The controversial New Deal program not only provided low-income housing, it also put people to work and helped get the country on its feet again.

The quiet, blue-collar neighborhood oozed charm despite the uniformity of its four hundred brick houses, laid out in sets of three, each with a front porch, fenced backyard, and three small bedrooms.

The tree-lined streets were designated by letters of the alphabet. I used to say jokingly—but with some degree of truth—that I first learned the alphabet at an early age, not to be able to read, but just to find my way home.

If I misbehaved, no matter whether it was on R Street, or S Street, or T Street, word would reach Mama before I arrived home. She would be waiting at the door, her arms crossed, wanting an explanation of my conduct. I soon learned that mothers are genetically equipped with child-monitoring capabilities even when they are nowhere in sight.

Although children were always under the watchful eye of somebody's mother, I don't recall much house-to-house visiting between neighborhood women. Most interaction took place over the back fence or from the front porch. The men of the neighborhood worked government or blue-collar jobs; the women took care of the kids, pets, and shopping. We spent evenings listening to the radio or getting ready for the next day.

The monotony of this routine was interrupted by bill collectors, meter readers, peddlers, and tradesmen of various stripes, including Bible salesmen, magazine vendors, and insurance collectors.

Children and housewives alike welcomed the itinerant scissors-grinder man who toted a huge cast-iron sharpening device on his back. Walking through the neighborhood, swinging a metal gong in a monotonous rhythm, he would set up shop under a shade tree as housewives ran to gather their cutlery for sharpening.

Another regular in the neighborhood was the insurance man who showed up every few weeks to collect the 25 cents due on each of our two insurance policies. Those payments gave families such as ours the feeling that should something happen to the breadwinner, we would not be left in utter poverty. It gave us a false sense of security, but it was all that we had.

Our agent, Mr. Campbell (or "Bigfoot," as my father referred to him, because of the enormous wing-tipped shoes he wore), carefully recorded the payments in our account book and again in his large binder. Then, having completed his business, "Bigfoot" would down a glass of iced tea, engage in a few pleasantries, or share bits of gossip from his other stops, before going on his way.

For the kids, the favorite neighborhood visitor was, without question, the Good Humor man, driving his white, shiny enameled truck with an ice cream bar painted across the sides. His return each spring coincided with the end of the school year. He wore a white uniform, a visored cap, and a coin dispenser on his belt. Driving slowly down the street, ringing the bell atop his truck, he gave us ample time to run indoors to beg a few coins for an ice cream bar or a popsicle.

For me, a far less welcomed guest was the piano teacher. My mother had paid $500 for a Wurlitzer spinet. Although she didn't play, she polished the piano lovingly and enhanced it with a hand-crocheted doily and an arrangement of waxed fruit. She was proud of the piano and determined that I should learn to play. Mr. Thompson, who lived around the corner, was hired as my teacher. Dressed in his seersucker suit, bow tie, and Panama hat, he was quite a dandy in a neighborhood where most men owned only one suit and tie that was reserved for church, funerals, and weddings.

I was not an attentive student, nor was he an inspiring teacher, so we were a match destined for failure. Bored by his profession and despairing of my performance, he spent the half-hour lesson yawning or flossing his teeth.

My parents were shelling out $1.50 each week and expected results. They quizzed Mr. Thompson on his methods and my abilities. When he declared that I would never play as well as he did, my father, who had not a modicum of musical ability and little patience with Mr. Thompson, defended my talent and dismissed him on the spot, declaring the $1.50 could be put to better use elsewhere.

After that, my piano instruction suffered from my mother shopping the best price for lessons and from my preference for softball. My hands fitted much more adeptly around a baseball bat than they ever did across an octave. My passion for the game went uninterrupted until the onset of adolescence, when I discovered, sadly, that boys were not looking for girls with the largest batting average.

Mama bemoaned the fact that I was not the girl she dreamed of teaching to sew, cook, and play with dolls. She was stuck with a "tomboy"—competitive and boisterous. Making a "lady" out of me became her life's work. Having my three male cousins living next door only made it more difficult. She suggested tap dancing or charm school. I resisted any form of improvement until she finally hit upon braces to straighten my teeth. I jumped at the trade-off.

Braces, however, were a three-year commitment at a cost of $15 a month, plus an hour-long bus and streetcar trip to the dentist. I probably could have learned to tap dance and how to be charming for all she spent on my teeth, but there were no funds left for other improvements.

Besides trying to enhance my talent and looks, Mama worked hard to make me an obedient, authority-respecting offspring. I recall how upset she was when I removed my scratchy pillow label, the one that read, "Do not remove under penalty of law."

"Do you really think the 'pillow police' will knock on our door?" I asked.

Sensing the absurdity of the idea, but not wishing to admit it, Mama replied, "You really enjoy being defiant, don't you, Jean?"

I didn't admit it at the time, but yes, I did rather enjoy defying a ridiculous rule. It was a small matter. But I was pleased that I had questioned it nonetheless.

Generally, my childhood was blissful, as childhood should be. One of my early tendencies would remain with me for life. I was always a collector of something. I filled old cigar boxes with dried leaves, rocks, marbles, pins from Pep Cereal containers, stamps, autographs, postcards, and even tinfoil. I enjoyed humor in all its forms and kept scrapbooks of cartoons and jokes that I found amusing. My collection of war cards and military insignias was the envy of every kid on S Street. I once sent a Christmas card to Gen. Douglas MacArthur when he was Supreme Allied Commander in Japan, asking for his autograph. Six months later, the signed card arrived in a fancy official envelope that impressed both the mailman and our neighbors. On the other hand, I never heard from the King of England.

Regardless of the pastime in which I was absorbed, everything halted at five o'clock when my cousins and I were called to "clean up for supper." Each meal required well-scrubbed hands and a clean face. No one without a shirt, socks, or shoes was allowed to eat a bite from my mother's table. Criticism of a dish, playing with food, leaving a morsel on the plate was unacceptable.

My mother was especially keen on serving vegetables. It was a rare meal that didn't include several varieties, plus some form of potatoes. (I'm convinced that potatoes are to the Irish what rice is to the Chinese, and no meal is complete without these cultural staples.) Sunday's mashed potatoes were accompanied by either southern fried chicken or roast beef—and gravy, of course. Leftover potatoes reappeared on Monday evening as fried potato cakes.

The only steak served at our table was identified as Swiss steak, a cut of round beef that had been hammered, coated with flour, and fried to chewing consistency. Only after I was married did I taste the pricier, more tender beef. Was I ever surprised to find that there were steaks that could be sliced instead of "sawed."

My grandparents often ate with us, especially on Sundays after church. They still held their forks backward—European style—though their ancestors had been in America for more than two hundred years. I looked upon this mannerism as terribly old-fashioned and tried to do the exact opposite. Interestingly, my children, after living and traveling in Europe, have reintroduced this old, and now trendy, eating method to our family.

Any frivolous behavior at the dinner table brought with it a reminder to "show respect for your food." In keeping with that attitude, singing at Mama's table was strictly forbidden, though I never knew why. It might have harkened back many generations to a time of scarcity when the family meal was a sacred and thankful occasion.

As I grew older, I found that the quaint customs my family observed were not commonly practiced by others. After attending my first church banquet, I couldn't wait to get home to tell what had happened.

"Granny," I said, "we sang at the table!"

She scoffed at the thought.

"All I have to say is, it must not be much of a church."

Living in a row house with one exposed brick side offered a unique urban pastime. When no one was around for a ball game, throwing a tennis ball against the side of the house was a pleasant diversion, but a terrible aggravation to those indoors.

One horribly embarrassing moment came from my fondness for this activity. During Sunday school, my teacher, Mrs. Ellis, tried to illustrate the point that God bestows talents on each of us. She said that our talents could be found in those activities that we enjoyed and performed especially well. She then asked each of us to describe something at which we excelled.

I could feel the sweat break out on my forehead. I did nothing well. Nothing worth mentioning.

Mary Beth spoke first. Without missing a beat, she smugly declared herself an excellent seamstress and pointed to the skirt she was wearing as proof. Well, sewing sure wasn't my talent. I had nearly flunked apron making, a necessary skill for young ladies looking to move beyond the seventh grade.

Mrs. Ellis, pleased with her response, complimented the skirt.

Sylvia spoke next. "I can play the piano," she announced. "Now I'm taking lessons on the church organ."

Mrs. Ellis smiled approvingly.

Gloria responded by showing the blue ribbon she had just won at ballet school.

My turn came next, and there was simply nothing to say. I finally blurted out, "I can throw a tennis ball against the house and catch it a hundred times in a row."

The class dissolved in laughter.

Mrs. Ellis ended their merriment by concluding that for some people talents are revealed later in life.

I clung to that hope.

Stunned by my failings, I began spending less time playing ball and more time reading. When I wanted solitude, I could always find it under the Lombardy poplar in the backyard or on the front porch glider. Sipping a glass of cherry Kool-Aid and reading a Captain Marvel comic was one of the purest pleasures of childhood. In those days when allowances were fifty cents a week and comics cost a mere dime, I would blow my entire allowance on these treasures without a moment of guilt.

At four o'clock each afternoon, kids put aside everything, raced to the living room, and gathered around the radio. The daily serials featuring Captain Midnight and Jack Armstrong, the All-American Boy, whisked me and my friends into the world of high adventure where goodness and justice prevailed. I remember succumbing to one of Captain Midnight's "special offers." By sending in an Ovaltine label, plus 25 cents, I would receive a "genuine brass decoder ring" to decipher messages sent at the end of each broadcast. I couldn't resist. I felt like the good captain duped me when the ring turned my finger green, causing my mother to reprimand me for wasting half my allowance on something so worthless.

Life was not all fun and games; there were chores, the most time-consuming occurring on laundry day. My participation was limited to the summer months. Every Monday morning, Mama and I stripped the beds, emptied the clothes hamper, and hauled every washable in sight to the basement. Without admitting it, housewives competed to see who could get their clothes on the line the earliest, and I did all I could to see that Mama made a good showing.

Having first sorted the clothes into whites and darks, we filled the washing machine tub with hot water and a cup of Oxydol soap. After about ten to fifteen minutes of washing, I'd fish the wet clothes from the tub with a short pole and process each piece through the mangles atop the machine. This required a careful eye. Overloading could jam the roller or twist an item into a Gordian knot. For those, like myself, who wanted to hurry the process, there were tales of women who broke fingers or lost chunks of hair by carelessly feeding the mangle.

In the final stages, each item passed through a double rinse in the cast-iron laundry tubs—one with a dab of bluing to whiten sheets, shirts, and underwear. Shirts and blouses paused in a starch solution cooked to the consistency of watered-down paste. Together, Mama and I heaved the wet clothing into the wicker laundry basket, lugged it upstairs, and hung it in the backyard.

Unwritten rules governed the drying process, too. Items had to be grouped on the clothesline by size and kind. To do otherwise marked you as an inept laundress. Not wanting to bring shame on the family, I carefully strung my lines and propped them in place with long bamboo poles.

Folding the dried clothes that afternoon gave Mama great satisfaction. She would invariably sniff the sheets or towels and say, "Ummm . . . the clothes smell so good when they're hung outside to dry, don't they?"

I was glad she got some consolation from all that work, because I was convinced that the clothes, once indoors, would smell like the rest of us in a matter of hours. This fallacy associated with air-dried clothing kept Mama from investing in a dryer for many years.

Ironing started early on Tuesday morning. Sheets, handkerchiefs, shirts, blouses, work clothes, and aprons were dampened with the sprinkler bottle, rolled, and stacked for pressing. For a while, Mama hired Agnes, an elderly black woman, to do the ironing. Agnes, a snuff user, was also a great storyteller. I was fascinated by both and looked forward to her arrival each week. Not only could Agnes weave a compelling tale, she had the unique ability to spit across the ironing board into the laundry tubs without missing a stroke or staining a garment.

In addition to washing laundry in the basement, Mama was frequently downstairs "fixing hair," as she called it, for a friend, neighbor, or relative. She achieved the well-set look, using a combination of metal wave clips and neat rows of pin curls. Without the benefit of hair spray, the skill of a beautician was in achieving a tight curl that would hold for a week. Elderly women emerged from our cellar with blue-tinted curls and pompadours much in vogue at the time.

Between appointments, Mama would be in the kitchen, whipping up a cake from scratch, baking cookies, or putting together a tasty meat loaf. Our basement customers were more like guests, often sharing a meal with us, after which Daddy would drive them home. Widows paid

Mama a reduced rate, while someone with a sick or unemployed husband was told to "pay when you can." By the time customers were treated to food, travel, and credit, I doubt that Mama made the cost of the shampoo she used.

An exciting innovation in hairdressing came with the introduction of the cold wave. Mama was enough of a businesswoman to understand that this was the "wave of the future." She attended classes to acquire the skills needed for this new chemical approach to curling hair that would replace the heated clamps then in use.

With the new curling technique came increased prices. Cold waves cost $15 to $30 at a time when finger waves were less than $2 and permanent waves, $10. Unfortunately, the cold wave had a nauseating smell—a displeasure that women endured for the sake of curly hair.

Much to Mama's delight, I was blessed with naturally curly hair, after having been nearly bald for the first year of my life. I had once worn long banana curls like the child actress Shirley Temple, the idol of every little girl in the thirties and forties. Even so, Mama convinced me to try the new cold wave. To my dismay, I was left with a blonde Afro look at a time when screen stars Rita Hayworth and Betty Grable were sporting long, loose tresses. I was mortified. Ruined for life, I thought. Mama tried to comfort me with assurances that my hair would grow out and that I would return to normal. After that, I never got another permanent, resisting even the more delicate body perms later developed.

When my hair grew out—long, lovely, and wavy—Mama urged me to enter a hair contest conducted by a Washington radio station. I would rather have had my head shaved than to participate in such a travesty. But Mama persisted. Contestants, all older than I, paraded around the studio like show horses waiting to be called to the winner's circle. I came in second. That suited me fine but disappointed Mama, who thought the first-place winner was too chummy with the judges.

Years later, after I had married and left home, Mama did two things that surprised me. She took piano lessons. (She couldn't bear having the $500 piano sit there unused.) And despite her tendency to avoid either economic or personal risk, she bought the beauty shop in which she had then worked for years and later purchased another.

For the first time in her life, Mama had an income, not just from her own efforts, but from the efforts of those she employed. She kept a close eye on the business and worked side by side with her employees, expecting as much from them as she did from herself. Her hard work and attention to detail paid off. Mama became a stock market investor and watched her savings soar during the bull market of the eighties. Having made the transition from the working class to the investing class, she became increasingly attracted to Republican candidates and, despite my protests, voted for Ronald Reagan.

In the forties, beneath the veneer of normalcy in our neighborhood was a hard reality that could not be ignored: our nation was at war with the Germans and the Japanese. We accepted the inconveniences and made the necessary adjustments to support the effort. President Roosevelt described the war as, "One front and one battle where everyone in the United States—every man, woman, and child—is in action." It was everybody's war, and we all took part as FDR told us we should.

Mama left her daytime hairdressing and went to work as a file clerk for the Navy Department—though she still kept a few basement customers in the evenings and on weekends. Daddy, too old for the draft, took on several jobs in addition to serving as a volunteer air raid warden for our block. During the practice drills, he would don his white helmet and patrol the streets armed only with the nightstick that was standard civilian defense attire. His mission was to see that everyone remained indoors with lights extinguished and blackout shades secured—the point being that in the days before precision bombing a darkened city made it more difficult for the enemy to see its targets.

Our family also looked out for our next-door neighbor, whose husband was serving in Europe. In her front window hung a small banner with a blue star, indicating that a member of the household was on active duty. Several of my teenage cousins marched off to war . . . one didn't come back. When that happened, the star on my great-aunt's banner changed. She became a "Gold Star" mother.

Wartime also brought shortages and rationing that limited sugar, coffee, meat, butter, cheese, tires, and gasoline. Daddy planted a victory garden that kept our family and neighbors supplied with fresh vegetables each summer. "Can all you can" was the wartime slogan, and we did. Mama lined our basement shelves with jars of tomatoes, green beans, beets, sauerkraut, pickles, and chowchow—enough to see us through another Thirty Years War.

Meatless Tuesdays became a regular part of our wartime menus. We made do with three gallons of gas per week, unless Daddy was able to trade some sugar stamps for fuel stamps. When we did travel, we did so at the victory speed of 35 m.p.h. to save fuel. Butter was replaced with the new oleomargarine that, at the time, looked and tasted much like lard. For those who found it disgusting to spread on toast, the ugly lump came with a packet of yellow coloring to improve its appearance.

Mostly, I missed sleeping on real cotton sheets. In a fervor of patriotism, my mother made sheets from feed sacks. Six of these bags, split along the side, bleached to remove the printing, and sewn together produced a sturdy but scratchy bed covering. When I complained, Mama let me know that it was a small sacrifice to make, knowing that our soldiers were sleeping in foxholes and on cots.

One of the happy occasions following the end of the war was seeing Mama pull out the old percale sheets she had been saving. Those indestructible feed sack sheets survived the war and went on for decades to serve as camping gear, drop cloths, and dust rags.

Kids did their part on the home front, too. I collected old newspapers that I sold to the scrap yard for 50 cents a hundred pounds; magazines fetched 75 cents. I'm not sure just how all this scrap paper was recycled in the interest of the war effort. Still, my sales provided me with ample money for comic books and enough to invest in some $18.87 war bonds that held the promise of a $25.00 repayment a decade later.

At my grade school, Benjamin G. Orr Elementary, students were fingerprinted for identification purposes as we prepared for the possibility of an air attack. Regular air raid drills—much like tornado drills—required students to sit along hallway walls, heads down, until the "all-clear" signal sounded. Of course, the nation's capital was never bombed, but each Saturday at the theater we saw newsreels of air battles and bombings on the other side of the world. Our parents and teachers soothed our fears by reminding us that we were "an ocean away" from any battlefield and, thus, insulated from such horrors.

Even so, we kept our spirits high, singing songs about the heroism of Pvt. Roger Young, the infantryman who "fought and died for the men he marched among." Traditional baseball cards were replaced by ones featuring war heroes and military equipment. My favorite "flip card" featured the handsome, young Capt. Colin Kelly, who died when his B-17 went down during one of the first bombing missions following Pearl Harbor.

My most creative defense project was organizing the kids into an army prepared to defend the neighborhood in the event the Japanese should reach the shores of the Anacostia River and march on S Street. Like the patriots of old, we each brought our own arms, which in our case consisted of toy rifles or wood poles. I supplied them with insignias from my prized collection in hopes of instilling some military spirit in the ranks. They were a frustrating bunch to command, inept at following orders, marching in step, or even showing up on time.

I finally decided I would have to go it alone. If the war would last just seven more years, I could join the women's Marine Corps. In the meanwhile, I would go back to collecting scrap paper and expanding my insignia collection.

I never got over the patriotism that we felt during those years of uncertainty and sacrifice. We were at our best as a people, confident of our national purpose. Tom Brokaw would later capture the spirit of the era. In his book *The Greatest Generation,* he recalled the civic virtues—duty, honor, and citizenship—that stirred our nation during freedom's darkest hours. Perhaps the poet Carl Sandburg described the time best. He said, "Nothing like us ever was." He was right. With each generation, we prove it anew.

Besides the influence of home, community, and wartime, there was another important force influencing the S Street kids of the forties—the public schools. My grade school was several blocks away from home and only big enough to hold one class each of kindergarten through sixth-grade students. According to the engraved stone over the front door, it was built in 1906, which accounted for it having no "unnecessary" embellishments, such as a gymnasium, cafeteria, library, or auditorium.

Its large front hallway and wide staircase served as a makeshift assembly area with students sitting on the floor and stairs for special programs. The playground, too, was primitive by today's standards, its most memorable feature being its cinder-covered surface. During those grade-school years, my knees were always stone-pocked or scabbed from scrapes acquired in a robust game of kickball or a fall from the monkey bars.

With so many school and neighborhood windows within range, playing baseball in the schoolyard was out of the question. The boys contented themselves with swapping "flip cards" or engaging in a game of mumblety-peg with their pocketknives. No one questioned the boys having a "lethal weapon" in school, and I can't recall anyone using a knife in a threatening manner.

Girls engaged in more delicate pastimes. They lined up to either jump rope or play hopscotch along the chalk squares drawn onto the one small patch of available concrete. I avoided those genteel activities in favor of playing kickball with the boys on those occasions when, out of desperation, they were willing to admit a girl to the team.

Playground activities were not always fair or even kind. Some degenerated into fistfighting, name-calling, and other cruelties that children often unleash on each other. I was stunned one day watching kids torment Rosalind, a new girl in our school, pelting her with bitter, hateful words, testing their ability to hurl ethnic slurs. Caught up in the frenzy of the moment, I joined the crowd. That is, until poor Rosalind lifted her downcast eyes and looked directly at me.

Startled by the hurt in those young eyes and the pain that I felt in the pit of my stomach, I ran off quickly, vowing to myself that I would never be a part of anything like that again. Rosalind moved shortly thereafter, so I never had the chance to make amends. But I remember her eyes . . . and I remember how I felt.

The old playground chant, "Sticks and stones can break my bones, but words can never hurt me," was simply not true. I was young, but I was beginning to learn that words, like blunt instruments, were powerful tools for good or for harm.

Fortunately, there was more camaraderie than cruelty on the playground. One such time was our May Day observance when we frolicked around the flagpole to mark the arrival of spring. This gala event was well attended by mothers who had spent hours baking cookies and creating long, ribbon-bedecked dresses with matching headpieces and nosegays for their daughters. Those with sons got by with a sash and a starched white shirt. My mother was one of the few women in our neighborhood who held a job, so her participation took a little more effort. However, she was a great seamstress and cook and always did her part when called upon.

At least the parents attending our activities got to use the big front doors of the school, which were otherwise off-limits. Students had to enter through one of the two "trap doors" located to the side of the front steps. Each morning at nine o'clock the boys lined up in front of one portal and the girls in front of the other, awaiting the entry bell.

Getting through the door required bending down slightly and stepping over a ledge designed much like the entry to a Chinese pagoda. Once inside, it took some care to maneuver down the creaky wooden stairway, built without risers. Although this exercise was potentially dangerous, no one was ever injured.

Our morning routine took us past the dingy boiler room where the janitor could often be seen stoking the coal-burning furnace that kept the old building quite cozy. I never figured out why we performed this daily parade down the basement steps and up another flight to our classrooms. But it did expedite our entry, since no one wanted to linger too long in the dark underground passageway.

Once we had reached our desks, the day began with a passage from the Bible, followed by the Lord's Prayer and the Pledge of Allegiance to the Flag. Nobody complained at what we called the Opening Exercises. There was a war going on, and we needed all the prayers and patriotism we could muster for our side.

Unfortunately, there came a time when even the classroom was uninviting to me. It happened during the third grade. I had "skipped" a half year of kindergarten after being delayed a semester in starting school because of a long bout with whooping cough. Later, a kindly second-grade teacher, thinking me too precocious for her classroom (or too pesky, I don't know which), "skipped" me again.

I could have done without the honor. This untimely promotion separated me from my teacher, the lovable Miss Johnson, and catapulted me into the hell pit across the hall in Miss Strayder's third-grade classroom.

I arrived there at midyear, not knowing anyone, and terrified by all I had heard. Miss Strayder fulfilled my every fear. Within weeks, she turned her wrath upon me, announcing before the entire class that she did not understand why I had been "skipped" instead of Mary Beth—a rival of mine who was under consideration at the time and to whom I would gladly have given my slot in third grade had I known.

I began showing signs of the stress created by the transfer. My hands would sweat so profusely that I had to place a handkerchief or a folded piece of paper under my writing hand when I did my assignments. Miss Strayder further added to the strain by standing over me, peering at my work. Without warning, she would lunge at my paper with her red pencil, making a huge X across the page.

"THERE'S NO MARGIN ON THIS PAGE!" she'd yell. "I DON'T WANT TO SEE ANOTHER PAPER WITHOUT A MARGIN!"

Her words ripped through me like a sharp knife.

I dared not ask what she meant. Obviously, I had missed out on some "secret" that everyone else knew. If I asked, it would only confirm that I should not be in third grade. Worse yet, I might be "put back" to second grade and my family humiliated by my failure.

I finally got up enough nerve to ask the boy next to me for advice.

"A margin? It's just an imaginary line," he said, and ran off to recess.

I ruled out asking my parents because I knew they wouldn't understand anything as complicated as an "imaginary line."

As the demand for margins continued, the red X's and the sweaty palms became more frequent. I started getting sick to my stomach on the way to school. Then the "sickness" started on Sunday evening in anticipation of Monday morning.

My parents became concerned. I eventually had to divulge my "margin" problem to them. And I was right. They didn't know what it was either. Nor did my aunt or next-door neighbor. Obviously, this was no big deal in the one-room schools they had attended.

Despite my pleadings, Mama stormed off to school to get to the bottom of the situation. It was horrifying to think of my dear mother having to go toe-to-toe with the evil Miss Strayder.

I would probably be expelled! My life ruined!

Surely, I was too young to be sent off to parochial school, where crusty nuns rapped students on the knuckles with a wooden ruler for poor performance—or so I was told. Worse yet, I might be sent to reform school.

I waited and worried.

As it turned out, Mama's visit to the school had a softening effect on Miss Strayder's attitude. She did a full turnaround, taking time privately to show me how to maintain both a left- and right-hand margin as I wrote.

Still, I could never warm up to her. I stumbled through the year only because I knew that upstairs in the fourth-grade room awaited Miss Simon. Her classroom was literally a greenhouse where tender plants, such as I, could blossom and grow. Her warm smile and cheery manner would ignite within me a love for books that would never be extinguished.

My confidence soared. By sixth grade I knew that I wanted to be a writer—a decision I kept to myself to avoid ridicule. I had already made the mistake of divulging my interests to my parents, who had dismissed writing as an uncertain pursuit with little hope of return.

Most of my girlfriends avoided this confrontation by simply going along with what was expected of them. On one occasion when we were questioned about what we wanted to be "when we grew up," the girls uniformly said, "I want to be a secretary" or "I want to be a teacher" or "I want to be a nurse"—though I remember one sheepishly admitting that she was thinking about being an artist.

I even toned back my aspirations, saying, "I'd like to be a newspaper reporter." That was safe, I figured, with Superman's sidekick, Lois Lane, having made this an acceptable vocation for women of the forties.

Good old Mr. Mackey, my sixth-grade teacher, encouraged my deviation. He picked me to do the writing for the bulletin board, assigning me the task of covering the "European Front" of the war. It required that I read the newspapers—the *Washington Star*, the *Times-Herald*, the *Daily News*—and summarize my findings with a weekly report to the class. I took the job seriously and learned the wartime vocabulary, including the names of battles, military leaders, equipment, and ranks, along with a good dose of European geography.

When President Franklin Roosevelt died in April 1945, Mr. Mackey picked me to write a "special report." I had seen FDR several times as he was whisked from Union Station through the streets of Washington to the White House, sometimes by open limousine. My parents spoke of him in reverential tones and huddled about the radio to catch every word of his "fireside chats." Roosevelt came into office the year I was born, and now, eleven years later, he was the only president I had ever known. I trusted our president with childlike confidence to keep our country safe. For the first time, I felt a deep emotional attachment to the task of writing, shedding a few tears as I searched my limited vocabulary to express my sadness.

With the arrival of VE Day the following month, Mr. Mackey asked me to write and deliver a speech at the school assembly to commemorate our victory in Europe.

"Why me?" I asked nervously.

"Why not? You'll do the best job."

I blushed. I had undoubtedly impressed him with my journalism to evoke such a fine compliment. Still, I fretted over the speech.

The next day the entire school assembled in the front hallway. As the time approached, I wound my way to the front, stepping around sprawling bodies and wondering if the kids would ever settle down enough to listen.

They were still wiggling and giggling as Mr. Mackey raised his arms signaling silence. I could hear my heart beating in my chest. I faced a group of restless kids lining the stairway and sitting cross-legged on the entry floor. It was my first audience!

I took a deep breath. Mr. Mackey had said to speak loudly and slowly. I began.

"The war is over," I said with all the enthusiasm an eleven-year-old could muster on the topic. (That wasn't entirely true, we still had the Japanese yet to beat.)

I paused—mostly for air.

Every kid in the room stopped twitching, and they all turned their eyes toward me, waiting for what would come next.

I couldn't believe what a commanding effect I had just had on them!

It would be years before I was taught the importance of an opening sentence in capturing an audience's attention.

I continued.

"There will be no more fighting in Europe. Our soldiers will be coming home, some of them your fathers and your brothers."

Someone, somewhere, began to clap. Others joined.

I had never received any direct applause.

It caught me off guard.

I was on a roll!

I left the script and began to improvise.

"We beat the Germans; now we will beat the Japanese," I announced with gusto.

More bravado; more applause.

It was a short speech, maybe two or three minutes, but it did more for my emerging ego than anything I had ever experienced.

Once again, I had sensed the power of words.

This time it felt good.

You might say that I had two mothers.

Or so it seemed.

Because Mama worked much of the time, my grandmother frequently took care of me.

Granny was not especially active. Her disdain for exercise or exertion, in any form, made her the perfect candidate for all sorts of ailments. Yet she was quite hearty, her only exercise being the miles she logged in a well-worn high-backed rocker. She hummed a lot—usually old hymns—as she swayed to and fro, day after day, mile after mile.

Granny never revealed her age, mainly because no one had ever told her exactly when she arrived. That left the rest of us to guess—and her to deny whatever number was tossed out.

"You don't know how old I am. I don't know myself," she would say trying to end the discussion.

Her age was a shifting number on which we never settled with any certainty. But even allowing for a margin of error, she lived to be at least ninety-three.

I've tried to determine what contributed to her longevity. Hymn humming, well . . . probably not, though it undoubtedly was soothing.

Diet?

Maybe.

At age forty-something, Granny learned that she had high blood pressure and should abstain from salt. After that, she never ate another potato chip or slice of ham.

Unlike my mother, a bountiful southern cook, Granny stayed out of the kitchen. Mealtime with her was not impressive. Shredded wheat biscuits softened with hot water started the day. Lunch was often no more than a fried egg, or a slice of scrapple, and corn cakes made of meal and water—no salt. Dinner might be a lamb chop and greens that had been cooking all day with a piece of fatback for flavor and, of course, more corn cakes. No dessert, except fruit or a few graham crackers washed down with tea. Cups and cups of tea accompanied by salt-free crackers.

Granny avoided drafty rooms. The faintest breeze brushing against an open window would send her scurrying for a seat elsewhere. To be on the safe side she wore a light sweater nearly all year round. In the winter, she maintained good health by avoiding crowded rooms. Overnight visits were postponed because "changing beds" would almost certainly bring on influenza, or at least a chest cold, the remedy for which was a good shellacking with Vicks salve. If that failed, a stiff shot of whiskey (kept well hidden for such occasions), mixed with sugar and water, produced a cure, or at least made the suffering more tolerable. (Spirits were otherwise forbidden in my family, an absence that my grandfather often remedied by a stop at the neighborhood pub.)

Next to rocking and health care, Granny loved a Sunday afternoon ride in the country. For such occasions, my father lovingly polished the Merry Oldsmobile, bringing it to a high luster both on the outside and under the hood. He whisked the upholstery for any sign of lint. After much preparation, my grandmother would emerge from her bedroom looking for all the world like a grande dame on an outing along the Champs Elysées. On these occasions, she always wore her Sunday best set off with a two-strand pearl necklace from Palais Royale department store, white cotton gloves, a well-flowered hat with a veil, and a splash of perfume. The ubiquitous laced corset resembled plate armor and gave her a well-structured look from the waist down.

Despite the temperature, the car windows were cracked only enough to prevent the family from being overcome by heat—or the scent of perfume. My father, mother, and I sweltered, but we honored Granny's wishes, knowing that it was better to suffer some temporary discomfort than to bear the blame for causing whatever aches or pains might occur the following week. All these efforts must have had some salubrious effects, for I can never remember Granny being ill.

My attraction to words comes not from her but from my grandfather, a carpenter by trade. After a hard day on the job, he would arrive home on foot, wearing his porkpie cap and ankle-top shoes and with a copy of the *Washington Daily News* tucked under one arm. After supper, he would settle into his easy chair with a pack of Camel cigarettes and the tabloid-size newspaper.

By middle age, he had lost much of his hearing, so the radio had no appeal, and conversing with him meant shouting in abbreviated sentences. Upon finishing the paper, he would take out a pocketknife and sharpen a pencil to a fine point before tackling the crossword puzzle. When he offered to teach me the "ups and downs" of puzzle solving, I was elated and often spent hours with him until we had either completed the task or come as close as we could.

Granddaddy was a walker before it became a popular sport. For him it was a necessity. He never owned a car, and bus fare was scarce, especially before payday. When I walked with him, he would take my small hand and envelope it in his calloused fist. I felt completely safe.

If a funeral procession passed, he would pause respectfully, no matter how hurried we might be, or how cold it was, and stand with his cap against his chest in a show of respect for the departed. (Later I would see that same display of respect from farmers standing in their fields as Mel and Randy's cortege passed along the roads of Missouri.)

Probably of most value, Granddaddy Sullivan showed me how to use a hammer, a level, and a hand drill. He patiently taught me to measure, mark, and saw a board. I never had great occasion to use these skills, but knowing basic carpentry would later give me confidence in dealing with builders and repairmen.

My Irish grandfather couldn't resist a gathering of his coworkers at the local pub on payday and would occasionally come staggering along the sidewalk, winding his way home on foot. Fortunately, whether tipsy or sober, he was good-natured and soft-spoken.

Arriving home, he would slump into his easy chair and fall asleep, but not before my grandmother gave him a tongue-lashing for his waywardness. She added more guilt by rifling his pockets, removing the remainder of his pay before he awoke. The next day she would pounce on him for having lost his entire week's earnings.

Meanwhile, she had secured the hard-earned dollars in a small cloth bag with a drawstring that she kept securely pinned to the inside of her brassiere. No bank account. No sugar bowl. Just the safety of her ample bosom.

As a little girl, I can remember her giving me one of those well-protected bills for a birthday or other special occasion. The bills had a faint odor of sweat and were so tightly rolled that it was nearly impossible to flatten them out in a wallet. I would run a hot iron over my new dollar and spend it quickly. As far as I know, Granddaddy never figured out the scam. After all, she kept food on the table and paid the rent, a skill that he happily attributed to her good management.

But the "Bosom Bank" could not cover those times when construction work was down and layoffs inevitable. My grandparents had no worker benefits, health insurance, or savings account to prop them up during such times. Unwilling to bear the stigma of government relief, they would pick up their few possessions and move to cheaper quarters, often with no more than two rooms and a common bath.

Sharing a bathroom with another family was not as inconvenient for them as it might seem. My grandparents had grown up in an era when bathing was a weekly ritual reserved for Saturday night. They would never change that routine. I remember Granny's warning, "It's not good for you to take a bath so often. It will dry out your skin and could bring on a chest cold." Many of her health and financial precautions came from having endured flu epidemics, the Great Depression, and other deprivations—hardships that I could not possibly relate to generations later.

My grandparents had grown up in White Oak, Virginia, between King George and Fredericksburg. Granny, a member of the Armstrong clan, was one of seven children whose roots went back to the eighteenth-century Scotch-Irish settlement in America. She would occasionally use an old Scottish word seldom heard today. The word *gumption,* for instance. Gumption was a much-desired trait, and no good would come of your life without it. Robert Pirsig would later call gumption "psychic gasoline." He wrote, "A person filled with gumption doesn't . . . stew about things. He's at the front of the train . . . watching to see what's up the track and meeting it when it comes."

The Scotch-Irish in America did just that. Those early settlers were a hearty breed who tamed the frontier and contributed a large part to what we call the American spirit. They were typically clannish, independent, superstitious, deeply religious, and strong-willed. But most important, they were adaptive—a necessary trait for enduring the hardships of pioneer life. Those hearty survivalists had the stamina to stave off disease and starvation and go eye to eye with the American Indians. When tribesmen came after them with tomahawks, the Scotch-Irish retaliated in kind and displaced a few scalps themselves. Happily, they made their peace with the Native Americans and produced some descendants, giving me the opportunity to be a card-carrying member of the Patawomeck Indian tribe.

Although no violence was evident in the family in my day, Granny could still carry a grudge with the best. She remembered clearly that Mrs. Newton had failed to speak to her at the grocery store one day twenty years earlier. Her superstitions were real, too, having been implanted years ago, and no scientific evidence to the contrary could alter them. As a child, I can remember her stern admonitions.

"Don't rock that chair with no one in it," she'd caution.

"Why not?" I would ask tauntingly. "What's wrong with rocking a chair?"

"Just don't you do it. You never know what might happen."

She never said exactly. It was almost as though the curse was too horrible to reveal. I suspect it had something to do with death, but she never said for sure.

Any statement of future intent was always subject to divine approval, as in "I'm going to visit my sister next week, God willing." She also declared thunderstorms to be the "Lord's work," and an occasion to be revered. My cousins and I had to refrain from rowdy games or loud talking and remain respectfully solemn during such times. Ill omens also surrounded Friday, and nothing of importance was commenced on such an inauspicious day.

Sunday, too, had its special requirements. A needle and thread were never used on the Lord's Day, even if a button fell from the dress you were about to wear to church. The garment was changed and the repair work delayed until the next day.

Responsibility had befallen my grandmother in her preteen years. Her own mother, having become increasingly ill, was taken to town by horse and buggy to see a doctor. She returned home, had a cup of coffee, and died. Granny was left with the care of the younger children while her father, a tenant farmer, and the boys worked the fields. One of her vivid recollections was of fleeing the house to get away from the overwhelming task only to run into an apparition of her mother, standing in the doorway and insisting that she return. It was enough of a scare to keep her on the job for a few more years.

I realize now that it was not Granny's intention to teach me error. It was just that her mind brimmed with misinformation gleaned over the years and guarded tenaciously against anything to the contrary. Because she had only a few years of schooling and little exposure to the outside world, opportunity had passed her by just as it had so many women of her era. She never held a job, owned a home, or voted; never drove a car or traveled by train or airplane; never visited a museum or art gallery or attended a play; and never wrote a check.

I remember when I first discovered the secret that crippled her life. The summer that I was ten years old, my mother began working in the government in Washington D.C. It was the patriotic thing to do. World

War II was in full sway. It became my responsibility to accompany my grandmother to the grocery store.

Since Granny didn't drive, we walked the six blocks to the Acme Grocery each week. I still remember how much I disliked that task. But one day as we arrived at the store, I looked down the street and saw a man on a ladder painting letters on a plate-glass window. The outline read, "Public Library Now Open."

I was so excited!

I said, "Granny, is it all right if I go to the new library while you shop? I'll be right there to help with the grocery bags when you get through."

She reluctantly agreed. For the next half hour, I was in heaven surrounded by all those wonderful books—more books than I had ever seen in my life. I always felt like a misfit in a family that valued work more than words. There were no books in my home, not even a dictionary, unless you counted the musty set of Colliers Encyclopedias that filled a small bookshelf in the living room.

In a transcendent state, surrounded by hundreds of books, I forgot all about Granny and the groceries. A pecking on the windowpane jarred me back to my real world.

I looked up. There was my grandmother making beckoning motions for me to come help her with the groceries.

I quickly checked out three books, and we juggled books and bags all the way home. I spent the next week—every chance I got—with my newfound treasures. It was a hot, humid summer, before the days of air-conditioning, so I spent much of the time on the front porch of our row house. Sitting in the squeaky glider with a flyswatter and a glass of Kool-Aid nearby, I was in another world.

By the next week, I had finished my reading and was looking forward to the grocery-shopping trip and the chance to acquire more books.

As time went on, however, it troubled me that my grandmother showed no interest in the books that I found so compelling.

One day I said, "Granny, I wish you would read this book."

She said no, she wasn't interested.

I said, "But just read this part here, it is so good."

It was then that she told me something I couldn't believe.

She said, "I can't read."

I said, "What do you mean, you can't read? *Everybody* can read!"

She explained that, after her mother's death, there was never time for school or books. Work and daily survival mattered most. Time was wasted that did not put food on the table or hay in the barn.

In my youthful exuberance I said, "I'll teach you! What do you want to read?"

She said she had always wanted to read the Bible. Frankly, at the time, that was not my book of choice. But we read the Bible that summer, and I suspect it did me more good than it did her.

Later I joined the Dollar-a-Month Book Club and started getting pulp novels through the mail. After just one Frank Yerby southern romance, Granny was hooked on reading.

Even with her new skills, it was hard for her to accept information that didn't fit into her worldview. In 1969, when the United States first landed a man on the moon, we all sat glued to the television screen awed by the miracle in space.

Granny said nothing. She just kept rocking, one arm pressed across her waist and the other perched on it supporting her chin.

"Well, what do you think, Granny?" I asked.

"Nothing to it," she said disgustedly.

"What do you mean? That man is walking on the moon right now."

"No, he's not," she declared. "You can't walk on the moon. It's a bunch of nonsense and you believe it."

With that instant analysis, she left the room. We never got Granny to believe in moon walking or modern science, or anything that was at odds with the King James Version of the Bible. It was all too bewildering.

My memories are not so much of the misinformation she passed on as of her clutching me in her arms when I ran indoors, crying from some playtime wound.

"Let me hold you until the hurt goes away," she would say, pulling me into her lap as she continued rocking.

Although she's been gone for more than twenty-five years, I still think of her at strange times—when I put on perfume, when there's a thunderstorm, when I repair a hem on Sunday morning, or when I overindulge in potato chips.

But most often, I think of her when I make a pot of fresh tea and wish she were here to enjoy it with me . . . or to hold me, to help the hurt go away.

When asked who had the most profound effect on my life, I realized it was not any single person, but groups of people—my family, my community, my church. Growing up Baptist, particularly Southern Baptist in the forties and fifties, was life-shaping—it was intended to be.

When I first met Mel at church, when we were both fifteen, there was a sea of difference in our upbringing and families. Mine was urban, his rural. His parents were college educated; neither of mine had a high school diploma. His family loved politics; mine was indifferent to the political world.

But one area of similarity cemented our relationship and defined our values. We had both grown up Baptist. That meant that for all our lives we had attended Sunday school and church each Sunday morning, as well as Training Union and church each Sunday evening, prayer meeting on Wednesday, choir practice on Thursday, church socials, and carry-in dinners. It was just part of being Baptist on the East Coast, in the South, or in the Midwest.

Understanding Southern Baptists—or even being one—required a degree of tolerance and good humor. We were by nature a free-spirited people, not given to a lot of harmony among ourselves. Mel used to say that everything he knew about politics he learned in the monthly business meetings of a Baptist church. It was an admission that the pure democracy then practiced within the church was often unruly and unpredictable.

Baptists have no difficulty believing the story about what happened when the minister became ill and the board of deacons met to determine what should be done. After much discussion, they wrote him a note. "Dear Pastor, Upon hearing of your illness, we voted to pray for your recovery. The motion passed 9 to 3."

One Baptist specialty was the two-week spring and fall revival meetings. For the youth, it was the highlight of the social season. New love blossomed on the back pew and during the walk home after the service.

Revival meetings offered an acceptable reason to be out with your sweetie every night, though cautious families might not otherwise allow such frequency. How could parents resist a teenager pleading, "You don't want me to go to church tonight? Why not?" It was "spiritual blackmail" that left a parent speechless and ultimately agreeable.

The attraction of revival meetings was due in part to boredom in the days before television and the internet. There were not many entertainment choices in our neighborhood. Of course, you could spend the evening on the front-porch glider, talking with the next-door neighbor sitting in his.

These discussions were never very deep: the condition of your lawn, car, or rose bushes; the rising price of eggs, bus fare, or gasoline; or commentary on the president's latest speech. When the conversation, or the mosquitoes, became too unbearable, you could always go indoors and close out the evening with a radio broadcast of *Amos 'n' Andy, Fibber McGee and Molly, The Green Hornet, One Man's Family,* or the *Hit Parade.*

Watering the yard was a popular evening pastime, too, as was cutting the grass with the push mower, or crocheting doilies and handkerchief edges. For a real treat, we would take a ride in the car—just drive around for a half hour and end up at High's Ice Cream counter.

I remember that for several summers I was assigned the chore of removing the Japanese beetles from the rose bushes before they turned the leaves into lace. These pesky insects were thick enough that I could fill a quart jar with them each evening. I handled so many beetles that I can make a perfect anatomical drawing of one from memory.

Faced with these alternatives, it is easy to see how a revival meeting could add a spark of excitement to life. These biannual events featured a visiting minister, most often imported from Texas, where Baptists were plentiful and doctrine unblemished.

Some were flashy dressers, decked out in white suits and white suede shoes. "Solomon in all his glory was not arrayed as one of these." They invariably had a compelling story of their conversion from the "paths of sin" to servants of God. Their spiritual journey was related each night with great emotion and in vivid and sometimes gross detail.

These modern-day troubadours were splendid performers, prancing about the platform, waving their arms, moving their audience from tears to laughter at their leisure. Their unconventional behavior had its appeal, as did the loud, foot-stomping music that revved the audience for the main event much like a warmup band does at a rock concert.

Some of these visiting evangelists were sincere proclaimers of the faith, others mere Bible-thumping showmen. We took 'em as they came, figuring if they could quote Scripture accurately they weren't likely to do much harm to the flock. They gave us our money's worth and saved a few souls for good measure.

Two-week revivals are now outdated. Today's new breed of religious showmen is working in the more lucrative vineyards to be found in televangelism. Even so, I miss those old-time rascals.

Fortunately, as a counterbalance there were people like Mrs. Redman—one of the stalwart members of the church that I admired most. Each summer she taught handicrafts at Vacation Bible School—another two-week event that has diminished over time.

If there is a museum of Baptist memorabilia, I hope these innovative art objects are included. My earliest creation was a necklace strung from dried cantaloupe seeds. There were plaques shaped like a rooster and covered with gilded macaroni. We did the wildest things with oatmeal boxes, plastic Clorox containers, and popsicle sticks. All the while, we belted out choruses of *I've Got the Joy, Joy, Joy, Joy Down in My Heart*. Mama, bless her, found a place to display my art and even boasted of my handiwork to friends.

But Mrs. Redman's grandest contribution to youth came from the Bible stories she told using a flannel board to stick her cutout characters onto before the days of Velcro.

We loved her dearly, though there was little appealing about her personal appearance. She was an ample woman, with gold-rimmed teeth and a hairdo of tight sausage curls, who encased her body in a corset that gave an unusual tilt to her torso.

I was fascinated more by her creativity than by her looks. I watched Mrs. Redman closely, observing every nuance of her storytelling and flannel graph skills. Some day I wanted to tell spellbinding stories like that. But, first, I had to learn what was in the Bible.

I saved my money and bought a thick, zippered, red-letter Bible with my name etched in gold leaf in the lower corner. It became my fondest possession. I began to read my new Bible every night, underlining and memorizing the beautiful words of the King James Version that I would find meaningful for the rest of my life.

One New Year's Eve I had a chance to test what I had been learning. It was customary to have what was called a Watch Night Service, the idea being that one "watched" the New Year unfold at church among the faithful rather than engage in some "sinful revelry" elsewhere.

One of the highlights of the long evening was the Bible bee, which was much like the old spelling bee but with questions to the participants from the Scriptures. Each Sunday school class put up a contestant. Year after year the winner was Miss Farris, a middle-aged seminary graduate with a wide knowledge of Bible trivia. I was selected from my class, only to find that as a teenager I was the youngest participant.

That evening, the questioning proceeded down the row until there were only two contestants remaining, Miss Farris and me. We entered the final round neck and neck. The last question to her was, "What words of warning were written on King Nebuchadnezzar's wall and what did they mean?"

Well, Miss Farris knew the meaning, "Thou art weighed in the balances and found wanting." But she could not come up with the cryptic words. Time ran out and the question passed to me.

Frankly, I don't think a person in that room knew the answer. It was a tough question designed to weed out one, or both, of us and to get on with the refreshments.

"Jean, do you by any chance know the answer? If not, the game is over," the quizmaster declared, willing to settle for a tie.

"I think so," I said, causing a stir of surprise in the room. "I can spell it, but I'm not sure I can pronounce it."

"Well, give it a try," he said.

"Mene, mene, tekel, upharsim," I replied, stumbling through the mysterious words of a bygone era.

"That's close enough!" the questioner said excitedly. "Jean Carpenter is this year's winner!"

I won some little prize—a book, I think.

Not wanting to press my luck, I never competed again.

However, my recognition that evening led to an opportunity I hadn't anticipated. When Youth Week rolled around, I was asked to teach the Steadfast Sunday School Class on Palm Sunday morning. This class of adult women was taught by Mrs. Elmore, a wizened little lady with a squeaky voice and the biggest Bible I had ever seen. Her classroom was decorated like a Victorian parlor and enhanced with fresh flowers and reproductions of famous paintings. She had taught Sunday school for fifty years, and to stand in her "pulpit" was no easy task.

When I walked into class on my morning to teach, the women—including my mother—were seated in neat rows all bedecked in flowered hats, veils, and white cotton gloves. Mama beamed with pride. I could see her whispering "That's . . . my . . . daughter" to the lady next to her.

I had prepared for this moment for the last two weeks, reading commentaries and concordances, gathering far more information than I'd ever need for the thirty minutes allocated to me. I had rehearsed to the point of memorization.

However, in my overprepared state, I stumbled, making an embarrassing slip of the tongue. To show the extent of my research, I went into some depth describing the clothing of the religious leaders of the biblical era. Of particular interest was a small leather box attached to the forehead of a priest. It contained bits of Scripture that served as a reminder to keep the word of the Lord ever before him. The device was called a *phylactery*.

In relating this bit of trivia, the words that came from my mouth were, "The priests of the day wore *prophylactics* on their heads."

As soon as I said it, I prayed that the floor would open and swallow me. There was no going back, no explanation that worked. So I just kept forging ahead. No one winced, but behind a few veils I detected a smile as some in the audience conjured up a picture of just what a priest with a condom on his head might look like. It was enough of an embarrassment to take me out of the Bible teaching business for a while.

In the stress of the situation, I was able to deliver my entire half hour of material in ten minutes. After heaping profuse praise upon me, dear Mrs. Elmore took over the podium and spoke extemporaneously for the reminder of the time. It was a feat I admired and longed to duplicate.

Mrs. Elmore was good, the revivalists were entertaining, Miss Farris was well versed, but the real fascination for us home folks was the returning missionaries. Before the days of easy travel, our worldview came from *National Geographic* and missionaries on furlough. They always started out by saying "Hello" in Swahili or some strange language and then worked in the Lord's Prayer or John 3:16. They wore the garb of the country in which they served and displayed a number of fascinating trinkets. They always had slides showing themselves traipsing through jungles or visiting a leper colony in the outback. It was all mysterious and adventurous. Without a doubt, they were the heroes, and our church supported them enthusiastically.

Looking back on those years, I never regret having grown up Baptist. It was a great impediment to wrongdoing, a source of lasting strength, and a chance to develop a social conscience. I am saddened that so much of what was good about that experience has slipped away during the battles for power within the structure of the Southern Baptist Convention today.

When I think of the local church that meant so much in my formative years, I recall a line in the old pop tune "It Had to Be You." One of the lines goes like this: "With all her faults . . . I love her still."

The Early Years

My mother was a hairdresser; my father, a plumber. I was lavished with all the attention and restrained by all the safeguards that come with being an only child. Mama bemoaned the fact that I was not the girl she dreamed of teaching to sew, cook, and play with dolls. She was stuck with a "tomboy"— competitive and boisterous.

I was a preschooler when my family moved to S Street S.E. in Washington, D.C. The sign on the property read, "New FHA Homes for Sale—$5,990. No Money Down. Government Guaranteed Loans." These easy-to-acquire homes were designed for families like my own—all first-time homeowners in search of the American Dream.

You might say that I had two mothers. Or so it seemed. Mama worked much of the time, so my grandmother Lucy Armstrong Sullivan frequently took care of me. Because Granny had only a few years of schooling and little exposure to the outside world, opportunity had passed her by just as it had so many women of her era.

Besides the influence of home, community, and wartime, there was another important force that shaped the S Street kids of the forties—the public schools. Here I am wearing my first long dress, an outfit assembled by my mother for our school's annual May Day frolic around the flagpole.

My first introduction to horseback riding came while posing for a street photographer that roamed the neighborhoods of Washington. But on Sunday afternoons my parents took me to the roadside park where for only a nickel I could get an escorted pony ride around the track.

The three most important things in Daddy's life: Mama, me—and his Merry Oldsmobile. He kept the car shiny on the outside, immaculate under the hood, and spotless on the inside.

I wore long banana curls like the child actress Shirley Temple, the idol of every little girl in the thirties and forties.

Jean and Mel

Mel and I met at a church youth group when we were both fifteen years old. After that, he walked me home from school each day. We often sat on my front steps or the porch to talk or study.

In June 1951, we graduated from Anacostia High School in Washington, D.C. Mel and I had sat next to each other in classes throughout high school. With my name being Carpenter and his Carnahan, there was no one to come between us in the alphabetical seating.

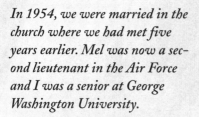

In 1954, we were married in the church where we had met five years earlier. Mel was now a second lieutenant in the Air Force and I was a senior at George Washington University.

Five

Magnificent Dreams
and Noble Plans

Life is either a daring adventure or nothing.

—Helen Keller

I tried to size him up as we sat parked in his '48 Plymouth outside my house. His hair was perfectly combed and smelled of the grooming lotion that held his blond pompadour in place. He wore razor-creased slacks, a crisp white shirt, and highly polished wing-tips that made him look like any other high school boy on a date during the late 1940s.

And I could have been any other postwar teenager with my chic scoop-necked blouse well anchored inside a sweeping ballerina-style skirt that barely cleared the top of my bobby socks and saddle oxfords.

My date, fifteen-year-old Mel Carnahan, was new in Washington. He had arrived from Missouri along with his parents some weeks earlier. His father, a rural school superintendent, had just been elected to Congress during a time when Harry Truman, another Missourian, would be leading the nation.

Just a week earlier, Mel had walked me home after we met at a church youth gathering. So this evening at a movie could be considered a first date, or a second, depending on how you counted it. That was important to know. It made a difference in the forties.

A kiss was reserved for the second date. A "nice girl" would never consent to such a thing any earlier.

As he reached out to touch my hand, my heart raced!

Does he expect a kiss?

Surely not.

After all, there are rules for first dates.

He must understand that, even though he's from way out in Missouri.

Besides that, I hardly know this lanky fifteen-year-old boy sitting beside me in the car. He could be twenty, or even twenty-five, from the way he acts.

He's so . . . so grown up. Obviously, he's counting this as our second date. I know he is. He's going to kiss me!

I would try a diversion.

"What are you going to do when you grow up," I asked nervously, interrupting the moment.

Still, he kissed me briefly before replying.

"I want to run for Congress. But I've never told anybody that before."

"Then why tell me?" I gasped, caught off guard by the boldness of the kiss and his declaration for office almost in the same breath.

"I thought you ought to know . . . because there's something else I want to do first."

"Really, what's that?"

"Get married," he responded coolly.

"Got anybody in mind?"

"Yeah . . . you."

"Me?" I laughed.

Was this a proposal? A declaration of some kind? This guy has more of a sense of humor than I thought.

"Come on," I said, reaching for the door handle. "Let's go in the house and watch the *Ed Sullivan Show*. My mother made some chocolate chip cookies today."

We dated from then on, throughout high school and college, but he never proposed again. After that, we just assumed that some day we'd get married.

Our budding teenage romance did not go unnoticed at the high school. Our principal, Mrs. Corkrey, was a crusty authoritarian given to playing favorites when it suited her purposes. Having several congressional kids in her school was a source of pride to her in what was otherwise a student body from local, middle-income families. She took a particular liking to Mel, calling him to the office to urge his participation in various student activities. She was also quick to inquire about "the new girlfriend," as though she had some screening rights. I had attended the school far longer than Mel but had never before appeared on her radar screen. But then she began speaking to me in the halls. I had no desire to be chummy with Mrs. Corkrey and teased Mel about being the "teacher's pet," or in this case the principal's.

Nonetheless, when it came time to select members to the National Honor Society, much to my surprise, I appeared among the chosen.

"I've been discovered," I joked to Mel.

"What do you mean? You've got great grades. Why not?"

"Well, I'm a little short on extracurricular activities," I said, having focused most of my time on our church youth group. Knowing that the requirements for admission to the honor society were scholarship, leadership, character, and service, I was pleased at being included in such a select group.

"The key will look good on my charm bracelet, and the listing will be great for my college application," I said.

Ah, college. Now that would be a prickly point for both of us over the next few months. Mel was eyeing George Washington University, but his father wanted him to attend the Naval Academy or to go to Australia as an exchange student. I was eager for campus life and had been accepted at Maryland University. But just a month before the school year began, my mother pulled the plug on my plan. She had not been keen on my attending a four-year college in the first place.

"You need to get a business school education, Jean, so you can become a good secretary," she advised. "You can always get an office job if you know shorthand and typing." There was no malice in her intentions. She was preparing me for the world in which she grew up, and not the one in which I would be living and working.

To my parents, it wasn't so important whether you liked your job or not. Any honorable, steady work was worthy of your best. Both my parents had survived the Depression with menial, low-paying jobs. My father had found employment at St. Elizabeths Hospital, the federal mental institution. In the days before psychiatric drugs, it was his job to "work a gang of patients." This was the mental health therapy of the time that put patients to work doing farm chores—milking cows, feeding animals, cleaning barns, and planting crops. For Daddy, it was like being an "urban farmer," with hours that required him to get up at 4:30 a.m. each day.

He was well acquainted with the routine. He had lost his mother early in life, and later a widow took him in after his family home burned. The foster mother sent her own children to school but kept him at home to do the farm chores. As a result, he wound up with about three years of education, barely enough to read and write. However, I can't recall him ever mentioning his lost childhood as an excuse for anything. One of his favorite sayings was, "No use crying over spilled milk." It was his way of accepting that bad things happen. You survive. Life goes on.

During the twenties, Mama had begun her work career as a clerk at a Woolworth's dime store. Looking to upgrade her skills, she signed on as an apprentice in a beauty shop to learn hairdressing—a job that earned her $3 a week at the height of the Depression.

By contrast, my first employment was a summer job with the U.S. Navy Department. I had taken the Civil Service test and scored well enough to get a GS-3 rating as a clerk-stenographer—a job paying $2,600 a year. Although I dutifully banked my paychecks, I had only saved enough for college tuition and books, not for room and board. Mama began advocating for the more reasonably priced Strayer Business School in downtown Washington.

I was over a barrel with only weeks before school started. After much negotiating, Mama and I reached an agreement. I would commute to George Washington and live at home. As a concession, I would major in business administration, which Mama mistakenly thought was like business school. I didn't tell her differently. I would use my electives for history, philosophy, literature—those subjects that stirred my soul. Our deal was something of a compromise; neither of us got what we wanted at the time. But neither of us regretted the outcome.

Meanwhile, Mel was cutting a deal with his father. He would not go to Australia or the military academy. Instead, he would commute to

George Washington University and promise not to marry until he finished college. While his father was thinking a four-year delay, Mel was
thinking three. He accelerated the timeline by going to school nights
and summers, enabling him to finish a year early. We scheduled our
wedding three days after his graduation.

I returned to school while he commenced his two-year stint in the
Air Force. Even wearing the bars of a second lieutenant, he was on
course for what he wanted to do with his life—run for public office. To
Mel, military service was not an interruption, but necessary preparation
for public service. In the wake of World War II and the Korean War,
no one would consider seeking elective office without having first served
his country.

My first introduction to campaign politics came with a presidential
rally in the fifties. I remember the sparkle in Mel's eye as we stood in
a hot, smoked-filled ballroom waiting an hour to hear presidential candidate Adlai Stevenson. One line we heard that evening, Mel would re-
peat in speeches for the rest of his life.

"Public service is a good and noble profession, one worthy of our
lives," Stevenson said. "For in no other way can you improve the lives of
so many." It was splendid idealism, and neither of us ever got over it.

In the years that followed, I learned that Mel was not motivated by
money or possessions. His heart and head were geared to public service. I grew to accept that. My life was now rolled into his. His goals
were my goals. In time, his victories would be my victories and his losses
mine as well. It would always be that way.

At the time, law school was the incubator for budding politicians.
Nearly all of Missouri's highest officeholders had degrees from the
state's university. Following that path meant a move to Columbia and
three years at the University of Missouri Law School. It was a heart-
breaking moment for my parents when we parted, separating them
from their only child and their new grandson, Randy, a chubby nine-
month-old.

My parents had not traveled beyond the East Coast, so the thought
of me pioneering westward with an infant brought with it scenes from
a Ma and Pa Kettle movie. Feeling that we were without essential serv-

ices in the Midwest, Mama would ship us "care packages," including apples from Winchester, our favorite apple-picking spot in Virginia. The postage was greater than the cost of the fruit. Still, I enjoyed her generosity and never let on that our stores were comparable to hers. But after my mother visited Missouri and discovered our supermarkets and shopping malls, I never received another gift apple.

With the birth of Russ, our second son, Mel felt a need to augment our income. In addition to his studies, he took a series of part-time and summer jobs: insurance adjuster, church choir director, stock clerk, airline refueler. Despite the distractions of fatherhood and employment, he graduated fifth in his class, good enough for the Order of the Coif, the highest of law school honors.

With a diploma in hand, the next question was where to settle. Mel wanted to run for Congress after his father retired from office. He talked only to family about this desire—and then only rarely—but it influenced his every decision. In keeping with his aspirations, we started looking for a town in southeast Missouri within the Eighth Congressional District.

Mel's only sibling, Bob, and his wife, Oma, lived in Rolla, a college town of some nine thousand people just two hours southwest of St. Louis. The city just happened to be in the Eighth Congressional District. Bob was building and selling prefabricated homes that were not much bigger than trailers, but at a cost of $10,000, the price was right. We snapped up one along with an offer for Mel to join an old, established law firm in town. Luckily, we landed in a neighborhood of young couples, several of whom became lifelong friends and ardent political supporters.

Mel's first taste of local politics came shortly after we settled in Rolla. During the Kennedy-Nixon presidential race, rural Democrats were divided largely because of Kennedy's religion. There had never been a Catholic president, and fear abounded in predominately Protestant south Missouri. One Sunday morning, during the worship service at the First Baptist Church, our pastor made some disparaging remarks about Kennedy. Mel was unaccustomed to political commentary from the pulpit. Knowing that Southern Baptists traditionally stood firm on the separation of church and state, he made an appointment to see the minister the following week to express his concern.

"I come to church on Sunday to hear about God, not about your political views," he said firmly. Although it was a stern declaration, it did not destroy their friendship. But there was never another political comment made from the pulpit of the First Baptist Church. Mel was twenty-six at the time.

The following year, Mel's first elective venture pitted him against the town's popular pool hall operator in a contest for municipal judge. It was a tough call for voters deciding between someone they knew and liked and a young man they didn't know, but who had a law degree. Despite his age and newcomer status, Mel won an easy victory largely because he was the only lawyer in the race—though a legal degree was not a requirement.

The part-time job consisted of handing out fines to careless dog owners and traffic violators, and jail time to the town drunks. Having a stable income allowed Mel the chance to open his own law office, an operation that would remain a one-man firm until our son Randy took over the business.

The more challenging election came the following year with a countywide race for state legislator. Like everything else he did, Mel took the contest very seriously. The winter before the election, he designed a six-week plan for knocking on every door throughout the district. The plan, of course, had to be carried out in the summer heat. The "knockin' and sweatin'" paid off, earning him a seat in the Missouri General Assembly and a chance to pursue his public service ambitions. The state capital was a little more than an hour away, but with the arrival of Robin, our baby daughter, Mel made it a point to drive home every evening to be with the family.

As Mel was taking on his legislative duties, his father was retiring from Congress, having lost a contentious primary battle for an eighth term. The elder Carnahan fell victim to the popular young speaker of the Missouri House, who conducted a more modern, vigorous campaign then had ever been waged in the district. Carnahan's backing of John F. Kennedy for president didn't help either in south Missouri. However, the new president remembered the congressman's loyalty and appointed him the first U.S. ambassador to the newly independent African country of Sierra Leone.

With the likelihood of his gaining a congressional seat diminished, Mel turned his full attention to state government. During his second term in the house, he was elected majority floor leader and earned an armload of silver plates and bowls for legislative achievement. Capital watchers agreed; Carnahan was on the fast track to the governor's office.

Mel's 1968 bid for the state senate started with a bitter primary battle—one of the toughest of the nineteen races he would run. Pregnant and with three kids to care for, I set up our low-budget campaign office in our dining room. I replaced the tablecloth and centerpiece with a telephone and an IBM Selectric typewriter. I moved in a file cabinet and our database of three-by-five cards and went to work.

Out of necessity, I was a "one-woman shop," writing the letters, handling the calls, creating the press releases and speeches, designing the literature, and dealing with printers, their deadlines and bobbles. (I would later say that every gray hair in my head was put there by a printer.)

My most exciting creation was the Caravan for Carnahan. The traveling road show of performers, family members, and supporters assembled each Saturday in a grocery store parking lot. Decked out in red cowboy hats and accompanied by a country band, our troupe would roll into small towns and stir up enough hoopla to draw a good-size crowd to hear Mel. In the end, our grassroots efforts made the difference in the close race.

During later campaigns, the size of our staff grew so fast that I was unable to keep up with who was working in the office. I knew things had changed dramatically from the days of my "dining room office" when I called for Mel and a "campaign receptionist" answered the phone.

I said, "Hello, this is Jean."

She replied, "Jean who?"

As we celebrated Mel's state senate victory on primary night in 1968, we were blissfully unaware that he had won the battle but lost the war.

We entered the general election with a deeply fractured party in a newly drawn district that proved to be less Democratic than anticipated.

The year ended with me losing the child I was carrying and Mel losing the election. Twelve years would pass before another opening occurred in state politics. But it would be less than a year before I was pregnant again. Tom was the baby of the family, but, as often happens with the youngest, he grew to be the tallest of us all.

Out of office and with no intention of doing anything that would hinder a later race, Mel returned to his solo law practice. The long interruption gave him a chance to raise a family, to build our farm home, to preside over the local school board and the building of a new high school, to head the committee building a new church auditorium, and to campaign for other office seekers.

Mel loved our new white frame home in the country with its gambrel roof and scenic view of both forest and rolling pastures. We later added a lake, several horses, and eventually a herd of black Angus cattle, thanks to Randy's interest. While some men find golfing, television viewing, or sports events relaxing, Mel preferred donning boots and a straw hat to operate the tractor, cut brush, build a fence, or make a hay crop. On snowy mornings, he would invariably pull on a pair of coveralls and a ski mask, hook the blade onto the tractor, and plow every driveway in sight.

Most often, he started the day with a three-mile run, or walk, along the dirt road in front of our house. He always returned with a plastic bag filled with debris that he had picked up along the way. I have noticed in recent years that our kids do the same thing. (Isn't it interesting that our children learn so much more from what we do than from what we say?) The ancient rabbis spoke of "tikkun olam," repairing the earth, as being the duty of each human being. I doubt if Mel had any formal introduction to that concept, but he practiced it in everything he did, whether he was walking a back road or advocating public policy.

Although he had farm chores, law clients, his family, and civic and church activities to occupy his time and thoughts, his political fire never burned out. There was no obvious reentry point into public life until

1979, when he rallied family and friends to seek an open seat for state treasurer. His advantage came in being the only candidate in the race to run television commercials. In a low-on-the-ballot statewide race where candidates have little name recognition, television can be the deciding factor. He won the four-year term, again placing him in the lineup of potential gubernatorial candidates.

But there was another "lineup" before that, one that I will never forget—the lineup for the Grand Ball on inauguration night. Elected state officeholders and their spouses traditionally gather in the governor's office to make their grand entrance down the stairway onto the floor of the Capitol Rotunda. Nervously awaiting our turn to make the descent into the crowd below, I took a deep breath. When I did, I felt the back zipper of my ball gown pop open. I reached around to feel exposed skin and a zipper attached top and bottom, but spread in the middle.

I was terrified!

I turned to the lieutenant governor's wife. "Geri, can you do anything about this zipper?" I said in a panic.

"Oh, my lord," she said, "come with me into the bathroom."

We made a hasty retreat to the nearby restroom.

"Hold on," she said, "I'm going to give this a yank. Either this is going to work or . . ."

She didn't finish the sentence.

I held my breath. I felt like the proverbial drowning man whose life passes before his eyes. After all our campaigning for state treasurer, at this moment of glory, Mel would have to descend the stairs without me. Or worse yet, with me pinned together like a ragged doll.

I felt a tug, followed by a swish.

"That did it," she said, "you're back together."

I breathed a sigh of relief and returned to the doorway just in time to hear the announcer say, "State Treasurer and Mrs. Mel Carnahan."

I grabbed Mel's arm, and we walked out onto the upper landing, smiled broadly, waved, and started down the stairway.

"Where in the world were you?" he muttered under his breath. "I thought I was going to have to make this entrance without you."

"I did, too. You don't know how lucky you are that I'm here," I said, continuing to wave, smile, and move cautiously so as not to catch a foot in my gown and stumble. We strolled graciously down the stairs as though nothing had ever happened. The following day I returned to our farm in Rolla and Mel took an apartment in Jefferson City. For the next four years, he would spend the workweek at the Capitol; I would keep the home fires burning.

During his four-year tenure as state treasurer, Mel proved himself a reformer, not given to politics as usual, when he insisted on ending the practice of awarding investment management contracts to political supporters and, instead, required that the contracts be competitively bid.

In 1984, Mel had the choice of running safely for reelection or plunging into the governor's race, involving a three-way Democratic primary, the winner of which would take on John Ashcroft, then the state's attorney general. Mel took the leap. That year we "wrote the book" on how to run a losing political campaign. The media had already decided the primary winner, written the story (at least in their heads), and didn't want to be bothered with the details. Wracked by staff and funding problems, the ill-fated venture stumbled along pathetically—its most memorable feature being Mel's desperate attempt to get media coverage by walking across the state.

Allowing for other scheduled events, the 325-mile meandering path from St. Louis to Kansas City took a month to complete. It was an epic struggle. Mel suffered shin splints much of the time but finished his walking-talking-listening odyssey hearty and well tanned. Although the press ignored the effort, it was a great opportunity for Mel to see the state and its people at ground level. But as one cynical observer noted, "You may *think* you're walking, but if it doesn't say so in the news, you're *not* walking."

Gov. Lawton Chiles, who had performed a similar feat, wrote Mel a letter and enclosed a copy of the journal he kept during his thousand-mile trek across Florida. His message was encouraging at the time and later proved to be true.

He wrote, "I've never known anyone who walked their state, who didn't eventually win." In my mind, that spoke more of sustained effort—the very quality that makes a good candidate and officeholder.

Despite the heroic attempt, Mel finished second in a three-way primary where he was outspent six to one. At least the loss came as no surprise. The election-night "party" was held in a hotel bedroom. Even that was too spacious for the few who bothered to attend.

I took the loss harder than Mel did. Not one to mope around or feel sorry for himself, he took his defeats in stride. Mel never expected life or public service to be without setbacks. He thought more like Charlie Brown, who once opined, "Life is a series of ups and downs." At the time, I felt more like Lucy: "All I want is ups, ups, ups."

The morning after the election, Mel arose early and went to work as if nothing had ever happened. I don't know how he was able to do it. Undoubtedly, having a routine to his life provided stability in good times and bad. He seemed to have a "road map" in his head for all occasions. He anticipated the delays along the way but knew that if you kept the motor running and steered in the right direction, you'd eventually get to your destination.

A few years later, however, his quest nearly came to a halt. When Mel suffered a mild heart attack, I wondered whether he would ever wage another political campaign. But like a prizefighter training for a comeback, he structured his life to include a healthy diet and regular exercise, whether he was at home or traveling.

Fully recovered, trim and fit, he reentered the political arena in 1987, this time seeking the office of lieutenant governor. The family cranked up for another statewide race, with Robin heading the campaign. Grandpa took on a few campaign chores, too. When I was away from home, he handled the phone messages and kept track of when our commercials ran on television. Because he was a diabetic, I checked on him regularly. I programmed the home phone so he could press the #1 button to dial me direct. I was amused when one of my friends called, wanting to reach me.

"She's easy to get hold of," Daddy explained. "All you have to do is press 1, and she'll pick up the phone."

With his victory in 1988, Mel became the sole Democratic survivor on the state ticket, making him the odd man in Gov. John Ashcroft's administration. That would change four years later. In 1992, Mel won the governorship by a landslide, sweeping the other statewide Democrats into office along with him and defying political pundits who frequently underestimated the mild-mannered, unpretentious Ozarkian, feeling he was unable to excite voters.

During his gubernatorial race, Mel took the biggest risk of his political career by advocating a tax increase to improve schools. Some Democrats were so frightened by the idea that they refused to appear on the same stage with him. But Mel felt that there was little use in being elected, or reelected, if you didn't stand for something. He was willing to venture all without hesitation.

Mel was fifty-eight years old when he was sworn in as governor of Missouri, having fought fifteen election battles, delivered hundreds of speeches, traveled thousands of miles, and raised millions of dollars. During his two terms as governor, he brought a progressive, common-sense approach to the state's problems. He felt it was the duty of government to provide opportunity for its citizens. You did that with good schools, not just for those in the silk-stocking districts, but for the inner-city kids of Kansas City and North St. Louis and for students in rural Missouri.

Mel had learned the value of education from his parents, both of whom were Ozark schoolteachers. Students living back in the hills, far beyond bus routes, stayed in the Carnahan home during the school week. As a school superintendent, his father was frequently faced with too many pupils and too little funding. When that happened, he would temporarily assume the role of coach or choir director to keep the music and sports programs intact. One of Mel's earliest recollections was of riding in their farm truck to the rail station to pick up government commodities for the school's hot lunch program, which his father had started.

Growing up in a family that placed such importance on education would later influence his priorities as the state's chief executive. During his first year as governor, Mel pushed for passage of his new school financing formula. But he insisted that any new funding be accompanied by educational reforms that included raising academic standards, reducing class sizes, establishing career paths for non-college-bound students, and expanding early childhood programs.

"We're not going to tax people and then give them more of the same old thing," he said repeatedly.

Although most onlookers thought the proposal had as much chance in the legislature as the proverbial "snowball," Mel insisted on making education the hallmark of his governorship. To him, it was a high-stakes gamble, but one worth the risk.

During the final days of the 1993 legislative session, as the vote neared on the education bill (Senate Bill 380), Mel and his staff—Marc Farinella, Roy Temple, D. K. Hirner, and Beth Wheeler—turned up the pressure on reluctant legislators with weekend calls from the governor and the home folks.

"The legislature is like a flowing river," Mel would say. "If you can just get them turned in the right direction, they'll do what they're supposed to do."

I suggested pinning proponents of S.B. 380 with a green ribbon as a reminder to vote the green light for education on the chamber's electronic voting board. Staffers in the governor's office liked the idea, bought some ribbon, and had several hundred pins assembled in no time.

I took to the Capitol hallways, pinning anyone who smiled approvingly in my direction. I even tried to pin Jim Wolfe, the gruff reporter for the *Joplin Globe*.

"Will you wear a green ribbon, Jim?" I asked with a twinkle in my eye as if I were about to invite him to the junior prom.

"What do it do?" he inquired, feigning an Ozark air.

"It marks you as one of the good guys for education."

Jim had to think about that.

"Well, maybe I'd better not be a billboard for anything today," he said cautiously.

I gave him an understanding pat on the arm and went on my way, mission accomplished. He now knew that Mel had all hands on deck for this one. That's what I wanted him to know. When I stopped to solicit votes in legislative offices, I raised a few eyebrows there, too. Secretaries were shocked when I popped in unexpectedly. They had never seen a First Lady walking the halls on behalf of a governor's agenda.

When it came time for one of the crucial votes, I joined Mel in the legislative gallery. He whispered to me that the vote was being delayed in an attempt to get a few more legislators on the scene who were favorable. The Republicans were holding their ranks pretty well, but some weak-kneed Democrats were in the no column with them.

As members of the General Assembly cast their votes, all eyes turned toward the front of the chamber as red and green lights began to dance across the two electronic voting boards. Lawmakers are well aware that someone is watching each vote, looking for the silver bullet to use on them in the next campaign. For many, backing S.B. 380 required courage. It seemed so politically virtuous to say—as many did—"Let's take this to a vote of the people." It was an excuse to delay or defeat the measure rather than debate and decide its outcome in the legislative arena. Now it was surprising to see how bold lawmakers could be when their governor was willing to stick his neck out and lead the charge.

The board flashed more than one hundred votes to reconsider. That was the first successful test of strength for the measure. The votes were there with some to spare. The next vote was closer. Green lights showing on the board totaled eighty-eight this time. Still, it was a good indicator of the final vote. The "river" was still flowing in the right direction.

Two days later, Mel and I stood in the side gallery for the final vote.

"Ring the bell and tally the vote," the speaker intoned as he had many times before. Only this time it marked a significant and costly difference for education.

"Where's Steve? Somebody get Steve," Mel said to nobody in particular, but with a concern that a vote he was counting was not showing up. Several staffers took off down the hall. In no time, Steve's light was flashing in the green column.

The electronic board stayed open a little longer than usual. The more fearful waited to see if their vote was really needed and, when it wasn't, jumped back to the politically safer red column.

The speaker announced the results.

"Ninety ayes. Seventy nays. The ayes have it."

They did it! With votes to spare!

A roar went up from the balcony filled with teachers observing the historic moment. Lawmakers gave themselves a round of applause. They had done their duty when it was tough. God bless 'em. Some signed their political death warrant with that vote.

As Mel made his way into the Capitol hallway, well-wishers and camera crews engulfed him. Many unable to reach Mel chose to convey their congratulations to me, our kids, or our weary staff.

Praise was unconstrained. "Historic . . . most productive session in decades . . . the *real* education governor" (Ashcroft had previously anointed himself with that title). In the final moments before leftover bills were flung into the air marking the end of the session, one legislator rose to his feet and inquired, "Now that we have given Governor Carnahan everything he wants, what are we going to do next year?" True, they had grappled successfully with a number of issues, including workers' compensation reform and health care, but there was still work to be done for higher education and mental health.

The newspaper accounts of the session were glowing, calling the outcome "long overdue . . . courageous . . . a session for the children of Missouri." Mel probably came closer in his own description. Knowing the hurdles they had faced, he called it "something of a miracle." He had worked hard on an issue in which he strongly believed and, because of the intensity of his belief, was able to bring others along with him. His ability to define a problem, determine the solution, and develop the backing needed for success was an essential element of his leadership style that served him well in every task he tackled.

Working with the same zeal, he secured better preschool programs and improved health care, providing coverage for more than 90,000 previously uninsured low-income families. He tripled the funding for in-home health care for seniors, led the fight for better regulation of nursing homes, and successfully pushed for stronger laws against senior abuse and neglect.

Anticrime measures were strengthened, including the state's sexual predator and juvenile crime laws. His job training program, welfare reform, and economic development policies helped create 300,000 new jobs, reducing welfare roles by more than 130,000. All the while, he balanced the budget and maintained the state's triple-A bond rating.

But because of S.B. 380, Republicans tried desperately to label him "Taxman Carnahan," despite his having cut annual sales, business, and income taxes by $630 million.

Perhaps the greatest disappointment for a governor who, as a child, spent countless hours in a backyard dirt pile constructing roads, bridges, and airstrips was his inability to gain consensus on upgrading the state's infrastructure. Building a modern transportation system was essential for the future he envisioned, but he was unable to convince a timid and divided legislature to take the risk.

Mel used to say, "Most of the time, you just sit in the boat, but every now and then you get to steer, and that's when you decide the direction." Direction was important to him in everything. Charting a course, doing your duty, making a difference—these defined his life.

Helen Keller was once asked, "Can there be anything worse than losing your sight?" She replied, "Yes, losing your vision." No one ever accused Mel of that.

During the spring of 1993, the forces of Mother Nature proved to be more formidable than a recalcitrant legislature. What started out as scattered springtime flooding in the low-lying areas turned into record high-water levels across the state. Thinking the rains would surely abate, Mel and I had proceeded with our plans to take a nine-day vacation to Italy after the legislature adjourned. We arrived at our hotel in Rome and had barely unpacked our clothes when word came that the situation in Missouri was worsening.

Mel turned to a security officer. "Find out when the next flight back to the States leaves."

The officer returned shortly. "There are no flights tonight," he reported, "but we can get on a flight leaving midmorning tomorrow."

"Good, we need to go home," Mel announced without hesitation.

We had canceled a trip to Rome five years earlier because of Mel's decision to run for lieutenant governor. By now, I was beginning to feel somewhat fatalistic about my chances of ever seeing the ancient city. Trying to salvage what we could of the trip, we squeezed in a tour of the Forum and Coliseum and arranged for a quick view of the Vatican the next morning. Although I would later joke about our "nineteen-hour trip to Rome"—most of it spent sleeping—neither of us had any doubt about our need to be back in Missouri.

In the months that followed, I learned more about the Missouri and Mississippi rivers than I wanted to know. We all did. Mark Twain called the Mississippi that "outlaw stream" that couldn't be tamed. "Cannot curb it or constrain it," he said.

Well, we tried. Sandbagged levees and flood walls did some good, while others washed away like sandcastles on a beach. Unlike hurricanes, tornadoes, and explosions that happen quickly, a flood can extend over weeks, continuing to wreak new havoc along its path.

Fortunately, the Missouri National Guard and the state emergency management team rose to the occasion, as did the federal government. Mel's contact with Vice President Gore drew immediate assurances that emergency funds were on the way.

Mel and I flew over most of the flooded areas by helicopter, accompanied by Gen. Raymond Pendergrass, head of the state national guard. On one trip, I recall that we ducked under the whirling blades as we made our way onboard the noisy chopper. The sound level was abated somewhat by the complimentary earplugs and headsets. I was literally lashed to my seat, with an awkward seatbelt unlike any other I had worn. My body was wound about with headphone wires that entwined my purse and camera straps. I felt as if I was part of a comedy routine with the governor, a general, and a guardsman all trying to save me from looking like a United Parcel package.

For me, getting into the helicopter was the hardest part of "flood patrol." "I fell out of the helicopter today," I told the mansion manager upon returning from viewing some high-water areas.

"You what?"

"Oh, it was still on the ground," I explained. "I slipped when I attempted the three-foot step into the helicopter without any assistance. It was not a pretty sight."

In the interest of better viewing, the side doors of the chopper were usually left open during flight. That meant that someone had to sit next to the gaping panel on each side. Mel always took one slot. I didn't mind sitting in one of those positions, except that it was the breeziest spot onboard. When I sat there, I would arrive at our destination looking like I had spent the morning in a wind tunnel.

Not until my visit to Ste. Genevieve did I fully realize the epic proportion of the flood and the heroic effort being expended by both victims and volunteers.

"We've got a million sandbags out there now," one weary guardsman said, pointing proudly toward the mound atop the levee. "But I don't know how long it can hold. Sandbags are just temporary and there's no telling when the water will crest, or for how long. We're working the hot spots all up and down the levee. I figure there's a 50–50 chance to save the town."

Other towns to the north—Augusta, Hartsburg—were already underwater. We saw them from our flyover: tops of house and barns, upturned trailers, stranded animals, and devastated crops. I wondered where the families were who once lived in what was now a watered wasteland. For most people the flood was just a news clip on evening television. But there were thousands of displaced people, and the number was growing daily.

The guardsman driving us to the levee parked his jeep near the river that runs along the city's historic district. At first glance, the gathering might have been mistaken for a beach party with lots of scantily clad people hovered together in the sand. Actually, it was hundreds of men, women, and children shoveling sand into bags that were then stacked on a loader and hauled to the levee.

The first man I came upon had traveled from St. Louis to join the bagging operation, along with his wife and six-year-old son.

"Show me how this is done," I said.

"Nothing to it," he answered, pressing a T-shirt sleeve to his face to sop away the droplets.

"You just put three shovelfuls into each bag."

"You mind if I give it a try?"

"Not at all," he said, passing the shovel to me and stepping back to watch my style.

His wife propped open the mouth of the next bag. I dug into the sandy mound. My first scoop nearly missed the bag but did completely fill my sandals. Not being as efficient as my mentor was, it took me four shovelfuls to fill my bag. Playing in the sand had long been a pleasure of mine, so I stuck with it while Mel shook hands and encouraged the volunteers. The nice couple from St. Louis tolerated my interference, since I was the First Lady and new at this kind of work. I probably filled twenty-five bags and came away feeling I had some small part in helping to save the levee.

In Jefferson City, I visited with flood victims, whose temporary homes consisted of cots shoved into one corner of a gymnasium. Interestingly, the women I talked to were coping much better than some of the men. The women found solace in each other, cared for the children, and managed the food distribution. Although many of the elderly women had preexisting medical conditions, they seemed to be taking their own debilities in stride as they turned to helping those in greater need.

"I'm worried about my husband," one told me, thinking I was a Red Cross volunteer.

"Where is he?" I asked.

"That's him," she said, pointing across the room to a man lying underneath a cot.

"He's so depressed. He won't talk. Won't do anything."

"I'm sorry," I said with a feeling of helplessness in the face of a situation I had never before encountered.

Her neighbor, leaning on a cane next to her, joined the conversation.

"I tell you what I'm concerned about: it's our apartments." Both ladies had been evacuated from the same rental complex.

The lady on the cane continued, "It's that sonabitch we rent from. He ain't going to replace our carpets. They're soaking wet. They need to come up and the floors scrubbed good. But he said he ain't going to do it. Said it was 'every man for himself' in times like these."

Before I could learn more, I was called away by a newspaper reporter wanting an interview.

"I saw you huddled with the women over there. What were they telling you?"

I expressed some of their concerns—but without the colorful language.

"Did you tell them who you are?"

"No, I didn't"

"Why not?"

"They didn't ask. And besides, I thought they would talk more freely if they didn't know."

I was to learn in the weeks ahead that listening to each other was one of the few ways we had to fight back. Just being there to listen and encourage meant a lot at this stage of the flood.

While helping at a Red Cross shelter in Hannibal, I talked to a seventy-nine-year-old woman who had no family. She had lost her home and all of her possessions in the flood.

With tears in her eyes, she said, "I even lost my cat."

There was no going home for her. Life would never be the same. She would likely go to a nursing home.

I put my hand on top of hers.

"Please, don't give up. Let's keep on fighting this thing," I whispered, squeezing her hand gently.

She smiled back, nodding her head in agreement.

About that time, her friend, impatient with hearing the travails of so many victims, stood up from the table, squared her shoulders, and said in a spirit that defied defeat, "This old river isn't the only thing that can rise. We can rise, too."

And with that said, she returned to dishing up food for a new round of flood refugees who had just arrived.

Over the summer months, the size, duration, and impact of the flood set hundred-year records. Before the waters subsided, the Mississippi and Missouri rivers would inundate croplands, swamp businesses, uproot communities, wash away cemeteries, and buckle highways, causing more than $3 billion of damage in Missouri alone. In an effort to lessen the effects of future flooding, the state purchased land in the flood zones and moved more than four thousand homes and businesses.

Despite the despair that we all feel in the wake of a natural disaster, I learned from the victims and the volunteers that you tough it out, you clean it up, and you begin again.

It has been a decade now since the Great Flood of '93, but I still remember the many grim but determined faces, smiling bravely against a flood of tears. Ordinary people emboldened by unexpected strength not only survive, they prevail.

• • •

One of the defining moment of Mel's governorship occurred during the January 1999 visit of Pope John Paul II. The previous November, the Missouri Supreme Court had unknowingly scheduled the execution of death row inmate Darrell Meese during the pontiff's two-day stay in St. Louis. Later the court drew attention to the case by changing the execution date without offering a reason, causing speculation that the move was meant to avoid a conflict with the papal stopover.

The historic visit set the stage for an extraordinary occurrence. Mel and I first met Pope John Paul in a Lambert airport hangar upon his arrival from Mexico City. President and Mrs. Clinton were also on hand for the welcome, along with a host of church leaders and local dignitaries. The panels of soft blue fabric forming makeshift corridors within the crowded hangar were posted with directions like lettering on a maze. One in particular caught my eye. Printed on computer paper and taped to the curtains, it read: "President's and Holy Father's restroom only." What a rare bit of signage! As the participants departed, my son Tom couldn't resist removing the "papal potty" sign as a souvenir of the day. Framed and hanging today in his law office, it still elicits fond memories of the papal/presidential visit to St. Louis.

The next morning, the governor's office received a call from St. Louis Archbishop Justin Rigali. He requested a meeting with Mel prior to the prayer service that afternoon at the St. Louis Cathedral Basilica. Mel agreed and showed up at the archbishop's residence about lunchtime along with his legal counsel, Joe Bednar, and assistant counsel, Angie Heffner. Bednar recalled the house being overrun by red-robed cardinals and bishops dining on what smelled like Polish sausage and sauerkraut. As the group assembled in the library, Rigali was joined by the Vatican's secretary of state, Cardinal Angelo Sodano, and communications director, Joaquin Navarro-Valls. Sodano explained that the Holy Father was resting upstairs in preparation for the prayer service. He then moved quickly to the point of the meeting.

"We have been placed in an awkward position," he explained. "Our visit has saved the life of Mr. Meese, but when we leave, he will die." Sodano then conveyed the pontiff's hope that the governor might grant clemency to the condemned man.

Mel explained that his office reviewed death penalty cases very carefully, but said that because of the pope's request he would take another look. It was a brief discussion, ending with an exchange of social pleasantries and a gift to Mel, a rosary commemorating the papal visit.

Later that day, I joined Mel at the cathedral, where more than two thousand people awaited the pope's arrival. Before the service began, Mel and I, along with Vice President and Mrs. Gore, were ushered to the front row of the church. The pontiff entered, his body stooped and frail, and sat solemnly at the altar flanked by dozens of splendidly arrayed cardinals and bishops. It was an impressive gathering of ecclesiastical and political power of the sort that most people never have the chance to witness.

At the end of the service, His Holiness came down from the altar and walked slowly in the direction of our pew. He paused, first, to bless those seated in wheelchairs in front of us and then stepped over to greet the Gores. Turning to Mel, he paused, reached out his hand, and whispered softly—only four words—"Mercy for Mr. Meese." Looking back, I realize that at that moment, their eyes, their hands, their hearts touched, though nothing more was said. Next, the pope greeted me, as I stood holding a handful of prayer beads that friends wanted to have blessed. From there, he proceeded slowly along the row of dignitaries and back down the cathedral aisle.

Upon returning to the capital city that evening, Mel called his top staff together.

"I'm inclined to grant clemency," he told them. "I was very impressed with the preciseness of the request. He did not ask me to commute the sentence of every death row inmate or to overturn the death penalty. He asked for something that it is within my immediate power to do." During the discussion that followed, all agreed to that assessment, but each knew that in the months ahead they would pay a heavy political price for the decision.

The next day, Mel announced that the death sentence of Darrell Meese would be commuted to life in prison without parole. He cited "the extraordinary circumstance" of the papal visit, saying, "I continue to support capital punishment, but after careful consideration of his direct and personal appeal and because of a deep and abiding respect for the pontiff and all he represents, I decided last night to grant his request."

Capital pundits, who base their views on polls and perception, could not believe that a governor facing a tight U.S. Senate race would do anything so politically inane. It didn't make sense. Meese clearly deserved the death penalty for the grisly shotgun slaying of his former drug partner, the man's wife, and his handicapped grandson. Mel had allowed twenty-six other scheduled executions to proceed, having commuted only the death sentence for a retarded man whose jury was not informed of his condition. Our political consultants felt that Mel had handed his opponent, John Ashcroft, an opportunity to cast him as "soft on crime."

One commentator called the decision "a simple gesture of largely irrational kindness." In a way, I suppose he was right. Mel never tried to make a reasoned argument for what he did, feeling the act needed no explanation. He would later describe the encounter as "a very moving moment for me," one he would never have expected. "I felt my response was appropriate," he concluded.

But for many, it left unanswered the age-old question: how do you reconcile mercy with justice? Are they in some way linked, as Shakespeare would have us believe? I later received a note from my friend Nick Knight, a Shakespearean scholar. He included a copy of Portia's words from *The Merchant of Venice* (act 4, scene 1)—words from another era, but still rich in meaning.

> The quality of mercy is not strain'd,
> It droppeth as the gentle rain from heaven
> Upon the place beneath; it is twice blest:
> It blesseth him that gives and him that takes;
> 'Tis mightiest in the mightiest: it becomes
> The thronèd monarch better than his crown;
> His sceptre shows the force of temporal power,
> The attribute to awe and majesty,
> Wherein doth sit the dread and fear of kings;
> But mercy is above this sceptred sway;
> It is enthronèd in the hearts of kings,
> It is an attribute to God himself;
> And earthly power doth then show likest God's
> When mercy seasons justice.

Six

Mansion on the Hill

We shape our buildings; thereafter they shape us.

—Winston Churchill

While Mel pursued his agenda at the State Capitol, two blocks away, at the Governor's Mansion, I was taking on a less defined role as First Lady of Missouri. I was not surprised to learn that Jackie Kennedy never liked the term *First Lady*. She said it sounded like the name of a racehorse. True, it is not a perfect description. In an earlier, more genteel era, the term *Mrs. Governor* was used to designate the wife of the chief executive. In the future, the term *First Spouse* may be necessary. For the time being, impudent legislators have coined their own label: "First B - - - - " (it rhymes with witch).

Regardless of the name, it's a position that generally comes with no pay, job description, or rules. At first, my new duties seemed like a cross between a hotel manager and a museum curator. I soon discovered that it was a job that could be shaped into whatever the First Lady had the gumption to attempt and the community would accept.

Some First Ladies on stepping into office get little more than a title—no residence, no security officers, and no budget. By contrast, the Missouri Governor's Mansion is outfitted with a chef, house cleaner, mansion manager, docents, security officers, preservation employees, guards, and the traditional prison inmate workers.

Despite the fringe benefits of "firstladyship," my transition from our two-story frame farmhouse to a four-story Victorian mansion with thirty rooms took some adjustments. With the first floor opened for tours and the living quarters on the second floor, it was like "living over the store," as one First Lady described it. But what a store! I fell in love with the old home from the moment I walked through its massive double doors. The 1871 Renaissance Revival mansion, sitting atop the bluffs of the Missouri River, is itself a symbol of strength, having survived the indignities inflicted on it by many decorators, neglectful occupants, and stingy legislators, as well as one attempt to tear it down!

I fondly remember my first night in the stately home. Following the inaugural ball, after everyone had left the mansion, I did something that the "child" in me was longing to do. I took a short, cautious slide down the rail of the Grand Stairway. The wide, curved steps, floating gracefully upward to the second floor, had attracted the young and the young-at-heart for decades. My performance was not stellar, but it would improve some years later with help from my grandsons.

While Mel was upstairs unpacking for our first night at the mansion, I walked alone through the cavernous first-floor rooms. Like Cinderella, I was mesmerized by the finery of the "castle"—its rich carpets, elegant Victorian furnishings, and ornate seventeen-foot ceilings.

Standing silently in the dimly lit parlor, I had the uneasy feeling of being locked inside a museum after-hours. I was certain that someone would come from around the corner and ask me to leave. Instead, I ran onto a security officer setting out motion-detection devices. I apologized for being there. "Stay as long as you like," he said, realizing the prerogatives of the First Family better than I did at the time.

The next morning I woke up to the sun glistening on the crystal chandelier high above our bed.

"I need a cup of coffee," I said to Mel, who was already dressed and eager to go to the Capitol to take up his new duties.

Not knowing that I could simply pick up the phone and place my order to the kitchen, I got up, dressed, and started for the elevator.

Seeing the Grand Stairway, I turned back and opted for a more elegant descent. I then wound my way through the back halls and into the kitchen, where the chef and prison inmates had already arrived.

As I picked up a paper cup and started pouring my coffee, one of the inmates spotted me and hurried over.

"Please, don't do that!" he said excitedly.

"Why not?" I asked, hoping I had not made some terrible blunder my first day on the job.

"Oh, the First Lady doesn't drink out of a paper cup," he said with great authority.

"I didn't know that," I said sheepishly.

Advice given me by the previous resident, Janet Ashcroft, had not included coffee cup etiquette.

He returned with a Lenox china cup, one of those with the wide mouth that cools the coffee too quickly.

I explained the problem. "What about a mug? Will that do?" I said.

He smiled, sensing that he had gone too far already in suggesting changes to my behavior, and happily agreed on the mug.

However, one thing Janet had noted stuck with me.

"Everyone wants to please you," she had said. "Sometimes people will even try to anticipate what you want."

The concept sounded good at the time. After living in a house full of teenagers, this would be a welcomed turn of events. That afternoon I discovered what Janet meant. I had noticed a blank area on the dinning room wall and was told that a portrait of an earlier First Lady once hung there, "but a former governor didn't like the facial expression."

"That's a shame," I said, "something needs to be hanging there to balance the room."

An hour later when I passed through the dining room workmen were on ladders, returning the "offensive" painting to its place. Like the "Princess Bride," my wish had become their command.

After the painting incident, I was careful about making casual statements or even voicing my displeasure. I found it difficult to joke or tease—as I otherwise would—because those around me took what I said more seriously than I intended. I quickly recognized that people really were trying to please me. I couldn't be wishy-washy, domineering, or critical. I had an eager team on board, wanting to do my bidding, and it was up to me to give direction to those feelings. I recalled reading J. B. West's book *Upstairs at the White House*. The chief usher of the White House commented on the "command style" of First Ladies for whom he had worked. "I soon learned that Mrs. Kennedy's wishes, murmured with a

'Do you think . . .' or 'Could you, please . . .' were as much a command as Mrs. Eisenhower's, 'I want this done immediately.'"

Only once, that I recall, was I angry enough to be uncharacteristically harsh. Soon after I moved into the mansion, I was looking out the window, watching a rain shower that had just started, when I noticed a group of people crowded about the front gate. I called a security officer.

"Why are people standing outside the mansion gate in the rain?" I asked.

"Oh, they're waiting for the one o'clock tour to begin."

I looked at my watch. It was about 12:50 p.m.

"You mean that you don't unlock the gate until exactly one o'clock?'

"Yes, ma'm. That's what we always do."

I was infuriated.

I assumed my most commanding voice.

"I want you to open that gate now and let those people come in out of the rain. This house belongs to them, and whenever any of us forget that, we're in bad trouble."

Mel laughed when I told him what I had done. He knew it was so unlike me to get that upset.

"It just takes a little while for people to figure out what you expect of them and how you feel about living here," he said. "Now they know."

In the weeks that followed, I continued searching for ways to bring meaning to my new role. My head was still awhirl as I nestled into bed one evening.

"How do you think I should approach this job?" I asked Mel.

"With great gusto," he said, only somewhat jokingly.

"Seriously, I mean what should I do? I have a title and a great opportunity. What do I make of it?"

"You don't have to decide right now. Give yourself time. It will become obvious as you go along. Just learn the ropes for now."

I knew he was right. His advice was always good, thoughtful, and reasonable. But I was impatient. I clicked off the television with the remote, leaving Jay Leno to finish his show without us. The backyard security lights seeping between the shutters reflected in the ornate, gilt-edged mirror above the marble fireplace. I wondered what my mother, or my grandmother, would think of all this grandeur and service. Each morning, my bed was made up before I finished breakfast. Clothes dropped into the hamper returned clean, ironed, and folded. Shoes set on the fireplace hearth reappeared shined to a high gloss.

I laughed to myself, recalling Mama's admonition, "Pick up your clothes, Jean. Straighten up your room. You're not going to have somebody to clean up after you all your life."

She was wrong—at least for the time being.

My grandmother would undoubtedly be saying, "Don't let this high living go to your head."

I wasn't so much concerned about that as I was about missing the opportunity to do something of value when I had the chance.

I had been reading what little history there was of the mansion and its previous families. We were the thirtieth family to live at the mansion. But I wanted the home to be more than just our residence. It could also be a "launching pad" for whatever I chose to advocate.

I reached for the "idea pad" that I kept on the night table. At the top of the list, I wrote, "Make the mansion a warm and hospitable place." That was a good starting point. People truly enjoy visiting the historic home and have a high level of expectation regarding its upkeep and openness. However, during the Ashcrofts' eight years at the mansion, access had been curtailed beyond what many legislators and townspeople thought reasonable. I felt that there was a precedent for greater openness that was worth following. I had earlier read of the first social event held at the mansion in January 1872, when the four-story, pink-brick building replaced the wood-frame home that guests had refused to visit because of it rundown condition.

The opening of the new mansion was a proud moment for the City of Jefferson, as the capital city was then called. Two thousand people traipsed through the home of Gov. and Mrs. B. Gratz Brown. Those fortunate enough to reach the dining room were treated to a pyramid of pitted snipe—a highly regarded delicacy of the day. Despite the gridlock on the stairways, the event was reported to be "one of the most magnificent entertainments which ever occurred west of St. Louis."

In keeping with the lusty traditions of the past, I flung open the doors of the executive home for visitors—schoolchildren, legislators, tourists, and civic groups. The mansion architect and decorators call the Victorian renovation a "living restoration." I'm sure that there is some definition of that term more complex than one that I offered a group of elderly ladies.

"It means you can sit on the furniture," I explained with a smile. And they did, delighted by the opportunity to enjoy tea and sweets in the splendor of yesteryear. Between fifty and sixty thousand people would visit the mansion annually—people from all walks of life and from many countries.

Within two months, we had served seven hundred people at receptions, teas, or meals, not including the two thousand served on inauguration day. Following one dinner for a group of business leaders, mansion manager Joyce Bunch and I kicked off our shoes and sat down to review the day over a cup of coffee. Our families had known each other since college days in Columbia. In recent years, she had managed the chancellor's residence but left there to help me get started at the mansion.

Mel walked through the dining room on his way upstairs and stopped to join us.

"You've got to tell me about this room and the pictures. I still don't know the history of the mansion."

Mel spent most of his time at the Capitol and missed much of the mansion lore that I was beginning to gather.

Pointing to the sideboard I said, "All you have to know is the story about Gov. Robert Stewart and the sideboard."

"You mean the horse story?"

"That's the one."

"Well, tell me again so I can get the details straight."

"Okay. There are several versions, depending on your audience. But as the story goes, when the sideboard was in the previous mansion, Governor Stewart rode his horse up the front steps and ordered the servants to feed the animal a peck of oats from the sideboard. He said that his horse was just as good as the lawmakers who ate there."

Mel chuckled, "Sounds like one of those days when he had had his fill of the legislature."

"Or fill of something," I added. In explaining the incidents, docents always drew a laugh from tour groups by noting that Stewart was considered "a stranger to thrift but not to alcohol."

I also related a few of the mansion ghost stories, including one of the party-loving First Lady Maggie Stephens. Her portrait hangs at the turn of the stairway, and guards speak of hearing songs and laughter late at night when she "returns" to entertain her guests again.

The tales, traditions, and history of the old executive home fascinated me. I was trying to learn all I could, as fast as I could, and enjoying every minute. But it had been a long day for all of us. Joyce left for her home in Columbia. Mel and I turned off the lights in the dining room. I was still having trouble finding the light switches, but I was doing better. Our steps made a hollow sound on the parquet floors as we walked hand in hand across the Great Hall.

"Well, does it feel like home yet?" he asked, as we wound our way up the curved stairway.

I smiled. "Yes, I'm adjusting very well."

"I can tell," he replied with a gentle hug.

Feeling increasingly confident, I next invited members of the legislature—Republicans and Democrats—to dinner. A former First Lady had said, "I tell my mansion guests to hang up their politics when they hang up their coats," and that sounded like a good policy to follow. Like a kid wanting to try all the toys in the store, I designed a formal, multiple-course meal with lots of silverware, candles, and crystal. We were halfway through the meal when I realized that this was a terrible mistake. The discussion at my table concerned the sorbet course.

"Why are we eating dessert before the meat gets here?" one lawmaker asked another, who didn't know the answer either. I started to say that it was to "cleanse the palate" for the main course, but knew instinctively that any defense would meet with ridicule. When the waiters served the salad European style, following the main course, that brought another round of comment.

"Kitchen must 'ave forgot the salad," one snorted.

When the final course arrived, everyone seemed pleased at getting a "second dessert." After that experience, I entertained the legislators on the lawn under a tent. The colorful theme parties with music, enter-tainment, and door prizes were well received. Best of all, there were no embarrassing questions or explanations required.

However, there was one question that friends and visitors frequently asked: "What's it like living at the mansion?"—the implication being that amid such splendor and service one must be affected in some way.

Most often I would respond with a comment that emphasized the size of the home. "I spend a lot of time trying to find the light switches," or "I feel like I need a pair of roller skates to get from place to place."

I had read Janet Ashcroft's answer to the "what's-it-like" question in the local newspaper. Reflecting on her eight years at the mansion, she explained that the abnormal living style imposed on the First Family could cause loneliness and isolation. Friends, she said, didn't call because they feared to "bother you." In a similar observation, Gov. Forrest Smith had called the home "a glorified jail." I was determined not to let my-self be trapped in that mentality. But later I, too, realized that friends had not called for months and that I had allowed myself to be "locked" indoors with my duties for days. When that happened, I would imme-diately pick up the phone and make a few calls to Rolla. I would then get out of my "mansion clothes" and dress more casually for a long walk on the Katy Trail. I always felt better afterward.

I began to understand what Mrs. Kennedy meant when she said that being First Lady is a "role." Sometimes I felt as if I was on a movie set or caught up in a drama. I was one of the performers, finding the proper costumes for the part, walking on at the right time, and saying the ap-propriate lines. But always I had the feeling that I would walk out of the "theater" and back into the real world for yet another role, then un-known.

In the meantime, I wanted to do something worthwhile during my time "onstage." I researched the activities of former First Ladies, both state and national. I was amused by Eleanor Roosevelt's *Seven Rules for First Ladies,* two of which dealt with riding in open-top cars.

"Lean back so as not to obscure a good view of your husband," she advised. And, "don't get so overweight that it's hard to sit three in the backseat." I tucked those thoughts away for whatever value they might have later.

I knew there was one task that I wanted to get over with early in my tenure as First Lady—having my portrait painted for the mansion. It is a tradition for each First Lady's portrait to hang in the entry hall during her residency. Not long after moving into the mansion, I spoke with Mary Pat Abele, the executive director of Missouri Mansion Preservation.

"I want to have my portrait painted this year. I'm not getting any younger, so it's better now than later," I said.

"Do you have anyone in mind?"

"Well, I'm looking for a 'true' artist—one that will paint me twenty pounds thinner and ten years younger," I joked.

I had always admired the work of St. Louis artist Chick Early. When I told him of my requirement, he smiled and assured me that the brush was more flattering than the camera lens. I could tell right away that we were going to get along swimmingly. Unlike the other First Ladies on display, he portrayed me with something in my hand—a dogwood branch. In reality, any flowering plant that I touch instantly wilts. It would have been truer to life had my hands been draped over a computer keyboard. By taking a series of photos from which to work, Early was able to keep the number of sittings to a minimum. That was good, because I was impatient to get on with other things.

At first, I spent much of each day dealing with requests, hammering out staff problems, making decisions, scheduling events, and greeting visitors, all the while watching the budget and expenses of the house.

Many of the questions put to me had to do with entertaining and maintenance at the mansion:

Where do you want the hors d'oeuvres served?

When can the water be turned off for plumbing repairs?

Is it okay to put up scaffolding to clean the chandelier?

Do the new docents meet with your approval?

The chef is on vacation and we have inadvertently scheduled two parties. Should we count on the inmates to prepare the meal (the cheaper, but riskier course), or pay a caterer and relax?

Which wine shall we serve, the Seval or the Vidal?

Now that was an amusing question to ask me. I know absolutely nothing about wine. I never drink more than a half glass of wine, and Mel was a teetotaler. Even so, we offered our guests the products of Missouri's fine vineyards, using wines donated for an event or purchased from private funds.

In my attempt to provide dining guests a unique experience, I searched cookbooks and closely observed the meals served in Washington restaurants or at the White House.

"The asparagus at a dinner party we attended last night was limp and dark," I said to our chef Sheri Wolf, who would soon be retiring. "It was not at all like what you serve."

She beamed.

"It's the steamer," she said proudly. "That's the only way to get it right."

I remembered how proud Mrs. Ashcroft had been of the steamer when we toured the kitchen on my pre-inaugural visit. It was her legacy to me like the beaten-biscuit machine was to earlier First Ladies, who passed it along from one administration to the next. Up until the sixties, the ubiquitous beaten biscuit, calling for pure pork lard, showed up on mansion tables, both for company and for everyday fare.

Now with changing tastes and diets, dining expectations were far more challenging. Whenever I returned from a trip, my staff knew that I would be brimming with ideas for new entrees or a novel food presentation. Our ever-patient chef, Jerry Walsh, could often replicate a dish merely from my description or drawing.

I even tried to replicate musical presentations. After watching Marine Corps violinists encircle the dining tables at the White House, filling the room with stereophonic sound, I determined to give our guests a similar treat. Not having the Marines at my disposal, I achieved much the same effect with a talented group of high school violinists.

The mansion manager, Paula Earls, added to the dining experience by choreographing the waiters, teaching them to set the plates before guests on cue. It took some military-style training from her, but the inmates were very proud of their "delivery" and pleased by the approving smiles of guests.

In being around a dozen or more prisoners each day, I found that they had many commendable traits. What they lacked was judgment—which usually accounted for their being in prison in the first place. One of our model waiters decided he would veer from the usual after-dinner procedure of emptying glasses of leftover wine into a bucket to be poured down the kitchen drain. He decided to correct the wastage by empty-ing several glasses himself, an offense that resulted in the loss of his mansion job and our loss of a well-trained server.

As time went on, I began delegating many of the day-to-day deci-sions to staff. I had capable people working for me, or available to me, eager to carry out my ideas for menus and decorating. Still, my desk was "papered" with worthy causes—causes whose advocates wanted me to speak at an event or to promote their organization. "How shall I ever find the grains of truth embedded in all this mass of paper?" Virginia Woolf wrote. I knew the feeling.

I continued to look for direction. I feared being fragmented, like the shirt of some pop star tossed to a demanding audience—too many pieces of me scattered about, resulting in nothing of substance.

Then it happened. As Mel had promised, the next step became clear.

A mansion visitor casually mentioned that there was a benefactor, a widow, who would like to see the fountain restored on the mansion lawn. I had no idea what he was talking about, but later I sought out Mary Pat Abele. As director of Missouri Mansion Preservation, she had amassed a wealth of institutional knowledge during the nearly twenty-five years she had served under four First Families.

"Was there ever a fountain here at the mansion?" I asked

"Oh, yes," she said, "there used to be one in front of the house. It was put there in 1900, but all that remains now is the pool. That was filled with dirt years ago and turned into a flower bed. I have a picture of the original fountain in my files."

In a short while, the photograph appeared on my desk, showing three children of the mansion playing in a waterless fountain. During the next few days, I looked at it often, inspecting its features and pondering the possibilities.

Rebuilding the fountain was not enough. It had to have a theme . . . a reason.

"Fountain . . . water . . . mansion . . . children," I mused. "What can you do with that?"

Then one day, it came to me.

I jumped up excitedly!

"That's it!" I shouted aloud, though there was no one around to hear. "A fountain tribute to children!" I was as excited as Archimedes discovering the moons of Jupiter.

I picked up the phone and called Jill, my assistant.

"Get hold of the state librarian and tell her I want anything she can find on fountains."

"Drinking fountains?" she asked.

"No, no, decorative water fountains, like Rome . . . like Kansas City."

"Gotcha," she said. By now, the staff was getting used to my unusual requests. By the time the books arrived the next day, I had my mission well in mind. I would build the fountain and focus my time at the mansion advocating for children. It fitted perfectly with Mel's education agenda and the work I was doing already with early childhood immunization and domestic violence.

For the moment, I reveled in delight, ignoring the two big hurdles that lay ahead in building the fountain: cost and design. I was not mentally prepared when the mansion architect estimated a project cost of $200,000. The "sticker shock" nearly sent me back to planning dinner parties and rearranging the furniture—the usual pastimes of First Ladies.

Rather than ask the legislature for money that it was unlikely to appropriate, I decided to seek private donors. The early benefactor was still interested, as was another widow, but that still left $150,000 yet to raise. I wanted to get on with the project and not spend the summer raising funds in small amounts. Within weeks, the stars began to align when another woman, a child advocate and philanthropist, opted to put us over the top.

With just three donors, I was ready to build the fountain—though more would be needed to later complete the plaza. The next step, selecting a sculptor, proved more difficult. Artists from around the country submitted drawings or visited the site with samples of their work, but nothing clicked. There was no "yes-this-is-it" feeling.

Disappointed by this interruption in my plan, I unloaded my woes on Jamie Anderson, an old friend and artist from my hometown of Rolla.

She listened patiently.

"I'd like to make a proposal for the fountain," she said.

Her offer caught me off guard.

"Have you ever done anything in bronze?"

"I once sculpted a small bust. It's just a matter of making molds and working with a foundry," she said with a confident air.

"You don't get the point, Jamie. You're my friend, so you'll have to be ten times better than the others before I'd consider you."

She understood.

I called a meeting of the Fine Arts Committee to share the decision-making process with me. I enjoyed working with architects, designers, decorators, artists—creative people who were not afraid of venturing into the unknown. I was cursed with a creative gene that frequently caused me trouble, making me the oddball even in my own family. Mel joked that I had "fifty ideas a day—most of them before breakfast."

Still, I often had trouble working on church or civic committees. I was too impatient. The solution to a problem would pop into my head in a series of steps that I would blurt out early in the discussion process, scaring everybody to death. After being met with blank stares much of the time, I figured out that committees prefer working slowly and methodically. I learned to control my enthusiasm or to introduce my thoughts more cautiously, or not at all.

As First Lady, I no longer felt restrained. I was now among people who thrived on the exchange of ideas, the grander the better. When discussing Halloween decorations with designers from Six Flags amusement park, I suggested that we put a thirty-foot inflatable gorilla on the roof of the staid, old mansion. There was no prolonged silence or raised eyebrows. Instead, everyone at the table jumped into the discussion. We talked about how it *could* be done, rather than the difficulties involved. In the brainstorming session that followed even more outrageous ideas came forth, many of which I happily included in my annual Halloween Spooktacular for children.

Jamie arrived at the mansion for our meeting with the Fine Arts Committee several weeks after our initial conversation. In so brief a time, I was expecting no more than a paper sketch. Instead, she arrived with a cloth-covered basket, looking much like Little Red Riding Hood. From underneath the cloth she slipped a clay maquette of her creation and placed the pieces at the center of the table. Her classical design included elements from the previous fountain and featured children in timeless garb playing about the water.

As members perused the model, walking about the table to view it from every angle, I feared to show how much I thought of her rendition. After all, Jamie was my friend, and a sculptor of no renown.

"I like it," one member said boldly.

"I do, too," another joined in.

I breathed a sigh of relief. Our search had come full circle and back home. I had wanted a Missouri artist, preferably a woman, but held faint hope that we could find both. Jamie's sculpture would be the first permanent work of a Missouri woman at the mansion. I was excited.

As Jamie wrapped the clay pieces and returned them gently to her picnic basket, I could not hide my pleasure.

"Jamie, you made a great presentation today. The best we've had."

"You couldn't see me shaking?" she quipped.

"Of course not. You talked their language and made them feel very confident about the project."

"Well, I was scared to death," she said. We both laughed. There were major hurdles ahead, but I felt we were on the right track. The project was a leap of faith for both of us. I trusted her to deliver, knowing that she had never before undertaken an artwork of this dimension, one requiring both artistry and engineering. It could be a high-cost failure permanently marring the mansion lawn as well as my credibility. Jamie felt the pressure, too, but it only made her stronger and more determined.

A year later, on Valentine's Day 1996, when the completed work arrived from the foundry, everyone at the mansion or in the vicinity turned out to watch—workers, prisoners, docents, schoolchildren, passersby. As the finely sculptured fountain was hoisted into place, it snuggled into the yard, like a lost treasure returned after many years to its rightful location.

The Missouri Children's Fountain is more than an appealing artwork; it is art with a message. The figure of a little girl tiptoeing into the water depicts a child who died at the mansion and is a symbol of the health care needs of children. Another depicts a nameless African American youngster who once stayed in the mansion barn. He is a reminder that no child should be left out when it comes to education and opportunity. The third figure, modeled in my grandson's likeness and surrounded by Missouri foliage and wildlife, depicts the need to preserve the environment for future generations.

It is still my hope that each governor who lives in the mansion will look at the fountain and be reminded of Missouri's children—their health, opportunity, and environment.

Building the fountain was a personal growth experience for both Jamie and for me. Together we had tested our strength, pushed our limits, found our wings.

The fountain was a showy bit of restoration work, but there were other, less visible areas crying out for attention. The state did basic repairs, but the finer, more costly embellishments to the house came from private donations to Missouri Mansion Preservation, Inc. But MMPI was broke and struggling when I arrived at the mansion. If I wanted to make significant improvements, I needed to raise the money. My first restoration project was unexpected and unplanned. During a pre-inaugural visit, I had observed a huge crate at one end of the third-floor ballroom.

"What's in the crate?" I had asked First Lady Janet Ashcroft.

"Oh, it's a mantel mirror for a fireplace that was supposed to go on this floor. It was here when we arrived eight years ago. I think the restoration project in the seventies ran out of money."

"What can be done with it?" I asked.

"Whatever you want. It came in through that window," she added, pointing to one of the large bay windows.

During the mansion reception that followed the inauguration, the unsightly crate was a point of conversation. I was delighted when a half dozen or more supporters agreed, without hesitation, to contribute toward getting the mirror in its rightful place.

After that, I took on more projects, one at a time, ultimately raising more than $1.5 million in behalf of the mansion. I felt it was wrong for the First Family to live in the historic home, using the historic resource, without making repairs and improvements. The Missouri Governor's Mansion ranked as one of the finest Victorian restorations in the country, and I wanted to keep it that way.

Working with architects, decorators, MMPI, and the state, we refurbished the public restrooms, the basement entry, office and security areas, the elevator, and the back stairway. We replaced the roof, threadbare upholstery and carpeting, and broken china and glassware, and we completely restored a second-floor room and another on the third floor. By computerizing the mansion, it became possible to print our own menu cards and to create a pictorial inventory of all mansion furnishings. For the first time, the chef was able to plan meals and to store and retrieve recipes on a kitchen computer.

To keep the work moving, I designed fund-raising letters and held benefit dinners, urging support for the ongoing restoration. One generous gift that greatly enhanced the home allowed for the purchase of a beautiful Lyon and Healy harp for the double parlor.

The old house bustled with activity year-round. Each spring we held an Easter egg hunt for children with disabilities. The year it rained, forcing us indoors, saw wheelchairs whizzing through the halls and a baby lamb tottering across the parquet floors.

Ten thousand people showed up on the mansion lawn each year for the Halloween Spooktacular provided by Six Flags amusement park. Our entire family dressed in costumes to greet visitors. Old and young alike were on hand for the arrival of Batman and the Batmobile. As the simulated smoke cleared, revealing a masked figure standing atop the mansion roof, my grandson, Andrew—dressed like a bumblebee—grabbed my hand excitedly and said, "Now, that's the *real* Batman!"

A few months later, the home took on quite a different look. Decked in holiday splendor, the mansion opened its massive double doors to several thousand visitors who came for the annual candlelight tours and choral celebration. Each year I selected a different theme, ranging from "Toyland" to a "Victorian Holiday" to "Winter Wonderland." Fortunately, I had some highly talented "elves," Chris Carr, Cindy Singer, Jill Bednar, and Mary Pat Abele, who willingly worked twelve hours a day for a week to make the ideas come alive.

My mind raced with other possibilities for using the mansion for more community activities. A grant from the Walt Disney Family Foundation that I solicited from Diane Disney Miller made it possible to create the Walt Disney Children's Arts Festival, a hands-on art experience for both rural and intercity students. I assigned a long-time educator, Micca Ruffin, and her committee the task of conducting the Children's Hour at the mansion one Saturday morning each month. MMPI offered classes in manners and etiquette for children, a course that concluded with "graduates" inviting their parents to lunch at the mansion to show off their newly acquired skills.

As construction, decorating, and entertaining went on at an accelerated pace, I turned to an even more consuming project: writing. My first literary effort had come at age fourteen with the submission of a love story to *True Confessions* magazine. At that tender age, my fictional romance didn't merit even a rejection slip from the editors. After that disappointment, I turned to writing skits, poetry, and satires for church programs, fellow workers, and friends. But the urge to write a book never faded.

As a reminder of my intent, I kept a cartoon on my desk. It showed a surgeon hovering over a patient on whom he had just performed an operation. With a scalpel in one hand and a book in the other, he looks down at the patient and says, "He was right! He *did* have a book in him!" I knew that, someday, I'd uncover the book within me. At the time, I didn't realize that—like giving birth—it would be such a magnificent agony.

The idea of writing the story of Missouri's First Families came after discovering that there was no compiled history of those who had served the state over the last 175 years. A mansion cookbook with a condensed history had sold well for the past decade, but it was no longer in print. I spoke with Mary Pat Abele, who had been involved in the earlier book project.

"I'm considering writing a history of the families who lived in the mansion—how they got here, what they did once in office and after they left here."

She responded cautiously.

"It's a lot of work," she said with a sigh. "It takes planning. I'll bring you a flow chart of how the cookbook was designed."

When she produced the chart, I was horrified. It looked like the systems grid for an electrical power plant. All the preliminary maneuvers were discouraging. Form an outline, determine the primary and secondary sources, hire a research assistant, raise the money to underwrite the book, find a publisher. . . .

"I've never written a book before and since I don't know any better, I'm going to put something on paper," I explained, knowing I was not proceeding properly. "I need to sit down and start writing," I said. "I can get this done in six months, if I work at it."

She smiled that Mona Lisa I-know-something-that-you-don't smile. It was just as well that I didn't know what was ahead. I was exuberant with the idea of producing an important historical work. I plunged onward, writing and rewriting, designing and redesigning, stopping and starting. The book would be entitled *If Walls Could Talk* and tell the story of the mansion, its First Families, and the times in which they lived. "We shape our buildings; thereafter they shape us," Winston Churchill once said. That seemed especially true of those who lived in the old home. Each family made of the experience something different, but I became convinced that they were never the same for having lived at the mansion.

As the scope of the task grew, I hired Lisa Heffernan Weil, a journalism graduate student who was willing to put aside her studies and postpone her family to be a part of the venture. Lisa did the library research, bringing me copies of old newspapers, articles, books, and pictures that she uncovered. I pored over them, extracting stories and historic tidbits to frame a chapter for each of the state's fifty governors.

When Lisa called to share some small fact that filled a hole in our research, we were made as giddy as schoolgirls by the discovery. Despite my earlier plans, after six months of researching and writing the end was nowhere in sight. Like Br'er Rabbit, I was stuck with this "tar baby" and couldn't get loose. Completing the work before leaving office became an obsession. I carried the manuscript everywhere I went—from the jungles of Costa Rica to the sandy beaches of the Dead Sea.

Knowing I lacked the credentials of a historian, I was careful to have my manuscript read by my friend Kenneth Winn, the state historian. Five years into the task, I asked him, "How do I know when I'm finished?"

"Oh," he said, "writing is never finished, it's just abandoned." I discovered that truth too late, as the manuscript grew to 436 printed pages with more than 600 pictures. My book came off the press weighing in at five pounds per volume. I made the old joke: "This book has a *resistible* quality. Once you put it *down*, you can't pick it *up* again."

I quickly got off two more books. The first was *Christmas at the Mansion: Its Memories and Menus,* a recounting of holiday celebrations and an illustrated collection of recipes used at the mansion and in my home. The final book was a paperback compilation of my speeches, aptly entitled *Will You Say a Few Words.* When filling out a form, I would no longer be embarrassed at having nothing to place on the line that asked, "Occupation?" I was a published writer!

There were other unique opportunities for Mel and me during his term as governor, but none more memorable than a 1995 invitation to spend the night at the Clinton White House. As a child, I used to ride the streetcar in front of 1600 Pennsylvania Avenue on my way to the orthodontist or to my piano lesson in Georgetown. But I had never toured the historic site. When I passed by, I always stared at the windows, hoping to catch a glimpse of Harry Truman, or even Bess or Margaret, but I never did. I couldn't imagine—not in my wildest dreams—that I would ever attend a social event at the White House, much less spend the night.

When we pulled into the driveway on the appointed day, my head was still spinning at the thought of a sleepover in such historic quarters. I had been to formal dinners on the first floor during the National Governors Association meetings, and Hillary had entertained the spouses at lunch on the second floor, but this was my first visit to the more casual third floor where we were to eat that night.

Joining us in the comfortably furnished solarium were Gov. and Mrs. Tom Carper of Delaware. Hillary was getting in later from a speaking engagement, but not in time for dinner. The buffet for five was very non-French as compared to our earlier meals at the White House. Being more health conscious, the new chef had replaced the calorie-laden cuisine with less artery-clogging dishes.

Our waiter started us with a heavenly asparagus soup. We remained seated as he filled each plate to order with roast beef (no gravy), an oversized baked potato, garlicky carrots, broccoli, green salad, and sourdough bread. A fruit-decorated flan capped the tasty, but unpretentious, meal.

Not surprising, current political issues dominated the conversation, ranging from welfare reform to teen pregnancy to gays in the military. On all topics, the president spoke freely, exuding the compassion and sincerity he conveys so well. Dressed in a sports shirt, he appeared up-beat and relaxed in spite of the abuse he had taken that week at the hands of congressional Republicans.

When a telephone rang during the meal, Clinton reached for the receiver on a nearby table. I was excited, thinking that I might overhear the president of the United States dealing firsthand with some world crisis.

I listened.

"No, Chelsea's not here right now. Who's calling?" There was a pause. "This is her father," he added. "I'll tell her you called."

Turning back to the table, the president beamed mischievously.

"It just mortifies Chelsea's friends when I answer the phone," he laughed heartily.

Governor Carper took the break in conversation as an opportunity to address some of his state's problems. Having the ear of the president, he could not resist pulling a note card from his pocket and launching into his prepared "want list." We all understood what he was doing. To-morrow he would be able to tell several important constituents, "I spoke directly to the president about your concerns."

Following the meal, we roamed about the third floor. The upper-story bedrooms have the feel of an old downtown hotel with their low ceilings and no-frills furnishings. We took the elevator to the second floor, where the family quarters are located at one end of a hall and two formal guest bedrooms at the other. The long, wide hallway serves much like a drawing room with its built-in bookshelves, Steinway grand piano, and presidential mementos. A large abstract painting, a colorful Chihuly glass bowl, and other art objects added a pleasant ambience.

I was surprised that the president took the time to show us to our rooms and to explain their historic features. The Carpers were assigned the Queen's Bedroom, which had lodged royalty and such notables as Winston Churchill and Russian leader V. M. Molotov. It's the room that Mrs. Kennedy pronounced "incredible . . . fit for a queen." Mel and I were given the much-venerated Lincoln Bedroom, containing one of the five original copies of the Gettysburg Address.

Before retiring for the night, like a good host, the president inquired if we needed anything more and pointed out the button that would summon help. Having discovered that I had only two shots left in my camera, I took the opportunity to request a new roll of film.

Upon seeing the Lincoln bed, I understood what Jackie Kennedy meant when she described its headboard as looking like a "cathedral." The eight-foot-long, six-foot-wide rosewood bed dominates the room. Actually, Lincoln never slept in the bed; it belonged to his wife, Mary. However, their eleven-year-old son, Willie, died in the bed when the family lived at the White House.

Although the bed is considered a national treasure, for many years overnighters complained of its notoriously lumpy mattress stuffed with horsehair. Finally, First Lady Barbara Bush, thinking more of the comfort of her guests than of authenticity, upgraded the bedding.

Some say that the spirit of Lincoln still pervades the room that served as the president's office and cabinet room during the Civil War. Presidents Eisenhower and Theodore Roosevelt both claimed to have felt the presence of Lincoln in the room. Maids and butlers tell of sightings. Ronald Reagan's dog often barked outside the door, but would not enter.

Wanting to enjoy my sleepover at the White House, I dismissed the "spirited" encounters. After all, the Missouri Governor's Mansion has its own weird sounds and ghostly sightings. Because Mel and I slept so soundly there, we apparently missed the alleged "wanderings" of former First Families, but security guards working the night shift could spin some spine-tingling tales. Without any qualms about the Lincoln Bedroom, I jumped into my nightgown and snuggled into the massive Victorian bed.

As Mel prepared for bed, he realized that he had neglected to pack his pajamas. Being of the "old school" when it came to nightwear, he was uncomfortable at the thought of sleeping in his underwear in the Lincoln Bedroom—*of all places!* I told him I doubted there was any protocol requiring pajamas and that worse breaches of etiquette had no doubt occurred at the White House. Sensing my lack of sympathy for his plight, he climbed into bed. Our kids, aware of their father's strong sense of propriety, would thereafter refer teasingly to the incident as "the time Dad spent the night in the White House without his pajamas."

The next morning I inspected the room further, snapped off a few photos, and jotted notes to friends on the elegant White House stationery. As I passed the window, I saw the White House press corps assembling on the lawn for an early interview with the president.

Minutes later a porter—as the servants at the White House are called—appeared at our door. The evening before I had filled out a menu card indicating what I wanted for breakfast and when and where I wished to eat. I was offered the choice of being served in an adjacent sitting room or in the sun-drenched atrium at the end of the hallway. It was a tough decision, but I opted for the cozy sitting room where the ghost of Richard Nixon might still linger. I am told that President Nixon often came there on summer evenings, cranked the thermostat down, lit the fireplace, and enjoyed a good cigar.

After Mel left to join the president for breakfast at Blair House, I nestled into a comfy chair beside the "Nixon fireplace" with a copy of the *Washington Post* and a cup of tea. Happily, I did not detect the presence of any former residents. But ever alert to Victorian decorating ideas, I was surprised to see that the ceiling paper of the Lincoln sitting room was the same as I had unknowingly picked for my mansion office.

Before leaving, I pulled back the curtains and took one last look onto Pennsylvania Avenue, where tourists and government workers filled the streets. A child outside the fence spotted me and waved. I smiled and waved back, recalling my own scanning of the White House as a youngster in search of a face in the window.

Knowing how much Mel and I had delighted in the visit, I returned to Missouri determined to invite more people to spend the night at the mansion. With four unused and beautifully restored bedrooms, we had a number of guests share the Victorian home with us during our tenure. Entertaining visitors and friends turned out to be one of the greatest joys of living in the Governor's Mansion.

As time went on, I realized that Mel's years of service in state government were drawing to a close. I was saddened at the thought. We would be moving to an as yet undetermined location. At this point in our lives, we had no children or family members to relocate, but we did have Beaumont, our lovable 150-pound Newfoundland. He had enjoyed the benefits of being the "First Pooch," relishing the attention given him by workers and visitors alike. He even suffered the indignity of being "dressed" as a skunk for Halloween with a white stripe sprayed down his back. Prison inmates working at the mansion volunteered for "doggie patrol," taking on the extra task of watching over the "big black bear"—as one youngster called him.

I doubt if Benny, his last caregiver, had ever owned a pet. The two became great friends, each looking forward to the other's arrival. Beaumont outweighed Bennie, making it difficult to determine who was in command at which end of the leash. Beaumont was beginning to show his age, and Bennie saw to his comfort by putting buckets of ice into his pen, providing him a cool bed during the summer heat.

When Beaumont died, we had him cremated and buried on the side lawn, marking the nearby stone wall with a small plaque. That same day, I met Bennie in the hallway with tears in his eyes. Sensing his hurt, I gave him a hug and thanked him for the loving care he had shown our family pet. I'm sure the security officers would have been frantic had they seen any contact between a prisoner and a member of the First Family. But for the moment, our labels didn't count. We were just two human beings sharing the loss of a loved one.

As I began my final year as First Lady, I had the warm feeling of having made some worthwhile improvements to the mansion. I had done what I set out to do—make the stately Victorian home more hospitable and accessible, build the fountain as a tribute to children, and complete a history of Missouri's First Families.

Whether Mel won or lost the Senate race, the two of us would be able to walk from the mansion, hand in hand, knowing that we had given our all to the task of serving the people of Missouri. Whatever new duties came our way—well, we'd take those on together, as we always had.

As it turned out, on my final day at the mansion, I walked down the Grand Stairway alone. The huge parlors were strewn with flowers, baubles, and ribbons—all part of the decorations for the annual Christmas tours that I had planned months earlier but would never see. This year the new governor, Roger Wilson, and his wife, Pat, would greet the thousands of visitors to the residence. The Wilsons, who would occupy the mansion only briefly, said to me repeatedly, "Stay as long as you like." It was a most gracious offer and one that I tried to honor by leaving as soon as possible so they could enjoy their few months in the wonderful old home.

On the day of my departure, I made my final descent of the Grand Stairway with the same sense of wonder I felt that first night in the mansion. As I stepped into the Great Hall, I noticed that my portrait was no longer in the spot traditionally reserved for the residing First Lady. The painting had already been moved to the double parlor, as I had requested. I hugged and thanked each staff member assembled to bid me farewell. With tears streaming down my face, I walked across the Great Hall, through the massive double doors, and into a waiting car. I had come to the mansion less than eight years earlier, a housewife assuming the role of First Lady. I was leaving as a widow and a United States senator.

The happiest decade of my life was over. Now, at age sixty-seven, I was taking on a new task, one that I had not sought, but one that I would not refuse. I had no idea where the next road would lead. But deep within, I felt the same Presence that Abraham spoke of centuries ago. Acting on faith alone, the ancient biblical wanderer "rose up, and went out, not knowing where he was going."

As the car moved from the driveway, the mansion's heavy iron gate closed slowly behind me, marking an ending to my time as First Lady. I did not look back.

Political Family

Ten-year-old Russ Carnahan first learned to woo voters as he handed out campaign matchbooks during Mel's 1966 race for the state senate.

By age ten, Tom Carnahan was an eager campaigner for his father during the 1980 state treasurer's race.

With four children to care for, I came home in the evening feeling much like a mother bird returning to a nest of hungry, chirping offspring requiring immediate attention. There was a big dinner to cook and dishes to be washed afterward. Fortunately, Mel would pitch in and help with whatever needed doing, whether it was dishes or diapers.

In the sixties, a political candidate would paint his name on the side of a station wagon, load the back with posters, and travel the district shaking hands and passing out campaign literature. Here, the Carnahan clan poses with Mel's newly painted vehicle. At the left are Mel's brother Bob and his wife, Oma,

and daughter Mary Ann; Mel's parents A. S. J. and Mary Carnahan; Mel and Jean with daughter Robin. Sitting on the fender are more members of Bob's family: Karen, Bobby, Katy, and Betty. In front of them are our two sons, Russ and Randy.

Mel soaked his feet and signed a tennis shoe following his 325-mile trek from St. Louis to Kansas City during his losing 1984 bid for governor. Gov. Lawton Chiles (D–Florida), who had made a similar walk, wrote Mel a letter saying, "I've never known anyone who walked their state, who didn't eventually win." In my mind, that spoke more of sustained effort—the very quality that makes a good candidate and officeholder.

A news reporter once referred to Mel as a "straight arrow." This led a supporter to create an arrow-shaped campaign pin with Mel's name on it.

KANSAS CITY STAR

In August 1992, our family celebrated Mel's primary victory in the governor's race. My father, eighty-six-year-old Reginald Carpenter, made his stage debut with great enthusiasm. He would not live to see the final victory three months later.

WIDE-WORLD PHOTO

The Inaugural

quests the honour of y

at the Inaugural

Governor Mel

Governor of

he South Steps of th

Monday, the eleventh of January

thousand nine hundred and ninety-three

at eleven-thirty o'clock

followed by

The Inaugural Ball

State Capitol

at eight-thirty o'clock

In January 1993, as the bells of nearby St. Peter's Church tolled the inaugural hour, Mel was sworn in as Missouri's fifty-first governor. In a spontaneous and heartfelt moment, I couldn't help but give expression to my feelings

139

Mel and I paused on the stairway overlooking the Capitol Rotunda to welcome those attending the 1997 inaugural ball.

In 1996, family members showed their approval after Mel came in first in his reelection bid. The Carnahan family had grown and changed considerably since we posed for a similar photo thirty years earlier.

The tedium of posing for the annual Christmas card photograph was always lightened by the antics of Beaumont, our Newfoundland, or one of the grandchildren.

Campaign photographers were always looking for some interesting way to pose the family. I got a kick out of this one taken at the farm that looked much like a scene from The Sound of Music.

Mel's favorite exercise was biking on the Katy Trail. I occasionally joined him, but most often I preferred walking or jogging.

Of the many formal portraits of Mel throughout his political career, this was one of my favorites.

Ten thousand people showed up on the mansion lawn each year for the Halloween Spooktacular provided by Six Flags amusement park. Our entire family dressed in costumes to greet visitors—young and old—who came to enjoy the games, treats, and musical performances.

The 1871 Governor's Mansion sits majestically atop a hill overlooking the Missouri River. As First Lady, fascinated by the grand Victorian home, I wrote If Walls Could Talk, a history of Missouri's First Families and the times in which they lived.

The Missouri Children's Fountain by artist Jamie Anderson is sculpture with a message. I wanted it to be a daily reminder to every governor of the health, opportunity, and environment of Missouri's youngest citizens.

MISSOURI MANSION PRESERVATION, INC.

I always looked forward to the mansion Easter egg hunt for children with disabilities. The event featured a big, pink bunny so skillfully played by the governor's legal counsel, Joe Bednar, that even his young daughter didn't recognize him.

The January 1999 visit of Pope John Paul II to St. Louis coincided with the scheduled execution of convicted murderer Darrell Meese and ended with Mel commuting the sentence at the request of the pope.

Mel and I viewed the Flood of '93 from the air as well as from the ground. On those helicopter rides, I often looked like a parcel post package securely wrapped and tied for delivery.

Marc Farinella, Mel's campaign manager, explained what happened to staff and supporters after the plane crash: "We all began to understand that this election was not about Mel Carnahan. It was about the things he stood for, and we still had the responsibility to carry those ideas forward."

Our whistle-stop tour of the state was a four-day journey, with Mel speaking from the back of the train during our stops in two dozen cities. The trip was inspired by the one Harry Truman made during the final days of his 1948 presidential campaign.

WENDY L. WERNER PHOTO

Crowds were fascinated by the old-fashioned, grassroots campaign style. Of all the cities we visited, I will never forget how I felt when the train rolled into Independence—Harry Truman's hometown. There was not a dry eye on the back platform of that train. Before us was a sea of friendly faces, a lively band, and a train station decked with flags, banners, and posters. It could have been a movie set.

145

*This editorial sketch of Chris, Mel, and Randy was reminiscent of the
whistle stop tour we had made across the state just months earlier.*

*Mel and Randy were not
only father and son, they
were also best friends.*

Randy, "the renaissance man," as I jokingly referred to him, had traveled on six continents. He could fix anything, shoe horses, bag a Thanksgiving turkey, climb mountains, operate farm equipment, and give fine legal and political counsel. He is pictured here with his grandfather.

Those who knew and worked with Chris Sifford still get together each spring for a bass fishing tournament in Puxico. In August, they gather for the Sifford Scramble, a tournament for golfers, and nongolfers. Both events raise money for the Chris Sifford Memorial Scholarship Fund. It's a wonderful remembrance of a young man whose ingratiating smile and caring spirit still warm our lives.

The walk from the mansion to the Capitol for the funeral service replicated the procession to the cemetery 113 years earlier for Gov. John Marmaduke, the only other governor to die while living at the mansion.

JEFFERSON CITY POST-TRIBUNE

JEFFERSON CITY POST-TRIBUNE

Thousands of mourners lined the streets to pay their respects to the governor, many leaving flowers, photos, drawings, poetry, and candles along the iron fence.

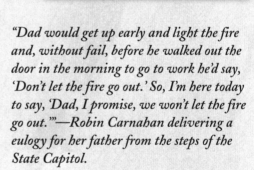

"Dad would get up early and light the fire and, without fail, before he walked out the door in the morning to go to work he'd say, 'Don't let the fire go out.' So, I'm here today to say, 'Dad, I promise, we won't let the fire go out.'"—Robin Carnahan delivering a eulogy for her father from the steps of the State Capitol.

I still see the small, gold torch being worn on the lapels of Carnahan supporters even now.

JEFFERSON CITY POST-TRIBUNE

Along with Mel, I had sat in front of the Missouri State Capitol several times as he was sworn into office. Now I sat there again, this time surrounded by ten thousand people, including President and Mrs. Bill Clinton. But for the moment, I felt very much alone.

KANSAS CITY STAR

Roy Temple and his wife, Stacie, join mourners at the funeral service. The plane crash was especially difficult for Roy, who lost the governor he admired and worked for so hard, as well as his lifelong friend, Chris Sifford. A lawyer and an accountant, Roy is an extraordinary political strategist and public policy analyst. Most important for anyone in political life, he is principled and loyal.

CHRISTINA DICKEN / SPRINGFIELD NEWS-LEADER

PAUL CHILDRESS PHOTO

Seven

One in a Hundred

The only true happiness comes from squandering ourselves for a purpose.

—John Mason Brown

When my family lived on our Rolla farm, I came home in the evening feeling much like a mother bird returning to a nest of hungry, chirping offspring requiring immediate care and attention. There was a big dinner to cook and dishes to be washed afterward. Heaps of laundry needed to be washed and folded. Fortunately, Mel would pitch in and help with whatever needed doing, whether it was dishes or diapers.

But by 1993, when Mel and I moved into the Governor's Mansion, our grown children had scattered, leaving fewer household chores and less frequent gatherings of the entire family. My home life again changed dramatically when I moved to Washington alone, leaving behind an eight-hundred-acre farm for an eight-hundred-square-foot apartment.

Even in Washington, it was difficult getting settled. Moving three times in two years, I was like Goldilocks trying to find the right fit. My first place, in Arlington, was too far from the Capitol; my next location, a noisy downtown apartment, was too expensive; but my final place, a small condominium a half block from my office, was just right.

Although I lived on Capitol Hill, getting home still took some effort. The printed schedule handed me each evening as part of my briefing book allotted every hour of my day to some activity with little personal time to spare. Evenings often called for one or more "stop bys," or "walk throughs" as my staff called them—a "stop by" being an event that required little more than a "walk through" while the car waited outside.

As I switched roles to take on household tasks, I often thought of the comment made to Lindy Boggs when she replaced her deceased husband in Congress. Lady Bird Johnson, who had urged Lindy to run, asked if she thought it was possible "to do the job without a wife." Mrs. Boggs replied, "Yes, but it will be more difficult."

Mrs. Boggs found—as I did—that being without a "wife" required more careful planning. I had to schedule, or squeeze in, time for shopping, even for groceries. For the sake of convenience, I often bypassed the supermarkets—once my second home—for the mom-and-pop grocery on the corner with its wide assortment of the trendy but costly foods demanded by Capitol Hill shoppers.

At the end of the day, I shuffled up two flights of stairs with an overstuffed briefcase and sometimes the dry cleaning or groceries. There was the juggle for the keys and lights . . . the unloading . . . the unwinding.

Sadly, there was no one awaiting my footsteps. At first, I pretended that there was. I caught myself wanting to yell out, "I'm home!" the way we each did in our family to announce our return. The refrigerator, usually the source of comfort food, offered little solace. Opening the door to a rack of yogurt, Diet Coke, and bagels was reminiscent of provisions found in a college dorm room during finals week.

Despite these feelings of "homelessness," I was grateful to get out of my shoes and relax. I wished for time to do more casual reading, as opposed to required reading. The stacks of books, magazines, and news clippings cluttering my night table, dresser, and computer desk were a daily reminder of my good intentions. In desperation, I asked my staff to underline articles I wanted to read so I could get the highlights, if not the full details.

I seldom turned on the television, knowing that it would distract me from my "homework." Most often, I headed for the bedroom, laid out my clothes for the next day, and jumped into bed. Then I reviewed my schedule and briefing material until I fell asleep.

In recent years, I had started my day with treadmill exercises, stretches, and weight lifting. When I lived at the Governor's Mansion, I got into a waiting car that took me to the local fitness center for an hour-long workout. In Washington, my treadmill and set of hand weights filled one corner of my bedroom. Although near at hand, they seemed more inaccessible than ever. In the interest of time, I often shortened my exercise routine and appeased myself with the promise that after the November campaign I would become more faithful.

I used the time I gained to scan the morning newspapers. Each day I read the *Washington Post* and the *New York Times* before going to the office. Because the Missouri newspapers came a day late, news clips were downloaded from the internet and ready for my review as soon as I arrived at work. Knowing that reporters lining the Senate hallways would be looking for a reaction to current events, staying posted on the news both in Washington and back home was especially important. A question could come from anywhere, on any topic, at any time. Because of that, I needed at least a thin layer of knowledge on a vast array of topics. I didn't like that situation. I preferred to have a deeper knowledge on a few issues, as other senators ultimately did. (McCain on campaign finance; John Warner [R-Virginia], military affairs; Kennedy, education). Again, my impatience was showing.

Given all my spontaneous interviews, seldom did I ever feel blindsided by a reporter. I attributed much of that to good briefings from my communications director, Tony Wyche. He was a master at developing and conveying a message and tracking what was important in both Washington and Missouri. He recognized, as I did, that as a newcomer I was allowed less margin for error. A mistake or lack of knowledge by my colleagues was more easily ignored. One blunder on my part would be blown out of all proportion.

Keeping current on Capitol Hill also meant attending the weekly caucus meetings. Each Tuesday at noon, the Democratic members gathered for lunch in room 211, just off the Senate Reception Room, while Republicans met down the hall in a larger, but less ornate, area. If the Senate can be compared to a high school class, than this would be considered homeroom time. Most members attended the caucus, it being one of the few times we saw each other as a group. Caucus meetings provided a place to discuss pending legislation, plot strategy as a party, listen to the complaints of members, or even celebrate a happy occasion such as a birthday.

Reporters staked out the halls to quiz members on any new or controversial comments coming from our discussions. Although the Democratic leader often cautioned against disclosures, one former senator declared, "Positions are leaked to the press before we've finished digesting lunch."

The 211 Caucus Room, or the Taj Mahal, as it was once called, is the legacy of Lyndon Johnson, who picked the room for himself as majority floor leader because of its proximity to the chamber. Johnson restored the shabby area with a stately green and gold decor, including the luxury of the day—a private bathroom that he walled off in a corner with rich mahogany paneling. It is said that Johnson would break from his visit with a senator or constituent to use the facility, but continue carrying on his conversation from behind the closed door.

While caucus and committee meetings were predictable, roll call votes were often unscheduled and could wreak havoc with the day's schedule. From my office, it took about five to seven minutes to make the trip by elevator to the basement, catch the Senate subway to the Capitol, and then ride the escalator and elevator to the second-floor Senate chamber.

Some days there were no votes at all, while on other days there were a half dozen. Members refer to rapid, back-to-back roll calls as a "vote-a-rama," an occasion that keeps senators away from their offices and confined to the Capitol. Those with seniority wait in their "hideaways"—small offices in the Capitol away from their main suites and nearer the chamber. It saves them travel time. Freshmen, on the other hand, get more exercise.

I made it a point to be present for every vote and every caucus, having missed only the day that I returned home to speak at a friend's funeral. I also attended and spoke at nearly all of my committee meetings, unless there were appointments or conflicts that came up at the last minute.

I had great committee assignments for a freshman: the Commerce, Science, and Transportation; Armed Services; Governmental Affairs; and the one I jokingly said I knew the most about—the Committee on Aging.

One of my assignments raised a few eyebrows in my family.

"I can't believe you want to serve on the Armed Services Committee," Tom said with a tone of surprise when he heard of my choice.

I knew it was time to unveil my hawkish youth, the product of a childhood spent in Washington during World War II. My father had taken me to view every piece of armament displayed in the nation's capital. We climbed into jeeps, tanks, and fighter plane cockpits. We boarded every navy submarine and ship that came up the Potomac for exhibit.

Now I was a member of the Senate Armed Services Committee—the fifth woman ever to serve in that capacity. I began reading everything from the escapades of Epaminondas to *New Soldier*. Within months, I could speak an entire sentence of meaningless acronyms and was well into identifying the various military weapons by name and function. With defense issues at the top of the news, this committee was more important than ever. Serving under both Republican and Democratic chairs during my time on the committee, I was favorably impressed by both. Senators John Warner and Carl Levin (D-Michigan) are gifted statesmen and true patriots. I also enjoyed the opportunity to work with the chair of the Governmental Affairs Committee, Joe Lieberman (D-Connecticut). His calm and reasoned approach to issues makes him one of the most pleasant and valued of lawmakers.

These top-notch committee assignments kept my days lively and my staff agile. There were no laggards. I quickly realized that I set both the pace and the tone for the office. As the old saying goes, "If mama ain't happy, ain't nobody happy." Well, it's the same for senators. There are many woebegone, browbeaten staffers on Capitol Hill, but mine were not among them.

My chief of staff, Roy Temple, a lawyer and accountant, is an extraordinary political strategist and public policy analyst, often expressing his ideas with rapid-fire speed and at a vociferous tempo. Most important for anyone in political life, he is principled and loyal. Having worked on the campaigns of three Carnahan office seekers, he seems more like a son than a staffer. A political junky from his youth, he had managed—and lost—three successive campaigns before coming on board with Mel. A lesser person would have given up and chosen another line of work. But not Roy. The plane crash had been especially difficult for him. In addition to losing the boss he admired and worked for so hard, he also lost his best friend, Chris Sifford. Both of them had been born and raised in the Bootheel town of Puxico. They were proud of those roots but still enjoyed tossing out one-liners about their small-town background.

"Why, when we were growing up, our idea of diversity was having a General Baptist Church, a Missionary Baptist Church, and a Southern Baptist Church," they often joked.

Another longtime staffer "adopted" by my family is John Beakley, a truly caring human being with a heart as big as the state of Texas from which he hails. John is by nature an encourager, and all those around him benefit from that attitude. He and his assistant, Ryan Rhodes, made it their mission to see that a frantic schedule worked for me and not the other way around.

Once when I balked at a fourteen-hour day and blurted out, "This is elder abuse!" he smiled reassuringly and pointed out that he had built an extra hour of "home time" into my schedule for the next morning.

Another Carnahan campaign veteran was my deputy chief of staff, Rachel Storch, an intelligent, talented Harvard graduate who never lost her ability to be a thoroughly pleasant and patient coworker under all circumstances. With David Schantzer as my legislative director, I had a well-seasoned policy expert, composed and focused, who was on top of every issue we tackled. His legislative assistants—Steve Neuman, Neal Orringer, Amy Barber, Sandy Fried, Stephen Sugg—poured themselves into their jobs, going beyond the call of duty to keep me informed and to keep our office active in the committee process.

And hats off to the hearty crew who opened, sorted, and read the mail in addition to answering the phones and responding to e-mails. In today's world of easy communications, constituent service has grown to be one of the biggest and most important operations in a congressional office. Years ago, when there was only one Senate Office Building, Truman enjoyed saying that he could be reached by simply writing to "Sen. Harry Truman, SOB, Washington."

After having assembled such a talented and diligent staff, it was difficult to see them dispersed after the 2002 election. They had worked more like a football team than a military squadron. From top staffers to interns to volunteers, we had something to prove. We were torchbearers for a cause. We felt that every day, and it showed.

Because I believe that the workplace influences our moods and efficiency, I tried to make our fifth-floor suite in the Hart Office Building as pleasant, colorful, and inviting as possible. Although its windows opened onto the inner core of the building rather than the street, the office was still light and cheerful. Brightening my room and attracting the most attention was a five-foot-round Missouri state seal cut from the carpet that was in the governor's office before its renovation. But much to the chagrin of several staffers, I also decorated the office with pictures and models of various military aircraft, some manufactured in Missouri.

"Why don't we put up pictures of children?" one staffer intoned.

She had a point. So we hung pictures of people along with display cases of my political buttons of Missouri governors and my collection of woman suffrage items. Also on view were autographed photographs of former Missouri senators, including Stuart Symington, Harry Truman, and Tom Eagleton.

Two oil paintings in my office were especially meaningful to me. One was a portrait of Harry Truman, on loan from the presidential library. On the opposite wall was an oil painting of Mel done shortly before his death. The St. Louis artist Chick Early had painted three identical portraits: one hangs in the State Capitol in Jefferson City; a smaller version is in my home; and the other I hung in my Senate office.

I had a strange feeling one day as I was meeting with constituents around the coffee table near the portrait. Although I was seated with my back to the wall, when I looked down Mel's image was reflecting in the glass-top table. I thought I was the only one who noticed it.

"Did you see what I saw?" Roy Temple asked after everyone had left.

I smiled. "You mean the reflection of Mel?"

"It looked like he was right here with us, didn't it?"

"Maybe so," I said. "At least that's a good thought to have."

I went back to my desk, but not before rearranging my display of Don Quixote figurines on the credenza just beneath Mel's portrait. The fictional knight-errant pursued impossible and costly dreams that others thought ridiculous. His quest to right wrongs wasn't always successful. Still, his ventures are a reminder to seek truth rather than self-interests.

Those are not bad ideals to cling to in Washington.

Within weeks of coming to Washington, I walked onto the Senate floor to cast a vote that I knew would be parsed, analyzed, criticized, reviewed, and held up for public examination by both friends and political foes alike.

President George W. Bush had nominated Sen. John Ashcroft for the position of U.S. attorney general, the highest law enforcer of the land. He was the last and most controversial of the president's nominees to be sent up to the Hill for approval.

Some months earlier, Ashcroft had been Missouri's own Republican U.S. senator, and the ardent opponent of just about everything that Mel Carnahan stood for. His campaign for reelection to the Senate was toughly fought and ended at the polls in defeat. Being cast by history as the candidate who "lost to a dead man" must be humiliating to someone who spent most of his adult life on the ballot.

Nonetheless, the day after the election Senator Ashcroft pulled himself together and followed his political instincts. Although some Republicans threatened to contest the election in court, there were no solid legal grounds on which to do so. And so they didn't. The circumstances were unusual, but the election had been held in accordance with state and federal law. Ashcroft made the best of it. He politely conceded defeat while trying to leave the impression that he was generously forgoing a court challenge merely out of sympathy for a widow. It was a smart move on his part. But it was the only thing he could do.

Now, in an epic turn of events, I was seated in the Senate chamber about to judge his fitness to serve as attorney general of the United States. There was talk around the country that, given the protracted and contested battle for the presidency that marked the election of 2000, the Bush mandate did not merit his choosing cabinet members whose records might appear extreme, as to many voters John Ashcroft's certainly did.

From the moment Bush announced the nomination, bitter debates flared around the country, on talk radio, in newspapers and magazines, and in coffee shops. In spite of—or perhaps because of—my long familiarity with John Ashcroft and his politics, I kept my own counsel.

When my new colleagues in the Senate asked me how I planned to vote, I kept my own counsel. When lobbyists buttonholed me in the halls, urging me to vote one way or another, I kept my own counsel.

When my staff informed me of the incoming opinions of my constituents—the final tally was about 6,500 opposing the nomination and 5,300 urging support—I took note of the numbers, but kept my own counsel.

In fact, I was spending much of the time during those stormy days meeting with TWA and American airlines officials and my colleagues on the Commerce Committee, discussing the proposed merger of the two companies.

The financial crisis left unresolved meant the loss of 12,000 jobs in Missouri and 20,000 nationwide. Clearly, this demanded immediate attention on my part as a new member of the Commerce Committee overseeing the transaction. However, there were those on the committee much opposed to any further mergers in the airline industry, among them the influential Sen. Fritz Hollings (D-South Carolina). I repeatedly spoke against the delays in approval that would have squelched the deal. I argued that this was not a "merger" in the traditional sense, but a "rescue mission" to save TWA from bankruptcy and our state and workers from great economic loss. Eventually, that opinion prevailed and the transaction went forward.

At the time, however, the confirmation of John Ashcroft seemed to be on the minds of most journalists and politicians. When the time came for the former Missouri senator to appear before the Judiciary Committee, he wrote me a note asking that I join Missouri's other senator, Republican Christopher Bond, in introducing him at the confirmation hearing. I had no problem with doing that. It is a courtesy traditionally extended by same-state senators.

During my introduction, I urged my colleagues to act fairly in the consideration of his appointment: "I ask you to look beyond any history of friendship or disputes, to look beyond the bonds or divisions of party, and to look beyond the urging of interest groups. Instead, let us base our decisions on the facts as they are determined by a full and fair hearing."

It was, nonetheless, to be a contentious confirmation fight with some groups even questioning Senator Ashcroft's views on race. They cited concerns about his comments at Bob Jones University and in *Southern Partisan* magazine; his fierce opposition to the court-ordered desegregation of St. Louis schools; and his single-handed fight to prevent Ronnie White, an African American jurist serving on the Missouri Supreme Court, from being approved for a federal judgeship.

Justice White agreed to testify against the confirmation. In compelling testimony before the committee, he pointed out the false allegations made about his record by Senator Ashcroft. Others pointed to what they viewed as Ashcroft's ideological extremism during his twenty-five years in public office on issues ranging from his approval of carrying concealed weapons to his unwavering opposition to abortion, even in cases of rape and incest.

I examined the evidence presented both for and against his confirmation. I listened to his testimony and read much of the extensive transcripts. I forced myself to be as objective as one can be under the circumstances and urged my Democratic colleagues to do the same. But ultimately, I concluded from the preponderance of evidence that John Ashcroft was unable, or unwilling, to separate his ideology from his decision making.

I knew that John Ashcroft had been a powerful Missouri governor and senator for many years, and despite his defeat at the polls by nearly 49,000 votes, he still had a great many supporters back home. But when the time came, I had to vote my conscience, regardless of the political consequences.

A. S. Puskin called conscience "the clawed beast scraping the heart." He was right.

I made the following statement on the floor of the Senate.

When the president said that he was a "uniter not a divider," I was deeply gratified.

This is someone after my own heart, I said.

I looked forward to working with him and the Congress in reaching across the chasm of our political differences to do some hard work for the American people.

Within the Senate, we have already reached out in a spirit of bipartisanship in structuring our committees. Saturday I had the chance to vote for the confirmation of all seven presidential nominees brought before us.

It was the beginning of a conciliatory course, a fragile alliance, but, nonetheless, one that I believe must mark any real progress in the 107th Congress.

But my hope of continuing in that spirit grows dim.

I am deeply disturbed by the nomination of John Ashcroft for the office of attorney general of the United States. I fear the unnecessary deepening of divisions in the Congress and throughout America.

It is not his credentials, or creed, or conservatism that bothers me, but the conflict and ill will that his nomination has generated.

Regrettably, perception is often reality, particularly in politics. The holder of this high and sensitive public office must be above reproach both in fact and in the minds of the American people. To settle for less is to risk disharmony and distrust in the land.

Because of this, we must be ever searching for new ways to strengthen our nation's wholeness. This nomination was such an opportunity.

Had the president wanted an attorney general who was a Missourian, a former senator, and one with solid conservative credentials, he would need look no further than to my state's own Sen. John Danforth—a man who could easily win confirmation by this body, as well as affirmation by the American people.

Mr. President, I feel compelled in the national interest to vote against the nomination of John Ashcroft.

My heart is heavy in doing so.

I was so looking forward to working with the president and Congress in healing our land.

Instead, it appears that a splinter will remain in the soul of America that will hurt for a long time to come.

Although this nomination may win a narrow victory, it will be at the cost of national unity and a damaged presidency.

However, there is still time to rectify this nomination.

In that hope, I respectfully call upon President Bush to withdraw the name of John Ashcroft from consideration in favor of one whose record and rhetoric are more consistent with the president's call to unify and not divide; to heal and not to hurt.

While I could not prevent the confirmation of John Ashcroft, I felt compelled to resist it. As I explained in my news release to the media, "The call of conscience must supersede all others. It is the only reliable anchor in the tempestuous sea of public life."

In the end, all fifty Republicans voted for the Ashcroft confirmation, along with eight Democrats. The final vote, 58–42, was the most ever cast against a successful attorney general nominee. Later that day, Supreme Court Justice Clarence Thomas swore in the seventy-ninth attorney general of the United States, John David Ashcroft.

In the months ahead, I would have only one other contact with John Ashcroft. It was unilateral. During the week following the 9/11 tragedy, with the burden of our country's safety and freedoms in such a delicate balance, I sent a brief, but sincere, handwritten note to the attorney general.

"During this perilous time in our nation's history my prayers are with you that you may be guided and strengthened in all that you do for America.

"Please let me know if I can be of help in any way."

There was never an acknowledgment; but, of course, he had his hands full at the time.

One of the requirements of freshmen members is to preside over the Senate. According to the U.S. Constitution, that is the task of the vice president. In fact, it is done by members on the assignment of the president pro tem of the Senate. Unlike the first woman senator, Hattie Caraway of Arkansas, who did not wield the gavel for twelve years, I was put to work during the first week of the session.

At first, I thought that the hour-long exercise three to four times a week was akin to freshman hazing. The senior members rarely preside unless they choose to do so—and few do. But in time, I came to look forward to those stints away from the usual office schedule. I could only be reached by Blackberry pager or a note delivered by a Senate page. Without distractions, it was a good opportunity to reflect and occasionally hear a rousing debate.

But whatever was occurring, the presiding officer had to use the correct parliamentary language. Fortunately, there's a professional parliamentarian, ever alert to what is going on in the chamber. Viewers of the Senate proceedings will see the parliamentarian seated at the long marble desk just below and to the right of the chair. The parliamentarian is sometimes turned toward the chair, giving the presiding officer the precise wording to use at a given time.

In most cases, the wording is routine. For instance, if there is a request made to include material in the record, the presiding officer says, "Without objection" or "Without objection, so ordered."

The most challenging part for newcomers is recognizing the senators not by name but by home state. For instance, John McCain would be recognized as the "senator from Arizona." Before I had all the names and states connected, I tried to anticipate who might speak next by scanning the chamber, noting who had requested a lectern or who was shuffling papers and charts. If memory failed, there was always the parliamentarian ready to assist.

If a senator asks how many minutes of allotted time remain in the debate, the parliamentarian, who keeps the time clock, passes that information to the chair, who responds, "The senator has two and a half minutes remaining," or whatever the time. If a member asks a question requiring a positive answer, the chair would reply, "The senator is correct," never using the more conversational second person.

Several animated conversations occurring on the floor at the same time can be disruptive to the proceedings. This is not always as apparent from the podium as it is on the floor. During such times a member may ask the chair (referred to as "Mr. President" or "Madam President") to call for order.

At that point, the presiding officer bangs the small ivory gavel and suggests that conversations be taken to the cloakroom. Sometimes it is necessary to make the demand several times or to delay proceeding until it is quiet enough to satisfy the member who is trying to speak or those trying to hear.

Often the Senate is in a "quorum call," which is just a parliamentary name for "time out on the field." Debate is suspended and work is conducted behind the scenes, allowing agreements to be reached.

Another suspension in proceeding occurs when a message is received from the House or from the president. On one of the most formal of occasions, two clerks appear at the front door of the chamber. Debate is suspended and the chair announces, "The Senate will receive a message from the president of the United States" (or from the House of Representatives). The bill clerk bows once to the chair as the envelope is received and again as he or she exits. It's an archaic and courtly proceeding, but very impressive.

Decorum has always been a concern of the Senate. Of the Senate's first twenty rules, half involve conduct in the chamber. In Thomas Jefferson's manual on form, he sounds much like a schoolmaster admonishing his pupils.

"No one is to disturb another in his speech by hissing, coughing, spitting, speaking, or whispering to another," he wrote.

There are attempts to seize the floor, however, with one member pressing, "Will the senator yield?" Most often senatorial courtesy prevails, and the speaking member yields the floor temporarily to either a foe or a friend of the position being presented. However, in the course of a heated exchange a member will often refuse the request.

Despite Jefferson's "schoolboy" warning, there have been times in history when tempers flared and fists flew on the floor of the U.S. Senate. During the heated decade before the Civil War, at least two personal attacks occurred in the chamber. In 1856, Sen. Charles Sumner of Massachusetts was "caned" by an irate House member using a walking stick.

A few years earlier, Sen. Henry Foote of Mississippi had pulled a pistol on Missouri's Thomas Hart Benton. Benton added to the drama by boldly stepping forth and shouting, "Stand out of the way and let the assassin fire!"

Quite by accident, I uncovered one of the traditions aimed at preventing bloodshed in the chamber. I was on my way to an evening event when a late Senate vote was called. Feeling a little overdressed for an appearance on the Senate floor, I threw my coat over my shoulders, cast my vote, and was about to leave when Lula Davis, a longtime clerk of the Senate, approached me.

"There's something you should know," she said cautiously. Lula had always been genuinely helpful and would continue to be throughout my time in the Senate.

"Oh, please tell me," I said.

"You are not supposed to wear a coat on the Senate floor."

"Why's that?"

"It's just a custom from the days when men wore cloaks and could slip in with a weapon that they might be tempted to use in the heat of a debate. That's why we call the outer room the 'cloakroom.'" I explained my dilemma. She seemed satisfied just to know she was teaching me some bit of trivia I needed to know.

It is only natural that an institution with such a long history has developed a number of quaint customs. One has to do with the mahogany writing desks, a number of which date to 1819, when the originals were replaced after the British burned the Capitol during the War of 1812. Each desk, with its pencil tray, inkwell, and shaker of blotting sand, is better equipped for a bygone era than it is for today's Senate. Ever conscious of tradition, the Senate continues to reject the use of computers and cell phones by members while in the chamber.

I was assigned Harry Truman's old desk (one of two he used during his time in the Senate). It is the custom for each senator using the desk to carve his or her name in the bottom of the drawer. I delayed performing this ritual until my final day in the Senate, when Lula insisted that I keep the tradition. She removed the drawer, gave me the required tools for the engraving, and then reinstalled the glass covering that protects the many signatures from further deterioration.

Another custom is the maintenance of the "candy desk." In 1968, Sen. George Murphy began keeping candy in his aisle desk on the last row and inviting senators to help themselves as they passed. After his departure, the custom seemed simply too "sweet" to discontinue. Today there are two "candy desks," one on each side of the chamber, both well stocked with mints, chocolates, and assorted hard candies.

One time-honored tradition was defined by former senator Norris Cotton (R-New Hampshire) in his book, *In the Senate: Amidst the Conflict and the Turmoil.* Cotton explained how members often encrypt their true feelings in their choice of words.

> One can usually tell from the degree of formality with which a senator refers to another what the nature of their personal relations may be. If the reference is made casually as "Senator Jones," they are probably close friends.
>
> If someone refers to a colleague as "the senator from Michigan," one may infer that they have a cordial relationship.
>
> If a senator refers to another as "the distinguished senator from Indiana," one may assume he does not particularly like him.
>
> And if he refers to him as "the very able and distinguished senator from California," it usually indicates that he hates his guts.

While members may be adversaries on the Senate floor, behind the scenes they often indulge in a more friendly rivalry, promoting a home state product or team. Before the 2001 Super Bowl game, I wagered on the outcome with the senators from Massachusetts, John Kerry and Ted Kennedy. If the St. Louis Rams won the game, they owed me a lobster dinner. On the other hand, if the New England Patriots won, I'd pay up with a St. Louis favorite, Ted Drewes Frozen Custard.

Upon hearing of my offer, Kerry said to me, "What the hell's frozen custard?"

I assured him that it was edible and that he should familiarize himself with this Midwest delicacy before considering a bid for the presidency. He said it appeared to him that a mere dish of ice cream was not equivalent to a New England lobster. I boasted that he would change his mind about that—in the unlikely event the Rams lost.

As it turned out, I had to "eat my words" rather than the lobster dinner. On payoff day, we gathered for the tasting of the custard. I have a great photograph of Kerry and Kennedy timidly testing the creamy mixture that had been packed in dry ice and shipped to Washington for the occasion. They loved it! Still, their New England pride would not let them admit that Missouri custard could compete with Massachusetts lobster. It was a priceless moment.

On a more serious side, Robert Byrd (D-West Virginia), guardian of Senate protocol and devotee of tradition, has written a four-volume collection on the history and proceedings of the Senate. He also offered an indoctrination course for new senators. Of special concern to him was the manner in which we presided.

"You must sit up straight," he insisted, like a teacher lecturing a class of students.

"You must not read, or answer your mail, while in the chair. You should pay attention. After all, you're presiding over the United States Senate."

These admonitions conflict with a senator's natural tendency to do more than one thing at a time. So there is a great temptation to pass the time signing mail, writing notes, or reviewing news clips.

After one of our classes in proper form, I was seated in the chamber next to Sen. Jon Corzine. Sen. Mark Dayton was presiding. He probably sits straighter and appears to listen more intently than does any other freshman. Corzine and I decided to shake him up a bit. We wrote a note and called for a page to deliver it to the dais.

Dayton opened the note and was noticeably startled.

It read, "Sen. Dayton, please sit up straighter, (Signed) Robert Byrd."

Scanning the chamber for Byrd—who wasn't there—Dayton seemed much relieved when he spotted Corzine and me, chuckling heartily at his gullibility.

Senator Byrd insisted on the correctness not only of the presiding officer but of decorum elsewhere in the chamber. During one of our freshman sessions, he spoke on the need for maintaining order.

"When necessary *bang* the gavel," he advised, his voice rising sharply.

"I don't mean a gentle tap. Give it a firm rap that gets attention!"

Whereupon the senator slammed the gavel down with such force that several of us at his conference table flinched in surprise.

"Don't worry about the gavel breaking. It's never broken before. Well, maybe once," he allowed, and paused to tell of an incident that occurred in 1954 when Vice President Richard Nixon was presiding, using the handleless ivory gavel thought to have been used by Vice President John Adams. The deteriorating instrument had been patched together with metal plates but was still being used despite its weakened condition.

Trying to maintain order during a late-night session, Nixon shattered the gavel beyond repair. The replacement gavel—a two-and-one-half-inch, hourglass-shaped piece of ivory—was a gift of the government of India. It is identical to the original, but with a floral design carved around the middle. Both gavels are housed in a wooden box that is ceremoniously placed on the dais each morning.

Unlike the instrument used in most legislative bodies, the Senate gavel has no handle, and thus is less likely to become airborne. Sen. Debbie Stabenow (D-Michigan) confided that in her home state she once sent the gavel flying off into the legislative chamber, doing no bodily harm but definitely commanding attention.

During one of our instruction sessions, someone mentioned the two lacquered snuffboxes in the chamber that rest on a ledge near the presiding officer. Byrd, who had devoted an entire page of senate history to the forms and usage of snuff, explained that these relics hold the finely ground tobacco once used for dipping or sniffing. In the interest of tradition, I am told, the boxes are kept stocked. Although there are no users among the members today, I suspect that some of the pages may have been tempted to test the potion during their tenure.

While the freshmen senators enjoyed the diversion of these old stories, Senator Byrd would draw us back to his "classroom."

"The point is, when presiding, you must demand order. Do not continue the session without having the body in order. You are in the chair and in charge. Don't forget that."

Senator Byrd was especially sensitive to the way in which the Senate opened each morning. At the appointed hour, the presiding officer would accompany the chaplain to the dais, being careful to remain one step below the clergyman.

Byrd explained, "There must be a proper respect for the chaplain as he delivers his opening prayer. He is God's representative for the moment, and his position should be elevated for the task."

The senator illustrated each of our duties in a memorable way, hammering his points home by sheer force of expression. He would sometimes fish into his inside coat pocket and retrieve a three-by-five copy of the U.S. Constitution. Our job, he would remind us, was to defend that sacred document even against those "rascals at the other end of the Avenue"—an obvious reference to those times when he thought the White House was usurping the legislative powers of Congress.

The aging senator still defends the Constitution and West Virginia with great fervor when he feels either is threatened, often striking a pose not too unlike that of Daniel Webster in George Healy's famous painting. Byrd also enlivens—and lengthens—the weekly caucus luncheons when he feels led by the spirit of Webster, Clay, or Calhoun to admonish his colleagues.

He has served in the Senate for forty-four years and is the top Democrat on the Appropriations Committee. In a body where knowledge is power, he is a master of the rules and their usage to gain a given outcome. He is also a master of the lost art of memorization. Following the swearing in of freshmen senators, he delivered a portion of one of his fourteen hour-long orations in the Old Senate Chamber. He was most impressive and a reminder of what the great political orators were able to do in a bygone era.

In addition to the group study sessions, a solo trip to Byrd's "citadel" is mandatory for Democratic freshmen. Even Hillary Clinton made the pilgrimage. The senator's advice to the former First Lady: "Be a workhorse, not a show horse. Accept being at the bottom of the totem pole, and go from there." In other words, do your committee work; don't just show up on the Sunday talk shows. That's good advice for any lawmaker, and New York's junior senator showed from the beginning that she understands that well.

Byrd presented all of the freshmen with a small version of the Constitution and urged them to carry it with them at all times, though I doubt that very many did. It was enough knowing that Bob Byrd "wore the Constitution" each day.

He also gave each new member an armload of books, including his history of the Senate and a copy of his orations. While others have written accounts of the Senate, Byrd's work is hailed as "the most ambitious study of the U.S. Senate in all our history."

As a writer, I am always appreciative of those who are more prolific than I. My writing is painfully slow and subject to many hours of revision and second-guessing. When I visited Byrd's office, I took along a copy of my history of Missouri's first families to exchange with him. I inscribed the book, "To Robert Byrd, the greatest Roman of them all."

He read the notation, obviously pleased. Turning to his assistant he said, "That's Shakespeare, you know." I felt that the inscription described the man whose presence in the U.S. Senate has contributed significantly in making it the world's greatest deliberative body.

From then on, we recognized each other's literary interests. He had a particular fondness for the hunting dog "Old Drum" and could quote the entire tribute to the famed Missouri canine given by Sen. George Graham Vest in 1870.

I loved it when he wandered from a prepared speech to quote some Scripture or poem that popped into his head. In two instances when he stumbled over a stanza, I found the poem on the internet and sent it to him. He always responded with a handwritten thank-you note.

I found in Bob Byrd a kind and kindred spirit.

I believe it was Sen. Zell Miller who told this story on himself. He had just finished making what he thought was a pretty good speech. As he and his wife, Shirley, were driving home, he pondered the events of the evening and the fine response to his speaking.

Feeling proud of his performance, Zell turned to his wife and said, "You know, there just aren't as many fine orators as there used to be."

Shirley replied, "Yes, and there's one less than you think there is."

In the Senate, I stood in "tall cotton," as they say in southeast Missouri. I was among some of the best speakers in the nation and, certainly, among the most verbose. The political dinosaur Sen. Strom Thurmond, though infirm and sluggish at nearly one hundred years of age, could still blurt out a robust "Aye" or "Nay" when prodded by an aide.

Understandably hard of hearing, Senator Thurmond had been known to interrupt a committee witness speaking too softly into the microphone by belting out, "Turn the machine on, sonny."

Thurmond, now deceased, holds the record time for a filibuster, twenty-four hours and eighteen minutes, against the Civil Rights Act of 1957. But the slow, steady march of racial justice could not be halted. Not even a United State senator could "talk down" an idea whose time had come.

Far on the opposite side of the Senate—and on the other side of the political spectrum from Thurmond—was the late Sen. Paul Wellstone (D-Minnesota), a former runner who struggled with multiple sclerosis. Even dragging one leg, he moved faster than most senators did as he hurried across the chamber to deliver a rousing speech on whatever topic stirred his liberal passions at the moment. He will be greatly missed, for every legislative body needs a Paul Wellstone to prick its conscience and remind it of the things that matter.

One of my favorite orators is the silver-tongued Fritz Hollings, a gentleman of the old school whose southern drawl and charming manner ingratiate him to voters and opponents alike. Although he is prone to rambling pleasantly, his well-made arguments and good-natured ridicule are a pure delight.

Another commanding presence by virtue of the timbre of his voice and the force of his ideas is Sen. Ted Kennedy. Like Daniel Webster, whose "voice could shake the world," Kennedy is a titan of power and persuasion on the Senate floor.

For sheer fluency and ease of speaking, I tip my hat to two Democratic senators, Dick Durbin of Illinois and Byron Dorgan of North Dakota. The velvet-voiced and easy-listening duo are the Frank Sinatras of the Senate, able to warble smoothly and convincingly on many topics.

Watch out for those "satin boxing gloves" on Sen. Barbara Mikulski (D-Maryland). Standing under the five-foot mark in height and built like a fireplug, when she stands next to Sen. Jay Rockefeller (D-West Virginia) her eye level reaches his bellybutton. Despite her size disadvantage, the quick-witted Marylander packs a wallop of influence with her punchy and pithy speaking style. Her stern and effective advocacy on behalf of women, workers, and the downtrodden gives her heightened political stature and respect on both sides of the aisle.

Mikulski's counterpart from the West Coast, Sen. Barbara Boxer (D-California), is as feisty as her name implies. (Her office baseball team was called the "Boxer Rebellion.") She can clobber an adversary at will, delivering a verbal karate chop to an obstinate committee witness or a quarrelsome colleague. California is served by another woman, Sen. Dianne Feinstein (D). She is a seasoned voice of reason whose words, either in person or on the floor, are measured, articulate, and trustworthy.

Senators Joe Biden, John Kerry, Paul Sarbanes (D-Maryland), Pat Leahy (D-Vermont), Pete Domenici (R-New Mexico), and Kent Conrad (D-North Dakota) are what I call the tough debaters. They are tough thinking, tough to ignore, tough to take on. Just listen to them and learn all you can. In addition to being laudable public speakers, Senators Harry Reid (D-Nevada), Blanche Lincoln (D-Arkansas), Conrad Burns (R-Montana), Charles Schumer (D-New York), Mary Landrieu (D-Louisiana), Evan Bayh (D-Indiana), and Chuck Hagel (R-Nebraska) would make delightful next-door neighbors, as would Jay Rockefeller.

When I first met Jay, I was tempted to say, "Hey, I know your family," but I didn't say that because I really didn't know his family. I just felt like I did. All my life, I had heard stories from my father about John D. Rockefeller Sr., the oil baron, philanthropist, and the first American to become a billionaire. Jay, his grandson, is an amiable fellow as well as a conscientious lawmaker not above teasing his colleagues, making fun of himself, or spinning some shaggy dog story. He would frequently inquire about my fund-raising. Aware that I was outstripping many of my colleagues in that area, he was always complimentary of my efforts.

"That's outstanding!" he would say, when I told him the results of a mailing or a fund-raiser. "I've never raised more then $10,000 at an event," he'd say with a twinkle in his eye.

I would laugh and say, "You never needed to, Jay."

He was used to such gibes and took them in stride. I often thought how much Daddy would have enjoyed swapping stories with Jay.

Any mention of speakers or storytellers would have to give kudos for rhetorical gimmickry to Republican Sen. Phil Gramm. The outspoken Texan often pondered how a piece of legislation would affect "little Dicky Flatt," his symbolic Everyman and the Lone Star state's version of Joe Six Pack.

I was told, however, that "little Dicky Flatt" is a real person, a printer, living in Mexia, Texas. I don't know. At least in the Senate, Gramm made him the embodiment of the average person. When speaking against some progressive legislation, the ultraconservative senator frequently asked: "Would little Dicky Flatt benefit more if we let him keep his money than have us use it for another federal program?" Even Democrat Fritz Hollings would occasionally reference "little Dicky Flatt" to make a point.

There is much evidence on both sides of the aisle that demagoguery is still the nation's number-one political pastime.

In my Senate office, I had an official speechwriter for the first time in my life. Dan Liestikow came to work for me knowing he would have the frustrating task of "writing for a writer." Dan tolerated my idiosyncrasies and learned to incorporate my material with his own to produce a text that I felt comfortable delivering.

Still, for the less frequent speaker, such as I, there were many pitfalls. I once forgot to number the pages of a prepared text, got them out of order, and began making nonsequential leaps from page to page. Oddly, my audience—which appeared to be listening with rapt attention— didn't seem to notice.

Several times, I was led onto a darkened stage with no podium light. When that happened, I found it best to abandon my text and launch into the "speaker's wonderland" of random thoughts.

One of the things I dread finding at a podium is the small "booster box" that someone has thoughtfully arranged to heighten the speaker. I have now learned to kick it out of the way, having dropped off the edge too many times. Besides that, when I'm using notes, the extra distance from the podium moves me too far beyond my range of vision. For my notes, I use a sixteen- or eighteen-point font to avoid using glasses when speaking—a lesson I learned from my colleague Sen. Max Cleland, who used what looks like thirty-six-point type.

Another distressing situation for a speaker comes from misjudging the makeup of the audience or the time allotted to speak. A group might be all young people or all seniors, or a mixture of Democrats and Republicans. What was pitched to the scheduler as a "brief welcome" could turn into a keynote address, or vice versa. To avoid such disasters, most offices insist that an extensive information sheet be filled out on each event.

Still, speaking as often as nine times a day—as I did once during the campaign—slips of the tongue are inevitable. I had only myself to blame for one embarrassing fiasco. While speaking at a school function I inadvertently changed the name from Stonegate school to Gateway school, a mistake I attributed to having the Gateway computer logo burnished in my memory from seeing it each day on my monitor.

The irony was that no one corrected me. I felt like the emperor who wore no clothes surrounded by people who wouldn't let me in on the secret. I would never have known except for an elderly man who made it a point to reveal my blunder as I was about to walk out the door. I was devastated and immediately wrote a letter of apology to the principal, who has—quite understandably—never invited me back.

One device for getting a speaker to an event is to offer an award that the grateful officeholder must receive in person. Some of these trophies are especially attractive and well designed. But I never receive one of these mementos without thinking of what Sen. Eugene McCarthy did when his collection of "Lucite tombstones" got out of hand.

"I hid them in hotel rooms," he confided to a reporter. "I discovered in my travels that if you pull out the bottom drawer of a hotel dresser there is space beneath it just the right size for a plaque." According to McCarthy, he has left plaques in Holiday Inns all across the country and has never heard of one being found.

As we know too well, most politicians will speak without awards or remuneration, their major fault being a tendency to "overspeak." Once started, a politician puts his mouth into overdrive and keeps rolling, the mellow and reasoned sound of his own voice erasing all boundaries of time.

Because my infatuation with words and storytelling tempts me to wander, I place hard limits on myself. Mel was an advocate of a few well-chosen words, and I have followed that path as well.

"No one ever complained that a speech was too short," he'd say when I asked if a talk I was preparing was long enough for the occasion. Once when the two of us were looking over our speaking requests, I made an observation, "I notice when people want a long speech they invite you, but when they want a short one, they ask me."

"Yes, and I notice you're getting more invitations than I am."

We both laughed. Of course, that wasn't happening, but it did make the point that program planners want a speaker, but not too much speaking. I still err on the side of brevity and whittle my text until it is seldom more than twenty minutes in length.

Unless I'm giving informal remarks or a campaign speech, I generally use notes or a prepared text, since my mind is seldom nimble enough for an eloquent, off-the-cuff performance. Nor am I comfortable writing my thoughts on a paper napkin minutes before speaking, as Mel often did.

Most often, I incorporate several stories into my speech. All speakers have certain quips, starters, and sure-fire lines on which they rely. I have hundreds of such stories cataloged in a database. But I still carry with me "My Little Green Storybook"—a loose-leaf binder of material gleaned over the years from articles and other speakers. I agree with Anatole France, who declared, "If a thing's been said—and said well—have no scruples, use it without apology."

If possible, I try to attribute a well-turned phrase to its creator, unlike Lyndon Johnson, who upon looking at a speech prepared for him that quoted Socrates, scratched out the philosopher's name and wrote in, "As my dear old Daddy used to say. . . ."

When I read or hear a new story, I think of how it can be adapted to convey a thought. If I want to urge an audience to speak out on behalf of an issue, I might weave the idea into a story, telling them not to be like the woman I heard about recently, whose son sent her a parrot for companionship.

He called a few days later and said, "How did you like the parrot?"

She said, "Why, it was dee-lish-ous!"

"You mean you ate the parrot? That parrot cost $2,000 and could speak five languages!"

"Well, why didn't he say something?"

I would then encourage my audience to "say something" or to work harder on behalf of their stated goals.

Because people often find politicians a bit pompous, they enjoy hearing some self-deprecating humor from a speaker. When addressing a group obviously better versed than I am on a given topic, I might start by saying, "Speaking to you today, I feel a lot like Charlie Brown did when he and his friends were lying on top a hill, looking up at the cloud formations."

"What do you see in those clouds?" Charlie asked.

Lucy responded quickly, "I see the southeast wall of the Sistine Chapel."

Linus replied, "I see Raphael's Madonna."

Charlie was silent.

Finally, Lucy spoke up, "Well, Charlie Brown, what do you see?"

"I was going to say a horsey and a doggie, but I don't think I'll bother."

Being from south Missouri, Mel could get by with telling stories from the Ozark region of the state. One I always enjoyed was about the helpless little lady who wrote to her husband locked away in the penitentiary.

"When do I plant the potatoes?" she pleaded.

He wrote back saying, "Not yet, but whatever you do, stay out of the garden. That's where the guns are hidden."

Her next letter to him revealed that the authorities had been reading his mail, just as he suspected.

She wrote, "I don't understand it. Two deputies and the sheriff came out here and dug up every square inch of the garden."

He answered, "Now the garden's ready, plant the potatoes."

Around St. Patrick's Day, I try to find an opportunity to tell my favorite Irish story. I told it in Washington, when I spoke at Sen. Tom

Daschle's annual "O'Daschle" Irish Breakfast. I have told it using an Irish dialect, but it works just as well without.

Many years ago, a king who disliked the local priest determined to find a way to dispose of him.

Calling the priest before him, the king announced, "Tomorrow you will die, unless you can answer three questions. First, how many baskets of dirt are in yonder hill? Second, how long would it take me to travel around the earth? And, finally, what am I thinking?"

Knowing he was unable to answer the questions, the priest went home, prepared to die. When told about the situation, the gardener asked permission to disguise himself and go before the king in the priest's place. The priest reluctantly agreed.

The next morning, the gardener, dressed in clerical garb, stood before the king to answer the questions.

"All right, priest, tell me, how many baskets of dirt are in yonder hill?"

"Sire, if you have a basket half the size of the hill, it will take two," he replied.

"Well spoken," the king replied. "Now tell me how long it would take me to travel around the earth."

"Sire, if you get up with the sun, and travel with the sun, it will take you twenty-four hours."

Finally, in disgust, the king blurted out, "Tell me, what am I thinking?"

"Ya think, ya talk'in to the priest, but cha ain't."

I find that a dash of humor or a heartwarming anecdote makes the message—and the messenger—more acceptable to the audience. I follow the advice of the witty and provocative Liz Carpenter, who worked in the Lyndon Johnson White House. She said, "Start with a laugh, put meat in the middle, and raise the flag at the end."

Good stories are like the proverbial "spoonful of sugar" that makes the medicine go down. I use them plentifully. Whatever the length of my speech or the occasion, I try to instill a nugget or two of truth, wrapped in a story to keep the listeners' attention.

As one speaker noted, "They may forget what you said, but they'll never forget how you made them feel." If the members of an audience go away seeing their duty more clearly and loving their county more dearly, then I have succeeded.

I was walking through the halls of the Senate during my first few days in Washington, gawking at the statuary and paintings of famous men that lined the corridors, when I was startled by one of the portraits.

The portrait of a woman!

I had no idea who she was.

When I inquired, I learned that she was Hattie Caraway of Arkansas, the first woman elected to a full term in the U.S. Senate. Back at my office, I pulled out some history books and discovered that Hattie's arrival in the Senate was somewhat like my own. She had come to Washington in 1932 after her husband, Sen. Thaddeus Caraway, died in office.

The governor of the state appointed Hattie to finish out the remainder of the term under what was called the "widow's mandate." The act of tokenism came from the Democratic governor, trying to atone for his earlier opposition to woman suffrage. It was also a way to keep the seat in safe hands until the next election.

Although she had graduated from a women's college, Hattie Caraway had never worked outside the home. Nor was she socially inclined. As a housewife, she seemed content to manage the family's small cotton farm in her husband's absence.

Making the transition to Washington was especially hard for Hattie, whom the press referred to as "plain Mrs. Caraway." At first, she was bewildered by the rules of the Senate, frightened by the idea of speaking on the floor, and consumed by her duties. Hattie showed her good humor when given the desk that had been occupied by Rebecca Felton, the Georgian who, a decade earlier, at the age of eighty-seven, had filled a Senate vacancy for one day. Caraway reasoned that the senators gave her the "female desk" because "they wanted as few of them contaminated as possible."

Visitors looking from the gallery to catch a glimpse of the former farm wife often found the primly dressed senator sitting at her desk knitting or making pencil sketches of her colleagues. When some of her arrogant, more talkative colleagues labeled her "Silent Hattie," she took a swipe back, declaring, "The men have left nothing unsaid." Despite the insults and innuendoes, Hattie got the last word with the publication of her journal, entitled "Silent Hattie Speaks," a revelation of the day-to-day behavior of her colleagues, including their attire.

As time went on, Hattie got into the swing of things and began to enjoy her new senatorial duties. Still, the politicians back home had no reason to believe that she would run for election in her own right. In fact, she had earlier indicated that she would not. Much to their annoyance, she changed her mind.

Not surprising, her sex became an issue in the campaign. One of her six opponents ran on the slogan "Arkansas needs another man in the Senate." Another predicted that Mrs. Caraway would be lucky to get 1 percent of the vote.

But Hattie proved to be a more astute politician than expected. During her early months in the Senate, she struck up a powerful friendship with her seatmate, the colorful Huey "Kingfish" Long of Louisiana. When it came to voting, she often sided with Long rather than with her Arkansas counterpart, Joe Robinson, the Democratic leader and a political foe of Long's.

The Kingfish did not forget her loyalty. In her first reelection bid, Hattie and Huey teamed up for a campaign tour of Arkansas, a week-long, two-thousand-mile caravan that included seven vehicles and two sound trucks. Pulling into a rural community, they would set up their road show on the town square, summoning folks to gather round to hear the political duo—though Long did most of the speaking and was clearly the main attraction.

Climbing upon a platform built on the roof of one of the sound trucks, Senator Long would introduce Hattie as the "brave little woman senator."

"We're here to pull a lot of potbellied politicians off a little woman's neck," he told his approving listeners.

Despite concerns about a woman being able to endure the rigors of stump speaking, with Huey by her side, Hattie proved to be a hearty and effective campaigner. On election day, she racked up 44.7 percent of the vote—twice the vote of her closest opponent. Overcoming her timidity, Senator Caraway went on to become the first woman to chair a Senate committee, and even gave the seconding speech for Franklin Roosevelt at the 1936 Democratic convention.

Hattie never had the chance to return the favor to Huey Long for what he did in aiding her election. The Kingfish could have used some help. For back in Louisiana, where political passion is the only thing hotter than the Cajun cooking, Huey had enemies.

Less than four years after their road show, the flamboyant Louisiana orator was gunned down in the halls of the State Capitol. Under the "widow's mandate" Rose Long joined Hattie in the Congress for a year. For the first time in history, there were two women in the U.S. Senate.

In time, other women came to the Senate, most to serve under the "widow's mandate" for two to six months, but for years there were never more than two women serving at the same time.

Hattie was no longer around when Republican Margaret Chase Smith of Maine arrived in the Senate. Mrs. Smith once served as an aide in her husband's congressional office. Following his death in 1946, she completed his term and was reelected three times before going to the Senate.

The soft-spoken but courageous senator is best remembered for a speech she delivered as a freshman in opposition to her fellow Republican, Sen. Joseph McCarthy. The Wisconsin senator was drawing national attention with his anti-Communist crusade that cast suspicion on innocent people. In her "Declaration of Conscience," Smith reprimanded the senator, who claimed to have proof that the State Department was riddled with Communists. Without mentioning him by name, Smith lambasted McCarthy for turning the Senate into "a forum of hate and character assassination."

Senator Smith's heroic stance earned her a place on the cover of *Newsweek* and favorable mention as a vice presidential candidate. McCarthy, condescendingly, declined to respond, saying, "I don't fight with women senators." Behind her back, however, he mockingly called Smith and the six senators who supported her "Snow White and the Six Dwarfs." It would be four years before her colleagues would have the

courage to censure the chairman of the Senate investigating committee for his incriminating tactics.

By 1987, only Sen. Nancy Landon Kassebaum (R-Kansas) was on
hand to welcome the Senate's newest female arrival, Barbara Mikulski
of Maryland. The daughter of a grocery store owner, Mikulski had el-
bowed her way onto the political scene fighting over a local road issue.
At last, the Senate "brotherhood" had met its match in the spunky, outspoken Polish woman from Baltimore. Not about to be sidelined with a
"widow's mandate," she was unmarried and as independent as they come.

"Happily, a woman's voice may do some good," Shakespeare wrote
back in the sixteenth century. Mikulski's certainly did. Still, by 1993,
women's voices accounted for only 2 percent of the U.S. Senate. Noting that, San Francisco Mayor Dianne Feinstein used the slogan "Two
Percent Is Not Enough" in her winning Senate campaign.

Mikulski nurtured each of the new women senators who came
trickling into Washington during the nineties. There was no hiding
her delight at seeing four more join the ranks at the turn of the new
century.

"We're now thirteen and exuberant!" she beamed. "We're in a league
of our own . . . ready to play major league ball," she told reporters at
one of her "Power Coffees" given for the new arrivals. She joked with
Larry King: "Some women look out the window waiting for Prince
Charming. I look out the window waiting for more women in the
United States Senate."

Even so, the number of women in the 107th Congress accounted for
only 13.6 percent of its membership, far behind the 50 percent makeup
of the population. Women fare better in the parliaments of the Nordic
countries, with more than 45 percent in Sweden, 38 percent in Den-
mark, and 37 percent in Finland.

Nonetheless, delighted by the gains, Mikulski had the earlier book
about women senators, entitled *Nine and Counting*, updated to reflect
the new numbers.

This time I was the one with the so-called widow's mandate. But
there was a difference. All the other women who served prior to Mikulski were appointed by their state's governor to fill an unexpired term.

Voters had no say. By contrast, voters actually knew that they were casting their ballots for me to serve. At least, in my own mind, I thought of it as the "people's mandate."

Of course, Senate Republicans did not feel that way. They saw Ashcroft's absence and my presence as a threat to the delicate balance of power in the Senate that teetered at 50–50 and ultimately collapsed with Sen. Jim Jefford's defection from the party to serve as an independent.

A few die-hard Republicans would not even speak to me in the halls or on the elevator. Plainly, they resented my presence, finding me unworthy of membership in their male-dominated stronghold. I still remember an early encounter with Frank Murkowski (R-Alaska). He sought me out on the floor, angrily waving his finger in my face.

"How dare you put a 'hold' on the White House Department of Energy nominees," he shouted.

To "hold on the calendar" or to "blue slip" is an informal request used to halt a nomination. Refusing to approve a presidential nominee is a senatorial prerogative and a power tool that senators wield to get what they want.

"I have no intention of delaying those nominees any longer than necessary," I said calmly. "What I want are some assurances that spent nuclear rods will not be transported across Missouri's major highway whenever it suits the Department of Energy to do so. I want assurances."

Up until then the White House had refused to acknowledge me in any way—a petty reaction that never changed. In its own self-interest, however the administration quickly responded, and I released my hold on the presidential nominees.

Dealing with Majority Leader Trent Lott of Mississippi was even more frustrating. When I was trying to get benefits for unemployed airline workers included in the airline bailout package, he condescendingly patted me on the hand and said, "Let's not put that on this bill, Jean. I'll put it on the next one." He did not intend ever to do it, and I told him as much.

One of the more meaningful comments that I received came just before I left Washington. I was on the Capitol subway with Sen. Daniel

Inouye (D-Hawaii), who thanked me for showing courage in coming to the Senate and for the good work that I had done. Dan is a true hero, a Japanese American who was at Pearl Harbor and later lost his right arm on a German battlefield. He said, "I have been on Capitol Hill for forty-three years, and I have seen widows come and go . . . but you're different from the others."

I was gratified by his recognition of my efforts. Because of what he stands for, his words were all the more meaningful. Certainly, I wanted to do more, much more, than was expected of me. I had always demanded a lot of myself. Like a marathon runner, I had tested my limits and found deep layers of strength in the physical, mental, and spiritual "muscle" that develops from persistent striving.

In speeches, I often told my audiences that what mattered in politics, or anything else, is *who you are* on the inside. I spoke of Harry Truman, whose seat I held and at whose desk I sat.

Few people realize that Truman came to the Senate as a political novice. He had never held an office higher than county commissioner. He had never done more than walk across a college campus. He never had a successful business—he was a failed haberdasher.

Even when he became president, few expected much of him, standing as he did in the shadow of Franklin Roosevelt. Still, Truman ended the war, rebuilt Europe, and integrated the government and the armed services at a time when 86 percent of the people said he was moving too fast.

The strength of Harry Truman was who he was and what he stood for.

In Washington, you are a *voice* and a *vote* for something!

Harry understood that.

Margaret Chase Smith understood it.

As does Barbara Mikulski today.

Not surprising, as time went on, I became the number-one target of the White House. Republican publications and websites referred to me as a "left-wing fanatic" not representing "Missouri values," despite my having voted for the positions supported by President Bush 70 percent of the time. Even so, I could expect a heavily funded opponent to use every weapon in the Republican political arsenal to discredit, diminish, and demolish me.

The easiest way to cast doubts on my effectiveness as a "real" senator was to plant such statements in print as, "Carnahan often looks lost on the Senate floor." No one would ever say that of a male senator. Such statements are a put-down designed and reserved to discredit a woman.

I had earlier heard some of the women senators referred to as "lightweights." That is a serious misnomer. Every woman—on both sides of the aisle—is a bright, forceful, and valuable contributor to the legislative process. They had to be extraordinary simply to break the "glass ceiling" in the political arena and wind up in the U.S. Senate. Interestingly, I never heard the "lightweight" expression used for any of the men who might have better fit the description. Men in Congress who don't measure up are more apt to be labeled as "working quietly, but effectively, behind the scenes."

Elizabeth Cady Stanton's prediction was right. In 1848, at the Seneca Falls Convention, she spoke to the women gathered in the hopes of someday being able to vote. She warned, "In the great work before us, we can anticipate misconception, misrepresentation, and ridicule." Knowing this has not deterred women in the least. Certainly not the women of the Senate.

The need for greater inclusion in governing is obvious from an illustration I read recently. Imagine that the world is a circle. Divide it into half men and half women. Then block off one-fourth on the male side to denote the number of white men. Mark a small sliver from that category to represent white men who are educated and, thereby, the primary decision makers in government and business around the world. For most of civilization, that "sliver" has ruled.

While we are moving to correct that imbalance, it is a slow, agonizing process. Eleanor Roosevelt pointed out the value of men and women working together in government: "I believe we will have better government in our countries when men and women discuss public issues together and make their decisions on the basis of their different areas of experience and their common concern for the welfare of their families and their world. . . . Too often the great decisions are originated and given form in bodies made up wholly of men, or so completely dominated by them that whatever of special value women have to offer is shunted aside without expression."

Because women do not get to the top by the same route as men, they often bring a new perspective to public policy. Still, we are not monolithic in our thinking. While the thirteen women senators in the 107th Congress—ten Democrats and three Republicans—shared a common interest in prescription drugs, gender equity, breast cancer treatment, and better schools, we were divided on labor issues, defense, homeland security, and reproductive rights. Nonetheless, the women of the Senate were a potent force when they chose to unite on an issue of mutual concern, legislative or otherwise.

I was amused on one occasion when the women put up a common defense. It happened when Floor Leader Tom Daschle spoke of staying in session until the day before Thanksgiving. The men saw no problem with that. The women were outraged!

"We have a meal to cook . . . family coming home," they protested. Daschle knew he had made a serious mistake and quietly moved the recess date forward a day.

Much has been made of a commitment wrenched from the women senators during a Larry King broadcast, stating they would not campaign against each other. For the most part that has been honored, although Sen. Kay Bailey Hutchison (R-Texas) stumped Michigan against the Democratic challenger, Debbie Stabenow, on the theory that Stabenow was not yet in the Senate. Before her visit to Missouri in behalf of my opponent, Hutchison tried unsuccessfully to salvage our relationship by telling me she wouldn't say anything against me.

It is unrealistic to believe that the sorority mentality that once united the women in a fragile alliance will continue indefinitely. As their numbers increase and they are less threatened by their minority status, solidarity will weaken. Still, it is worth the effort to form a common purpose whenever possible for the potential good it can achieve.

Senator Mikulski is insistent on keeping such a spirit alive and helps by scheduling monthly dinner meetings. She has a superb sense of humor that enlivens any social gathering. Whether we gathered at a Capitol Hill restaurant or at the home of Hillary Clinton, Dianne Feinstein, Barbara Boxer, or Mary Landrieu, it was a chance to let down our hair and enjoy each other's company as women, talking about our children or a sale at the local mall. I remember one evening devoted almost entirely to a "who dunnit?" analysis of the Chandra Levy murder case.

Interestingly, we never forgot our status as senators. One night we instinctively sat down at the table in the order of seniority. We all affirmed—and sometimes reaffirmed—that we would not divulge anything "juicy" that transpired at those meetings of the "Ya-Ya Sisterhood." Or as Barbara Mikulski put it, "No memos, no staff, no leaks." To my knowledge, all have kept the faith.

As members of what was once "the world's most exclusive men's club," we each had our favorite "female senator" story to recount. I especially enjoyed Sen. Patty Murray (D-Washington) telling of an elevator ride she took as a freshman senator. On board was the ninety-some-year-old Strom Thurmond, still recognized for his skirt-chasing antics. Strom looked at the petite, blonde-haired senator and said, "Who do you work for, honey?"

As Patty emerged from the elevator, she replied, "Senator, I work for the people of the state of Washington."

Although wheelchair-bound much of the time, Strom still had the capacity for making sexual innuendos. As I scrunched onto an over-crowded elevator one day, I asked, "Is there room for one more?" From his position in the corner Strom blurted out, "If not, you can sit on my lap, honey."

At some time or another, all of us were summoned to Strom's desk—first row, first seat—to receive a piece of hard candy from his coat pocket. Sometimes it was wrapped, sometimes it was slightly lint covered—it's the thought that counts. On opening day Sen. Hillary Clinton made the mistake of responding to one of Strom's beckoning calls. Leaning over to greet the frail senator, she was met with a hearty smack on the lips.

Maria Cantwell (D-Washington) tells of boarding an elevator when she first arrived that was reserved for senators only. The operator dutifully told her she would have to get off and use another elevator. Maria explained that she was the new senator from the state of Washington, to which the operator shook his head and replied, "They sure don't make you guys like they used to."

One of Barbara Mikulski's stories centered on an encounter she had with Max Cleland back in 1997 when he arrived in the Senate. The first multiple amputee to serve since the Civil War, Max found the men's room inaccessible to a wheelchair user, so he used the more accessible bathroom for women senators.

One day as he was leaving the ladies' room, he literally ran into Mikulski. The dean of women senators had worked doggedly to get a women's room near the chamber.

"What are you doing in here?" she demanded.

Max explained the situation and his efforts to get a wheelchair-accessible men's room.

Mikulski quipped, "Well, good luck, it took us eight years to get ours."

Certainly, Rebecca Felton, the first woman to speak from the floor of the Senate eighty years ago, would be right at home with the feisty women of the Senate today. She had campaigned across Georgia for more than fifty years, speaking out on suffrage, temperance, education, women's health, and prison reform.

Although she and her husband lost their sons, their farm, and their money during the Civil War, they continued their struggle. When Mr. Felton ran for Congress in 1874, she wrote with great enthusiasm about their joint efforts: "From the beginning to the end, I was in the thick of my husband's campaign. . . . I wrote hundreds of letters all over fourteen counties. I wrote night and day and for two months. . . . At one time, my health broke down, but I was propped up in bed with pillows and wrote ahead. I made appointments for speaking, recruited speakers, answered newspaper attacks, contracted for the printing and distribution of circulars and sample ballots."

Later, her one-day ceremonial stint in the U.S. Senate, at the age of eighty-seven, was formally opposed by those who cited the "irregularity" of her seating. During her only speech in the chamber, she made a prophetic statement that has since proved to be true. She told of seeing a newspaper cartoon depicting the Senate fully occupied with men and a woman walking in without a place to sit. In the drawing, some members rolled with sidesplitting laughter at the presence of a female, while others just looked off at the ceiling.

Felton commented on the illustration, "When the women of the country come in and sit with you . . . you will get ability, you will get integrity of purpose, you will get exalted patriotism, and you will get unstinted usefulness."

That day in 1922, Felton had a vision shared by few in the chamber who heard her but applauded by the many women who gathered in the gallery to cheer the new day that was dawning.

Eight

Be Not Overcome

Circumstances may appear to wreck our lives and God's plans, but God is not helpless among the ruins. Our broken lives are not lost or useless. God's love is still working.

—Eric Liddell in *Chariots of Fire*

It was so good to be at the farm after a busy week in Washington. Despite a stop to attend a fund-raiser on the way home, I had managed to make it to Rolla before the anticipated rainstorm.

The place looked inviting and homey. The farmhand who watches over the land and cattle had removed the fallen leaves, just as I had asked. Indoors I could tell that the weekly housekeeper had tidied up the rooms for my return. I felt secure and peaceful surrounded by familiar scenes and objects.

Still, it seemed strange. I was alone at the farm, a situation I had seldom experienced over the thirty-some years I lived there with Mel, the four kids, my father, and a variety of pets.

Silence can be distracting, almost haunting, especially after living all week in a noisy downtown apartment. At least, it would be cozy indoors, I thought to myself. No need to go anywhere. It was a perfect night to read and fall asleep listening to the gentle pitter-patter of rain upon the roof.

But first, I forced myself to deal with the mail that had piled up in my absence. There were always letters from constituents mistakenly addressed to the farm, bills to pay, catalogs to review.

As I sat at the kitchen table sorting through the stack, the storm grew more severe. I tried to ignore the shuttering vibrations and intermittent thunderclaps that pierced the quiet I was beginning to enjoy.

Moments later, I heard a violent snap of lightning that got my attention. I ran to the kitchen window to see if one of the many trees in the yard had been hit. Sheets of blinding rain falling upon the glass made it almost impossible to see out. Yet nothing seemed disturbed.

At various times, both the wellhouse pump and the computer had been knocked out by lightning strikes. I tested the faucets to make sure I still had water and then went upstairs to check the computer. When I walked into the room, I could smell a faint odor of singed wiring. Thinking that a nearby electric pole had been hit, I unplugged the computer and closed the door to lessen the smell throughout the house.

To be on the safe side, I returned later, but there was nothing more suspicious. Still, I felt uncomfortable as the storm continued to rage. Wanting to talk to someone, I called Bob Carnahan, my brother-in-law. He and his wife, Oma, lived just up the road. I told them what had happened and Bob suggested that I keep in touch if I needed anything. Later he, too, felt uneasy and drove down to see if everything was all right.

When he walked into the kitchen looking wet and worried, I knew that something was wrong.

"Do you know the house is on fire?" he said as calmly as he could, not wanting to alarm me.

"Where?"

There was no smoke . . . no sounding of the smoke detector . . . nothing.

"It's in the attic, just above Robin's bedroom."

I ran outdoors. For the first time, I saw the flames leaping from the roof eight to ten feet high!

I tried to stay composed. But returning to the house, I still fumbled pathetically, trying to find the number for the rural fire department. Finally, Bob came up with the number from memory.

"Come quickly," I said to the dispatcher, not knowing that all the rural fire departments for miles around were on call, fighting other storm-related fires that night.

I hung up and tried to remember what I had often rehearsed in my mind: what to save if your house is burning. The answer was always the things you can't replace. I immediately grabbed up the photograph albums on the first floor, knowing there were many others on the second floor, including all those from the funerals. As I moved the large oil painting of Mel to a safe location in my car, I suddenly thought of Dolley Madison retrieving George Washington's portrait from the burning White House years ago. By the time the volunteer firemen rolled into the driveway, I was ready to turn everything over to them and the neighbors who had arrived to assist. In my mind, I had given everything up for lost. Fortunately, my rescuers did not feel that way.

Drenched with rain, I stood in the driveway alongside my next-door neighbor, Sam Burton. As I watched the flames rise higher and higher from the roof, I dissolved in his arms.

"What have I done wrong?" I sobbed.

It was the same pitiful, faithless question Job had asked centuries earlier. I blurted it out instinctively. It was the lowest point in my "poor-little-me" state of mind.

Feeling useless in the presence of professional firefighters, I returned with Bob to his home. As I telephoned my three kids in St. Louis, I couldn't help but remember another call I had placed eleven months earlier following the plane crash.

More misfortune.

Another summons for help.

Despite the downpour, they all crammed into one car and started for Rolla, arriving about 1:00 a.m. to join the rescue effort.

Several of the volunteer firemen, taking a break, tromped through the woods to check on me.

"Yes, yes, I am doing fine," I'd say each time. "But you look exhausted," I said to one of the men encased in a bulky yellow fire jacket streaked with water and soot. His kind eyes and broad, sweaty smile peered out at me from under his helmet as we visited in the doorway.

"I know you," I said, sensing a vaguely familiar face behind all the protective wear.

"Yeah, I'm Danny," he said.

My thoughts immediately turned to a mischievous, round-faced kid with an ingratiating smile, growing up in our church. I knew his mother . . . his grandmother.

While my mind drifted to those associations, Danny went on.

"This is our third fire tonight. We're spread pretty thin. Got all the crews out for miles around." Danny went back to the fire after first assuring me that they were "saving a lot of things."

Having heard the news on the radio, people were showing up to help. Television trucks from Springfield and St. Louis, two hours away, found their way to the farm over the back roads of Rolla, filmed their story, and left. Firefighters and neighbors stayed until 4:00 a.m., salvaging and securing all that they could.

As I fell into bed dog-tired from the strain and turmoil, I tried to put the events of the evening into perspective. I was unharmed. Much of the furniture had been rescued, and damaged pieces, in many instances, looked repairable. A house could be rebuilt. I understood the difference between misfortune and tragedy.

The next day, Sunday morning, people were already at work when I arrived back at my house. Some I had not seen for years, having lived in Jefferson City and now Washington for nearly a decade.

"Why aren't you in church?" I said to one who I knew never missed a Sunday service.

She smiled. "I wanted to be here with you," she said, giving me an encouraging hug.

We walked through the house together. The roof was gone, but the first floor was intact. The wall studs framing the second-floor bedrooms were now charred timbers. I had watched those walls go up nearly thirty years before. It was our dream house in the country and the place where Mel and I had raised our four kids.

"Hey," my son Russ shouted, "I found some pictures under this fallen insulation!"

Sure enough, there were photos of Mel and Randy . . . the family, smiling out at us from under the debris. We took some comfort in the discovery. Pulling back the thick layers of soggy, fallen insulation, we uncovered more treasures—books, files, and clothing protected as though a wet blanket had been dropped over them.

We spent the day like archaeologists, uncovering small tidbits from the ruins. Those who joined us took on specialty jobs during the course of the day. A crew of volunteers—Martha and Ethel Burton, Lucy Sutcliffe, Katy Carnahan Jaronik, Tonia Stubblefield, and John and Mary McElwain—packed up everything in my kitchen cabinets. God bless 'em, that was a cruel task. My accumulation of many years as the family cook was extensive.

Alex Primm and his wife, Kathy, both of whom love books, sorted through my library, assigning each volume to a stack: "the survivors," "the savable," and "the trashed." Books thought to be savable were spread out on a blanket in the backyard to dry in the sun. Throughout the day, Alex worked with them tenderly, rotating each one toward the heat as he would a fine piece of meat on a barbecue grill.

In the end, we were both heartbroken that hundreds of books had to be placed in the dumpster. Some that I decided to pitch, Alex couldn't bear to let go, and he took them home for further treatment.

There was so much to do that I decided not to go back to Washington on Monday as I had planned. I hoped that a good night's sleep would bring a new outlook on the future. But that evening I was particularly unsettled. Everything I relied upon, the infrastructure of my life was gone. I felt stranded, scattered, and bewildered.

I had relied on the solace and strength that came from this farmland retreat. Now that was gone. My possessions of a lifetime were boxed and stashed in warehouses, garages, and the homes of friends and relatives.

While I was bemoaning the present, Russ, Robin, and Tom were planning the future. Even though each of them is a lawyer, living in St. Louis, they determined to do everything necessary to keep the farm. They could not walk away in defeat. This was the homestead. The boys would look after the financial matters while Robin would head up the cattle operation, learning to mend fences, to operate heavy equipment, and to breed and sell livestock.

But for the moment, all I could see were charred possessions and faded dreams. I wondered if there would ever be any certainty in my life again. On Monday night, I dropped into bed weary of searching for answers that didn't come and longing for something solid in my life that didn't keep slipping away.

"Tomorrow will be better," I said to myself with forced confidence. "I will see things more clearly in the light of a new day. I'll stay in Rolla for a while and get things straightened out . . . meet with the insurance company . . . think about rebuilding. And I'll write the thank-you notes to all those who came to help. Things are quiet on Capitol Hill right now. I'll take a few days to get collected."

Like me, people all over America were going to bed that evening rehearsing their plans for the future.

The next day, before noon, everything in the world had changed.

It was Tuesday, September 11.

I had just returned to my brother-in-law's house with a few more charred treasures. Oma and my neighbor Ethel were having amazing success laundering items retrieved from the fire. My mother's hand-crocheted bedspread that I had given up for lost was now blemish free. As we marveled over these salvaged heirlooms, the sounds and pictures flashing onto the television screen grabbed our attention.

We stood dumbfounded by the unfolding catastrophe—airplanes exploding! Buildings crumbling like a scene from some horror movie!

The Twin Towers . . . the Pentagon . . . attacked!

And perhaps more attacks meant for the Capitol and White House. What is happening?

Eventually, I turned away from the repeating scenes on the screen, trying to turn off the images that came to mind. I knew all too well what the families of these victims were feeling—families who had sent loved ones off to work that morning who would never return.

At only one other time in my life had I felt so frightened for our country. I was eight years old. The car radio that Sunday interrupted its broadcast to tell of the attack on Pearl Harbor.

I walked outdoors.

It was a gorgeous autumn day that belied the catastrophe occurring elsewhere. I wanted to go home, but there was no home. I walked through the yard where new patches of fallen leaves covered the ground after last night's rain. Our cattle grazed contentedly in the nearby field.

A squirrel ran so near that we both surprised each other. He scurried up the tree trunk with an acorn lodged between his teeth that he had clawed from beneath the freshly fallen leaves.

Yes, there are things to be found in the rubble of life.

"God is not helpless among the ruins."

My thoughts were still wandering . . . searching . . . when someone came with a message.

"There's a call from Washington . . . the Senate. They want to talk to you."

I picked up the phone, wondering if yet another calamity had unfolded.

"There a resolution of support to be voted on tomorrow," the caller said. "We want every senator present. We need a 100–0 vote."

"How can I get there?" I asked. "The airports are closed and no planes are flying."

"We'll send a military plane for you. Where do you want to be picked up?"

"Vichy is the nearest," I said, naming the old military airstrip from World War II that still served the area.

As I hung up the phone, I realized that life had refocused for all of us. My house fire was inconsequential. There were more pressing issues to address. That evening I picked up a book pulled from the rubble of my house. Flipping the pages, I found a quotation from Victor Hugo that I had underlined years ago.

He wrote, "Have courage for the great sorrows of life and patience for the small ones; and when you have laboriously accomplished your daily task, go to sleep in peace. God is awake."

I did just that.

Before leaving for the airport the next morning, I hugged my kids, already grimy from shuffling through the remains of their childhood home.

"I can't help but see some justice in my leaving you here with this incredible mess after the many you've left behind for me. This has got to be a mother's ultimate revenge," I laughed, finding some pleasure from the role reversal. They smiled back, willing to allow me a moment of satisfaction at their expense, gave me a hug, and cautioned me to "be careful" in Washington. Obviously, that would now be a bigger task then just dodging muggers and traffic.

Once again, I got into a car and drove off into the unknown.

Boarding the plane, I felt something of the angst that Saint Paul showed when he wrote, "I go to Jerusalem not knowing what awaits me there." I tried to relax and enjoy the smooth, sunny skies. But I could only focus on those skies filled with smoke and horror that I had seen repeatedly.

As we flew over the familiar landmarks of our nation's capital, I could see the smoldering gap in one side of the Pentagon. Having been told that all planes were grounded, I was astonished when off our wing a jet plane appeared out of nowhere!

"Fighter escort checking us out," the pilot volunteered. "Just a precaution."

"Oh," I stammered, not yet realizing the extent of the heightened security that had been put in place.

When the Senate met later that day, it was in a somber and historic setting. Normally voting is done from the well of the chamber with members straggling in over a twenty-minute period and pointing one finger up or down to signify their position.

This day all members of the Senate voted from their desks—a formal procedure reserved for the most awesome times and gravest decisions. As names were called, each senator rose solemnly and responded "Aye." The vote announced was 100–0—a solid show of support in our country's defense.

The next day, still filled with emotion, I went to the floor of the Senate to speak these words, many of which had come to mind on that flight to Washington.

Today, all across America and the world, hearts are heavy with grief.
We mourn for the victims and families whose lives have been ripped apart

by yesterday's horrific and unprecedented attack on innocent men, women, and children.

Like all Missourians, I am deeply grateful to the rescue workers and volunteers whose heroism saved thousands of lives.

Tragically, many of those heroes are now among the victims.

Their sacrificial deeds stand in sharp contrast to the barbaric acts we witnessed during yesterday's air attack on a peaceful people.

The terrorists wanted to do more than destroy our buildings. They wanted to destroy our influence in the world, the core of who we are as a nation, and the values we stand for as a democracy.

They will not succeed.

I can remember as a young girl the shock and sadness we felt with the sneak attack on Pearl Harbor.

But I also recall the undaunted spirit of America and our resolve to win a victory over tyranny.

We dropped everything we were doing and devoted our full energy and resources to eradicating the threat to our freedoms.

That resolve is as firm today as it ever was.

The pursuit of freedom is our destiny.

We will not now, or ever, flinch in the face of any aggressor or threat to our homeland.

Let those who practice terrorism or harbor terrorists have no doubt about American's resolve.

We will find you.

And you will pay a heavy price for your acts against mankind.

We have withstood worse enemies than you.

We conquered the evils of fascism in Europe and Asia.

We rescued democracy and we built a better world.

We defied communism for decades, powered by the certainty that freedom would ultimately triumph over oppression.

You will not take these gains from us.

Admittedly, today's foes are different.

They are faceless fanatics with no clear address or even purpose who target innocent people, sitting in offices and airplanes.

Although they are sophisticated and well funded, make no mistake, their days are numbered.

We will stand united against their aggression.

And we will do so in a manner that is consistent with our Constitution that is the foundation of our greatness.

We stand behind our president and our national leaders.

We will make the necessary sacrifices, direct the necessary resources, and use American might, technology, and ingenuity to secure our homeland.

But most of all, we will rely on America's courage and faith, knowing that our country has been a source of progress for humankind for over two centuries; knowing that peace-loving people around the world will join with us to eliminate this evil that plagues us all.

To the families who grieve and the victims who suffer, I say we mourn and suffer with you this day.

There will be a dawn tomorrow.

And many tomorrows after that.

There will be many dawns for America.

And as we greet those dawns, we will prove again what the poet Carl Sandburg once said: "We are Americans. Nothing like us ever was."

When we left for the weekend on October 17, 2001, no one on Capitol Hill knew what was in store for us over the next three months. Two days earlier, an anthrax-laced envelope had been delivered to Senator Daschle's suite less than a hundred yards from my own in the Hart Senate Office Building.

We were not to be alarmed, however. The cleanup would be completed over the weekend, we were told. Fine. That would mean little inconvenience to the fifty members and their staffs who worked in the nine-story glass-and-marble building.

In anticipation of returning on Monday, many had left behind briefcases, checkbooks, files, and other personal items they used on a daily basis. No one could predict that the weekend disinfecting job would turn into a ninety-six-day quarantine and a $20 million cleanup operation. After the initial cleaning deadline passed, we were told it would take a "few more days," then a "few more weeks." After that, the time schedule was left open-ended.

Meanwhile, fear was spreading that these two grams of lethal anthrax spores, to which twenty to thirty people on our floor had been directly exposed, had the potential to spread dramatically. The periodic briefing of senators only enhanced those fears.

This was not the typical barnyard anthrax that falls to the ground and clumps, making it less likely to become airborne again. This Ames strain anthrax had been tampered with to make the particles small enough to stay suspended in air or even to become re-aerosolized once they fell. (*Re-aerosolized* was a new word to me, but there were many new and unheard-of things to come over the next months.)

With the discovery of other anthrax deliveries—one to newsman Tom Brokaw—and the death of postal workers, clearly, precautions were demanded. The Senate doctor set up a screening process to test for exposure. Senate staff members waited patiently in a long line that ran the length of two hallways.

The easy procedure consisted of swabbing the nasal passage with a Q-tip, followed by several days of waiting for the results. To be on the safe side, those in the vicinity of Daschle's office were given the option of taking the antibiotic Cipro until their reports came back. Those in the immediate areas of exposure were sentenced to three months on the drug.

In an effort to maintain business as usual, the Hart Building "refugees" scrambled for office space. For a while, I worked out of my car on a cell phone. Then I was assigned a "cozy" seven-by-ten-foot room in the Capitol basement that I quickly dubbed "The Bunker." Attempts to add furnishings further reduced the work space. But the worst feature of the windowless room was the inability to send or receive cell phone calls from so far underground. Despite the cramped quarters, I continued visits with constituents, as well as already scheduled meetings with business and government leaders.

In the meantime, my staff scavenged for computers and supplies, determined to keep our office operating in spite of the situation. We set up offices in three different locations around Capitol Hill, one of them in my son Tom's apartment next to the Supreme Court.

Having to make temporary arrangements for the Congress was not without precedent. The Fourteenth Congress met in a downtown hotel for more than a year after the British burned the Capitol. Its members later moved into the "Brick Capitol" on the site of the present Supreme

Court building, where they met for more than four years while the roofs of the Capitol were replaced.

The current displacement, though less disruptive, was certainly more stressful. Rumors began to surface that we would never be able to return to the building. Neither the EPA nor the Centers for Disease Control were prepared to handle this situation, described by a Capitol police spokesman as "the largest bioterrorism attack in the United States."

It soon became apparent that we were "learning to deal with bioterrorism on the fly," as White House press secretary Ari Fleischer put it. As the anthrax learning curve improved, scientists pumped a poisonous gas—chlorine dioxide—into the building to kill any spores in the heating and ventilation system. Using the chemical as a disinfectant on such a large area was a radical, first-time procedure. Doing so had the potential of discoloring carpets, artwork, and upholstery.

But there was no manual on what to do. Textbooks on the subject were old and dealt only with the traditional forms of anthrax. It was an experiment, and we all had our fingers crossed.

Before the fumigation process began, I had two oil paintings removed from my office: the one of Mel, and the one of Harry Truman on loan from the Truman Library. Sadly, in Daschle's office several historic Indian artworks could not be saved. His office was stripped to the concrete walls, totally rebuilt, and refurnished.

On January 22, one day before the opening of the new session, the building was declared fit for occupancy and reopened. It still had the faint aroma of a swimming pool, even though another chemical had been used to break down the gas.

Returning to my office after such a long absence was like entering a time warp. The calendars still showed October 17, 2001. Fax machines had spewed out their remaining sheets of paper and shut down. Correspondence, usually acted upon quickly, was three months old. Empty flowerpots sat where green plants once bloomed.

During those three months our mail had been detained and "crispy fired" at temperatures greater than those used for sterilizing surgical instruments. From then on, all mail would come like that, and with the added precaution of having one corner snipped to prevent the delivery of any powdery substances.

Capitol tours, temporarily suspended, recommenced. In the interest of security, construction began on the front lawn for a multi-million-dollar underground visitors' entrance.

A new entry procedure put in place for senators and their staff, at first an annoyance, became a regular part of getting to and from the office. Each time I drove onto the Capitol plaza, my car trunk was inspected, a mirror on wheels searched the underside of the vehicle, and, for good measure, bomb-sniffing dogs performed their routine.

Through all this turmoil and uncertainty, the Senate stayed the course and, unlike the House, refused to adjourn. In another time of turmoil and uncertainty during the Civil War, President Lincoln had insisted that construction work on the new Rotunda proceed as planned. It was a testimony that the Union intended to win and move forward regardless of current circumstances.

Despite the inconveniences, and thanks in large part to Majority Leader Daschle's calm direction, the Senate performed without a hitch. Whoever planted those lethal biological agents hoped to incite fear and chaos within our country. But they were unable to shut down the work of a determined democracy.

The uninterrupted functioning of government was a proud testimony to the resolve of our leaders and workers and a high point in the history of the U.S. Senate.

"You're going where?" Robin asked.

"I'm going to Afghanistan," I replied excitedly.

"In the winter?"

"Yep, in January."

"What's the occasion?"

"It's a CODEL."

"Talk to me in words, not Washington acronyms."

"It means congressional delegation. I'm going with the Armed Services Committee to Turkey, Uzbekistan, Tajikistan, Afghanistan, Pakistan, and Oman."

"Wow," was all she could muster in reply.

Clearly, my adventurous daughter was jealous, having traveled extensively in Asia and Europe, but little in the places I was headed.

Until recently, most Americans couldn't find these Middle Eastern countries on a map, much less pronounce their names. Now we couldn't learn enough. And what we learned, in some cases, was troubling.

Take the Texas-sized nation of Afghanistan, for instance. It has had four years of drought, five years of oppression under Taliban rule, and twenty years of war. It's a country where measles is a major killer, women must go shrouded from head to toe in burkas, and the national sport involves throwing the carcass of a dead goat over a goal line from horseback.

By contrast, Afghanistan's northern neighbor of Turkey is a modern, democratic, Islamic nation. Uzbekistan, another neighbor, still follows the Soviet model with censorship and imprisonment of human rights activists, and even poets. The tiny kingdom of Oman, however, is ruled by a benevolent sultan living in a Disneyland palace.

Led by Joe Lieberman and John McCain, we nine senators would be the first congressional delegation to visit the area since the hostilities began. At first, the Republican leadership was not keen on my going, because of any advantage it might give me in an election year. The trade-off was to enlist Sen. Susan Collins (R-Maine), who was also running for reelection, to go. That was fine with me. I was willing to go along with whatever inside game it took to make the trip possible.

For the flight, the military provided a DC-10, a spacious cargo carrier. Pallets of seats added to the front half of the aircraft left the rear compartment available for our stored baggage. When we arrived at Andrews Air Force Base, the crew had already loaded food and supplies, enough for the entire trip over and back. Three meals, several snacks, and nine hours later we land in Ankara, Turkey. We planned to continue on to Istanbul following our meeting with Prime Minister Bülent Ecevit, but that was struck from the itinerary after a heavy snow prevented the trip.

Already labeled the "CODEL from Hell" because of the shifts in schedule, excessive security requirements, delays, and bad weather, we were all a bit unnerved by the time we left Dushanbe, Tajikistan, for our flight into Afghanistan.

This time we were aboard a C-130, configured for air-dropping troops and equipment into hostile areas. There were no amenities. Like parachutists, we were strapped into the web seating, pressed hip to hip, toe to toe, along two tight rows on one side of the plane. The late-night flight was meant to diminish our chance of being the target of enemy fire. Even the interior lighting was reduced to two eerie green lights to lessen our visibility from the ground.

Flying along a mountain ridge, we nestled onto the darkened airstrip at Baghram Airbase thirty miles north of Kabul, Afghanistan. American forces had recently reclaimed the crumbling airbase, abandoned by the Soviets a decade ago. Our pilots landed with the aid of night vision goggles (NVG) that literally allowed them to see in the dark. Relieved that we had traversed the unfriendly skies of Afghanistan unharmed, we listened for further instructions as the huge jawlike doors at the rear of the plane opened.

"Go directly, and quietly, to the vehicles," our guide commanded. "You are surrounded by a minefield. Whatever you do, don't step off the path. A soldier lost a foot just two days ago," he declared, reinforcing his warning.

Looking out into the darkness, I could see little more than the outline of the vehicles. The dusty terrain and creepy shadows looked as menacing as a moonscape.

A few soldiers approached the plane clutching M-16 rifles.

"Watch your step, m'am," my escort whispered.

A short beam of light from his flashlight pointed onto the powdery ground that surrounded us. Seeing my shoes instantly coated with the fine sand particles, I wished that I had worn the hiking boots that I had packed at the last minute.

The only relief from this alien terrain was the panorama of stars overhead, all in their familiar positions, an assurance that there are some unchanging features to the universe.

From the faint light cast on his face, I saw that my guide through this minefield was about nineteen or twenty years old. He probably signed up to see the world, or to learn a profession, but didn't have in mind doing it in a war-torn dustbowl.

This area of the world was once far enough away that most Americans didn't have to think about it. Their problems were not ours. But suddenly, dramatically, that had all changed. Our being there—nearly a tenth of the U.S. Senate—was a testimony to that.

We moved quickly toward the makeshift headquarters, a dilapidated concrete building reminiscent of a bombed-out site in an old World War II movie. It was nearly midnight, though my internal clock was thoroughly confused. Following a briefing, we were ushered into an army tent about twelve feet square with one bare lightbulb hanging from the ceiling, the chill of the night dissipated by a corner space heater.

It was a strange time and setting in which to gather for a meeting with the new interim president of Afghanistan, Hamid Karzai. We shuffled about the limited space to make room for the camera crews and security guards that pushed their way inside, anticipating Karzai's arrival.

When the tent flap opened again, the president entered, accompanied by several cabinet members and wearing a soft green tribal robe and military-style cap. His quick smile and easy conversation showed that he was familiar with Americans and their ways. "I used to see you on television in the United States," Karzai told Lieberman and McCain, referring to the senators' run for office the previous year. The president reminded us that his brother owned a restaurant in Chicago that he enjoyed visiting. After the small talk ran its course, Karzai turned to the topic of the hour—our common cause against terrorism. He did not deliver a long monologue like the other heads of state we had visited, but instead engaged freely in a question-and-answer session.

The question of the hour was, "Where is Osama bin Laden?"

Karzai smiled and replied that he did not know.

"It would be difficult for Osama to blend into the population. He is unusually tall and for that reason would be easily spotted," he explained.

When it was my turn to pose a question, I asked what was being done to bring women back into government, education, and health positions. Karzai used my inquiry as an opportunity to draw in one of the two women in his cabinet, Dr. Sima Samar.

I had read about her in preparation for the trip. During the Russian occupation, her husband was taken away for questioning and never seen again. Since then, the soft-spoken physician and human rights activist had endured threats for her work in setting up clinics, hospitals, and schools for girls.

She once said, "I believe we will all die one day, so let's take the risk of helping somebody."

She was taking yet another risk in heading the new department of women's affairs in her country. Her calm resolve and buoyant spirit showed that she welcomed the task.

Dr. Samar had been seated with a white knit scarf closely wrapped about her head and shoulders, her plainness a sharp contrast to some of the chicly dressed Afghan women I had met in Washington.

Her response to the president's request startled me at first. She nodded to Karzai and said softly, "With your permission." While this seemed strange to those of us in the Western world, I realized it was a sign of respect rather than any expression of inferiority. Karzai, who did not seem at all threatening, smiled his approval, and she continued.

She spoke in halting English, telling of her new offices and the 140 women working in the public information bureau. Samar has her work cut out for her in a country where the female literacy rate is a mere 20 percent, a country where women bear six children on the average, and one in fifteen dies from the complications of pregnancy.

Yet there is a division among Afghan women, who are polarized by ethnic groups, speak different languages, and have contrary views about the pace of progress in their country. Most agree, however, that education, health, and safety are primary and immediate concerns for all women.

I asked Dr. Samar for her business card. She apologized that none had been printed and wrote her name on a scrap of paper for me. I would see Sima Samar twice more in the United States, at the joint session of Congress during the State of the Union Address and again when she visited with the women senators on Capitol Hill. During those visits, she would plead for more peacekeeping forces for the rural areas where there is still little or no protection for women.

In addition to these immediate problems, there are basic reforms to be addressed. Not just human rights reforms, but economic and political reforms as well. It's a long and difficult job fraught with frustration, but essential to any democratization effort.

Karzai left us with a final comment.

"Our people do not ask, 'Why are the Americans here.' They ask, 'Will they stay long enough to make a difference?'"

That was a recurring and unanswered question.

After another round of handshakes, Karzai departed to meet British Prime Minister Tony Blair, whose plane had just arrived at the airbase. As the president stepped back outside and onto the dusty, rocky pathway, I overheard someone say, "Mr. President, be careful, stay on the path."

Those were my thoughts exactly.

The path of freedom is always lined with danger. Our "minefield meeting" is symbolic of the volatility we can expect in this country and the caution we must take. Our nations' futures, tragically linked by the deeds of September 11, will remain so for many years to come.

As I moved toward the plane, I was again in the keeping of the soldier with the rifle and the flashlight. I shook his hand warmly.

"Thank you for all you are doing for our county," I said. "Tell me, how are you getting along here so far away from home?"

"I miss my family," he replied with a stiff upper lip. "But we know why we're here, m'am, and we plan to stay until we get the job done."

By this time, my lip was not so stiff. As I reboarded the waiting plane, my thoughts drifted to a line from one of Carl Sandburg's poems: "Such as we were we gave ourselves outright." I was moved by the devotion to duty evidenced by these young people. We had come from the other side of the world, hoping to lift their spirits, but as it turned out, we were the ones inspired.

I watched from the cockpit as the pilots adjusted their night goggles for takeoff, revved up the engines, and lumbered down the runway into the star-studded night. One pilot pointed to some mortar fire that flared in the distance.

Our late arrival into Pakistan allowed for no more than three to four hours of sleep that night. It had been a long, incredible journey—a day of faces and voices that I couldn't get out of my mind.

The next morning we headed toward Pasni, in the southern tip of Pakistan. If you closed your eyes, you could imagine the sandy beachhead transformed into a plush seaside resort. But for the time being, it was a barren outpost—a tent city with no indoor plumbing. The American troops stationed there provided support services for the aircraft carrier USS *Theodore Roosevelt*, on duty in the Arabian Sea.

For our flight we boarded a COD Carrier (Carry Onboard Delivery), essentially a supply plane for the five thousand military personnel on board the ship. The challenge, of course, was to fly the COD onto what looked like a postage stamp floating in the middle of the sea.

Sitting next to me was Sen. John Edwards (D-North Carolina), both of us strapped securely and helmeted for a landing that would involve snagging the tail hook on the carrier deck. It's a feat performed at full throttle in the event another fly around is necessary. To stoke our apprehension, Sen. Fred Thompson (R-Tennessee), the movie-actor-turned-senator, told us that his last carrier landing took three rounds before the plane was successfully snatched from the sky.

Our new pilot's name was Bridget. She pushed her long, red hair inside her flight helmet and told us to enjoy the trip that she made routinely. Within fifteen minutes, she was making her approach onto the carrier. Because the plane had only small windows, we were prevented from being visually prepared for the landing. Despite Thompson's gloomy recollection, all we experienced was a noticeable tug that stopped the plane abruptly, an indication that Captain Bridget had performed another successful mission.

We had the choice of dining in the officers' mess or eating with the sailors from our home states. Most chose to be with the sailors. The food was unusually good. I selected a hearty portion of lasagna but noticed that a great variety of other dishes were available as well. The sailors were in good humor despite having been at sea for a record-breaking 113 days.

I asked one young man, "What keeps you going, out on the ocean for such a long time?"

He replied, "Oh, we get mail. Mail from people and kids we don't even know."

He pulled a piece of construction paper from his pocket that had been folded into a card. On it were drawings of American flags and photos of children along with their names.

"Look at what it says here at the bottom of the card," he said. "'Take care of America for us.' That's what we're doing."

It was a message not lost on any of us.

The Senate

KANSAS CITY STAR

Eight days before the election, I made my first public statement about the upcoming vote. It was not from a studio or at a public event, but outdoors from the deck of our farmhouse in Rolla surrounded by my family. Those shown in photo include Austin, Robin, Tom, Russ, his wife, Debra, and their younger son, Andrew.

What should have been a moment of sublime celebration, the moment I could finally cast my vote for my husband, whose race for the U.S. Senate was a culmination of a lifelong devotion to public duty, was instead a moment of solitary reckoning and grave public import.

KANSAS CITY STAR

209

*The 2000 election increased the number of females in the U.S. Senate from nine to thir-
teen. Here, the entire freshmen class poses with the democratic leadership, including
Senators Harry Reid, Tom Daschle, and Barbara Mikulski.*

My assignment to the Armed Service, Commerce, and Governmental Affairs committees offered an opportunity for some of my most fascinating and important work.

SEN. CARNAHAN

Each month the women of the senate—both Democrats and Republicans— met for dinner at a local restaurant or in a home. This evening we posed for a picture in the home of Sen. Dianne Feinstein (D-California).

OMA CARNAHAN

OMA CARNAHAN

I stood in the driveway, disheartened and drenched with rain as flames leaped from the second floor of my home. Later I tried to put the events of the evening into perspective. I was unharmed. Much of the furniture had been rescued, and damaged pieces looked repairable. A house could be rebuilt. I understood the difference between misfortune and tragedy.

I was surprised at the number of speaking requests I received. Whatever the occasion, I found that a dash of humor or a heart-warming anecdote makes the message—and the messenger—more acceptable to the audience.

The first senate delegation to visit Afghanistan after 9/11 poses with one of their flight crews. Standing from left to right are Senators Joe Lieberman, Jean Carnahan, John McCain, Bill Nelson, John Edwards, Susan Collins, Fred Thompson, Jack Reed, and Chuck Hagel.

When Enron chairman and CEO Ken Lay appeared before the Senate Commerce Committee, he was admonished sternly for his behavior that had led to the collapse of the company.

DICK BERKLEY

Although it was difficult, staffers Ryan Rhodes and John Beakley made sure that a frantic senate schedule worked for me and not the other way around.

The family farm in Rolla gives us all a chance to relax and enjoy the outdoors.

I own a Browning 20-gauge shotgun that I use for skeet shooting. Because I had the stock shortened to better fit my arm length, my family calls it "Mom's sawed-off shotgun."

Nine

An Ember in the Soul

I would rather be ashes than dust! I would rather that my spark should burn out in a brilliant blaze than it should be stifled by dry rot. I would rather be a superb meteor, every atom of me in magnificent glow, than a sleepy and permanent planet. The proper function of man is to live, not to exist. I shall not waste my days in trying to prolong them. I shall use my time.

—Jack London

What most people don't understand—or learn too late—is that running for public office takes more than the desire to serve, or even the ability to serve. It takes a "fire in the belly." For some, the fire is evident in a brash, declamatory style. With others, like Mel, the fire is more of an ember in the soul, a constant pilot light that fuels a passion for politics.

Many people toy with the idea of seeking office, but they are not ready to devote the time and energy required or to expose their faults and frailties to public scrutiny. Running for office means tossing your *life* in the ring—not just your hat. It is a risky and consuming pursuit. Or, as one Chicago alderman put it, "politics ain't beanbag."

Most who engage in public service pay an enormous personal price for that opportunity. Those who stay the course are driven by reasons other than the dubious honors, titles, or fleeting recognition that come their way. The best of them, down deep, believe that they can make a difference. Discontented with the status quo, they see themselves as agents for change. They champion a cause and, in so doing, inspire others by their "can-do" approach.

I do not fault those without the political "fire in the belly." Many other callings can ignite the soul. I simply believe that whatever one undertakes should be done with enormous passion, or left to others.

Admittedly, some people burn out over time, while some never fire up at all. But others burn brightly all their lives. When I hire people, experience or education is not nearly as important to me as the "fire." That one ingredient makes the difference in politics. It makes the difference in everything.

In my own race, I wasn't worried about "the fire." It was there. I wanted to carry on Mel's fight for education, health care, and workers. I have to admit, though, that I sometimes felt like the young basketball player who scored one point in the game where Michael Jordan scored sixty-six. Forever after, the young man referred to the game as the one where he and Michael Jordan together scored sixty-seven points.

Mel had been the star. He sparked the political interests of the rest of the family and those about him. I had become the dream keeper, but I wanted to be more than that. If I had the chance, I wanted to fight some new battles on my own—battles for women, seniors, children, and the disabled, the most vulnerable in our society. To do that, I needed to have a full term in office. The real test was whether I could harvest the money needed for a high-profile Senate campaign.

Money is the mother's milk of modern political campaigns. That has not always been the case. Mel's father, A. S. J. Carnahan, served for fourteen years in Congress without ever holding a fund-raiser, running a television commercial, or hiring a political consultant.

In the forties, when Mel was twelve years old, the two of them drove throughout their Ozark congressional district attending church picnics, visiting on town squares, and nailing posters onto trees and fence posts. There are people today who tell me, with some pride, that Congressman Carnahan slept on their sofa, sang at their church, or ate their chicken and dumplings.

To win in south Missouri, a candidate needed only to capture the Democratic primary. The general election was just a formality. Since the Great Depression, there were barely enough Republicans in those hill counties to staff the polls on election day. Money or issues made little difference in campaigns. Whichever candidate had the best reputation and shook the most hands came out the winner.

A half century later, in a statewide campaign against the incumbent Sen. John Ashcroft, Mel raised $8 million—the most ever raised by a Missouri Democrat. Ashcroft, as expected, garnered even more. But that didn't bother Mel. He had a philosophy that reflected his focus about running and raising money.

"You don't have to beat everybody, just one person," he would say if any of the family showed doubts about an impending race. "You don't have to raise more money than your opponent. You just have to be competitive." As the old song goes, "You've gotta accentuate the positive, eliminate the negative." That's what he did. It helped him get his head set straight for the race.

In my case, with less than two years before another statewide race, I had to get a fund-raising team in place immediately. I needed money in the bank just to be in a position to make the decision. I could back out later, but I sure couldn't go forward without a substantial war chest.

Back in Missouri, my Republican opponent, former congressman Jim Talent, had the political luxury of going to parades, picnics, receptions, and public gatherings while he counted on the infusion of large sums gathered by friends of the White House. I was stuck in Washington until the Senate adjourned just weeks before the general election. I had a 98 percent voting record and was determined to do the job expected of me.

Talent had missed 104 votes during his unsuccessful race for governor two years earlier. Surprisingly, that was never a big issue for him. But had I ignored that many votes, I would have been considered remiss in my duty. On the other hand, if I stayed in Washington, I was using a "rose garden" strategy. It was a no-win situation. I opted to make every vote.

Alongside my other duties—meeting with constituents; attending hearings, committee meetings, and receptions; preparing speeches; giving interviews; reading and answering mail; returning phone calls; voting; and presiding—I added a parallel track—fund-raising. At first, I set aside two hours several times a week. Later it would move to as much as four hours at a time and a national travel schedule that took me from coast to coast on weekends.

Without a doubt, one of my smartest decisions in the campaign was to hire Yael Ouzillou as my national fund-raiser. It took a while for me to pronounce her name, but she was patient. With a name like that, you have to have a sense of humor. Not only was Yael a pleasant and tireless worker, she was organized, methodical, and persistent—three essentials for a good fund-raiser.

She opened the Washington campaign office in a back alley garage near Capitol Hill. The two-story building also housed the fund-raising operation of Sen. Tom Harkin (D-Iowa). Ethics rules require the separation of official duties from the political operation, a distinction that I observed meticulously.

I met with donors off Capitol Hill and never made or received fund-raising calls in the Senate office. Mel always insisted on playing by the rules, and the members of my staff, many of whom had worked for Mel, were well trained to continue that tradition. Mel knew that the little things, so irrelevant at the time, had the potential for political ruin.

Examples abounded in Missouri to prove the importance of following the rules. In recent years, an attorney general and a speaker of the house had been sent to jail and a secretary of state impeached.

During one of Mel's earlier campaigns, a news article referred to him as a "straight arrow." This led a supporter to create an arrow-shaped pin that I see worn by Carnahan loyalists even today. Mel had worked a lifetime creating a squeaky clean political image. It was one that I wanted to keep.

Steve Neuman, a bright, politically savvy young man who worked for me in Washington, told of fund-raising with Mel.

> One day Mel came into the campaign headquarters for call time during the 2000 race. We were seated at a conference table in a small room where Mel frequently came to make fund-raising calls. I had a stack of call sheets ready and we began to work the phones.
>
> After about an hour, we came to a call sheet for a successful St. Louis businessman who had just recently won a state contract. Mel looked at the call sheet. Then he looked some more. He finally just

pushed it away and announced that he was not going to make that call.

I said, "What do you mean? That's a great call. Not only is the guy for you, he was just awarded a state contract."

Mel said, "That's exactly why I'm not going to call him. Because of that contract, he's going to feel obligated to give. I'm not going to do that."

To most politicians, that state contract would have been the reason to pick up the phone and ask for a check. To Mel, it was the reason not to. That's why his staff was so proud to work for him.

Knowing that I had big shoes to fill when it came to fund-raising, I traveled to the back alley garage for several sessions a day, squeezing in thirty to forty minutes of call time around my Senate schedule. Although the twelve-foot-square garage was no more than a hole in the wall, it had a reputation for housing winning candidates. Within weeks, we had a first-class operation in place despite the crude, makeshift surroundings.

I had a fondness for the fund-raising database that one has for things of their own creation. The file had grown from a few dozen cards on my desk to a well-designed computer program with a hundred and fifty thousand names. Mel always maintained a campaign headquarters even while in office. During that time, Scott Sorrell, our computer guru, had tended the database, refining the system and collecting twenty years of contribution data.

When I arrived at the garage for "call time," computer-generated sheets were already in place, along with ample amounts of junk food and "office toys," the kind you manipulate nervously to pass the time. Scott designed the call sheets to include the donor's giving history and notes of prior conversations. Knowing previous giving patterns helped me establish the amount of my request. A candidate does not want to ask for too much and be rejected or, heaven forbid, make a request for too little.

Every candidate and donor has his, or her, own style. Some candidates take a long time to get to the point, preferring to ply the potential contributor with small talk. But most donors are busy people. They know why you are calling, and they respect your ability to make "The Ask." Surprisingly, some donors feel honored that you think them capable of the large sum requested.

I once did call time with Sen. John Edwards. What a bundle of kinetic energy! Ignoring the chair and the junk food, he bounced between three telephones, garnering thousands of dollars for me from donors waiting online for the chance to speak with him. Senator Edwards's vigor and sincerity serve him as well in the Senate as they do on the fund-raising circuit.

The next day, I went back to my "fund-raising garage" knowing that my crew would expect me to match Edwards's performance.

"Do you think you can work three phone lines today?" Yael asked teasingly as I strapped on my headset.

"Well, maybe, but not without a chair and some cookies."

Not on my staff, but a great friend and legendary fund-raiser, is Ellen Malcolm of EMILY's List—the name is an acronym for Early Money Is Like Yeast. The unique and highly effective organization supports *only* pro-choice women candidates. My husband was the one exception to this rule, the only man to walk into their office and leave with a check. It was a tribute to his long and politically hazardous struggle in behalf of reproductive rights in Missouri.

EMILY's List continues to raise millions of dollars in small, direct-mail contributions *for* women and, largely, *from* women. Malcolm, the group's founder and director, is an extraordinary leader and a truly personable and caring human being. In the closing days of my campaign, when I did a door-to-door canvass, she came out from Washington and hit the pavement on my behalf. You won't find many in Washington political circles who would put forth that kind of effort for a candidate.

As time went on, the fund-raising phone calls that had started out as a vast intrusion became a pleasant interval in my day. I could relax and focus on just one thing—making those calls. Such single-mindedness was not possible in the Senate office. A day provided a host of divergent issues on which to concentrate. A visit with soybean farmers might occur on the heels of a briefing on Afghanistan from Secretary of State Colin Powell or Secretary of Defense Donald Rumsfeld. Reporters often pulled me aside to talk about a telecommunications issue before the Commerce Committee. A television interviewer might want the latest news on a bill affecting the Missouri River. I looked forward to the chance to dwell on one topic alone, even for a short while.

The lessons learned watching Mel evolve from being the "candidate who couldn't raise money" to one who overexcelled at the task were not lost on me. I knew from Mel's experience that fund-raising was a chore requiring a stern discipline.

If you can't raise money, no matter how dedicated you are to public service, you are greatly handicapped in getting your message to voters. I remember having this illustrated very vividly by an officeholder.

He said, "If I stand in front of Walmart during the last week of a campaign and shake hands with three hundred people, it makes me feel so good. But how many votes does it get me?

"In reality, half of those three hundred people will not be registered. Another half will not go to the polls on election day. Of the seventy-five remaining people, one-third will vote Republican no matter who's on the ticket. Another one-third will vote Democratic regardless. That leaves me with a mere twenty-five voters that I have any possibility of affecting."

That is why television plays such an important role in modern politics. It allows candidates who must reach vast audiences to deliver a well-honed message more efficiently than can be done in any other way. Because it is the most costly way to communicate with voters, huge sums must be raised. Long before the electronic age, Vincent van Gogh wrote, "There may be a great fire in our soul, but it becomes a mere wisp of smoke unless it's conveyed to others."

Knowing all this, there can be no excuses to duck the dreaded "call time" that appears persistently on the schedule of a well-organized campaign. Because fund-raising is a test of political will and stamina, it has to be a regular part of the candidate's life, like sleeping and eating. I know this sounds severe, but short of self-financing, it's the only way. Most people would rather undergo a root canal than to ask friends and strangers for money, but it's a job that can be learned.

My first systematic fund-raising efforts began while I was First Lady, drumming up support for the Governor's Mansion and other community projects that I initiated. Convincing people to give involves making them a part of your cause, whether it's political or charitable. People don't want to fund your ambition; they do want to fund a mission. My 71,000 campaign contributors, from all over the country, truly felt that ours was a worthy and common cause. They wanted to believe that there were ordinary people in politics motivated by principle.

The warm response to my fund-raising was personally gratifying. Of the hundreds of calls that I made, I can count on the fingers of one hand the number of people who told me no. Of course, not all followed through at the promised level, but they rarely gave me a flat refusal.

At first, I attributed my success to having a good call list, but I know now it was more than that. People truly admired what I was doing and wanted to express it in a tangible way. I would later learn that *one-half* the donors on EMILY's List contributed to me! Ellen Malcolm explained it this way: "When we feature you in a mailing with other candidates, your name has a giant sucking sound that draws donations mostly to you."

During my hundreds of fund-raising phone calls, only a few times did someone offer a contribution on the condition that I support an issue they favored. When that happened, I told Yael not to put them on the call list again and to return any donation that might be sent in the future.

My staff was ahead of the curve on the Enron scandal. Enron had sent an unsolicited donation to me in June, before its empire came crashing down. My chief of staff, Roy Temple, was already suspicious of the company from what he had learned of its activities in California.

"I smell a rat," he said. "We don't want any part of this outfit."

Roy had good instincts, so I had no trouble with his analysis. We returned the check immediately, long before any news of Enron's improprieties became known.

When the Enron story broke, the press, without bothering to check, announced the names of all the senators who had received checks from the company, including me. Later there were some minor retractions, but at the time the media were too busy painting everyone with the same brush to figure out that my office had responded differently from the rest.

Even with our cautious approach, we set a new record in fund-raising for a Missouri Democrat. Our budget called for raising $10 million, if we were lucky—$2 million more than Mel had raised. In the end, we took in $12 million in federal funds and raised another $8 million in nonfederal funds, the so-called soft money. And because I was the number-one target of the White House, my opponent was lavished with money to assure that I was turned out of office.

Obscene? Sickening? Yes. To think that one Midwest senate seat costs that much in today's political environment!

Would I have liked it otherwise? Definitely. But I had to play the same fund-raising game that is required of all those who seek higher office today.

Former senator Bill Bradley (D-New Jersey) says that campaign finance reform is the key to everything else we do in government. Yet for most voters the issue is a yawner. People feel, "That's just the way things are. Nothing can be changed." When faced with public financing as an alternative to private funding, voters are still unconvinced which is the better course.

I respect Senators John McCain and Russ Feingold (D-Wisconsin) for their tenacity in trying to achieve campaign finance reform. I told McCain when I first arrived in the Senate that I admired his work and wanted to help in any way I could. He has an uphill struggle, fighting most of the members of his own party, the White House, as well as the "boys on K Street," as the lobbyists are called because of the location of many of their offices. Having 12,000 registered lobbyists in Washington only aggravates the partisanship and gridlock in government today. Despite the roadblocks, after seven years of hard work, the McCain-Feingold campaign finance bill passed. Still, there are huge loopholes in the law and much left to be changed.

Because many big corporations pay little or no tax, and are further rewarded with huge government subsidies and lax regulations, they happily make enormous political contributions in the hopes of maintaining the status quo. When that happens, plutocracy, the rule of the rich, displaces democracy, the rule of the people. While I'm not ready to agree entirely with the cynics who declare, "Big money will never be defeated" or "People don't vote, money does," I do find political giving patterns disheartening. Less than one-tenth of 1 percent of Americans make 83 percent of the political contributions.

Even under the new campaign reform law, special interest groups are allowed to raise multi-millions in "soft money"—unrestricted amounts often coming from unidentifiable donors. You can recognize their handiwork in commercials that end with some ludicrous appeal, "Call Candidate X and tell him to stop beating small animals and children"—or whatever line draws political blood. Inflammatory ads are designed not to convey information or to show solid comparisons, but to excite political passion on a wedge issue known to move swing voters.

The need for campaign finance reform is an ongoing struggle. But until Americans insist that we reshape the system, the special interests will continue to reap the benefits that come from "buying" access to power.

Senator McCain says that he'll stand up for reform "until his last breath." Unfortunately, on his side of the aisle, he often stands alone.

Since 9/11, campaigning politicians have discovered yet another powerful "tool" with which to bludgeon each other: patriotism. Casting doubts on another American's love of country—his or her patriotism—is as despicable now as it was fifty years ago when Sen. Joseph McCarthy waged political sport on those he deemed "un-American." Yet it is done repeatedly in campaigns around the country in an attempt to divide people and to win elections.

Real patriotism does not divide, it unifies. Post-9/11 America showed us that. We rallied as we had in World War II in response to an enemy threatening our lives and freedoms. Patriotism, with all the passion that it ignites, can bond us together for good purpose or it can be "the last refuge of the scoundrel."

A political scalawag who signs on to a hot-button issue just to win an election does not have to bother with saving Social Security, getting a prescription drug benefit for the elderly, or seeing to the education of our children. A "correct" stance on guns and abortion, or a display of "superior patriotism," is often enough to carry a candidate to victory.

Single-issue voters, having been politically lobotomized by their leaders, respond like robots when their control buttons are pushed. True leadership in a democratic society comes not from fear-mongering, dictates, or coercion, but by example and consensus. Slash-and-burn rhetoric excites special interest groups, but it turns off young people and creates a greater distrust of public officeholders. We need leaders in search of solutions that work, leaders willing to draw us back to the basic problems plaguing our communities, schools, and workplaces.

Political courage is rare in an arena that values winning over principle. In 1993, when Mel proposed a tax increase to make historic improvements in education, he did so knowing that the issue would be hurled at him during the next election. He took the risk because it was the right thing to do for the future of Missouri's children. He understood the human and economic peril if Missouri continued to rank forty-something in support of education. It was an act of pure political courage with no personal gain, and no votes or dollars to be harvested.

Theodore Roosevelt had no use for what he called "tepid souls." He spoke of leaders engaged in "bold exploits, feats of courage, and nobility of purpose." Those who make principled responses to difficult issues will not always be rewarded at the polls. Nonetheless, they remind us of the importance of personal courage and moral leadership in shaping the future.

Congresswoman Barbara Jordan asked the perplexing question, "Who will speak for the common good?" In a political arena saturated by special interests and high-stakes divisive battles, who will put aside selfish pursuits and speak for the common good?

It's a question that won't go away. We must answer it again with each election.

It's always interesting to know what politicians do on election evening, between the time the polls close and when the outcome of the balloting is announced. So I was fascinated by a newspaper account of election night 2002 at the White House. According to one writer, President Bush, Karl Rove, and their political aides gathered in the family quarters to await the outcome of the nation's thirty-some Senate races. As they watched the Fox News channel tally up the votes, it soon became apparent that there was a Republican win in the making.

The president's multiple visits to Missouri and other key states, in addition to the many visits by his family, cabinet members, and high-ranking party leaders, had paid off. With the defeat of Max Cleland in Georgia, Walter Mondale in Minnesota, and me in Missouri, Republicans had wrenched three seats from Democratic hands and swung the Senate's delicate balance of power back to their side.

John Ashcroft's defeat had been avenged, as had Senator Jeffords's defection.

Savoring the moment, the president smiled broadly, leaned back in his easy chair, and lit up a cigar.

Meanwhile, back in Missouri, my supporters were having to accept the inevitability of defeat. I had run for the United States Senate against President George W. Bush . . . and lost. It had not started out that way, but that's the way it turned out. The name on the ballot next to mine was Jim Talent. But the name could have been "Spot" or "Mark Twain." It wouldn't have made any difference. Running against a sitting president with the highest recorded approval ratings of any chief executive since Gallup began polling is no easy task.

As the old Sioux medicine man once said, "The success of a rain dance depends a lot on timing." November 2002, was, indeed, the perfect time for George W. Bush, who had already taken on the aura of a wartime president. The long shadow of 9/11 had cast a pall over the election and the nation. Despite the president's astronomical ratings and media blitz, he won the Missouri Senate seat by a scant 1 percent of the vote.

As to my election loss, I didn't so much hurt for myself—though I would have liked the chance to finish the term. I had discovered the great potential for doing some worthwhile things that benefited real people and not just those with the biggest pocketbooks or the loudest voices.

My heart ached for the workers who had put so much of themselves into this campaign—knocking on doors, working phone banks, raising money, and stuffing envelopes.

I hurt for the kids, women, teachers, minorities, seniors, and disabled who believed in the message—and the messenger.

I hurt for the country that had lost the strong, solid leadership of Majority Leader Tom Daschle and with it the opportunity to divert the worst of the right-wing agenda.

It was 1:00 a.m. on election night before we faced the inevitable. Earlier in the day, I had written two speeches: one for victory, the other for defeat. On my way to the podium, I dropped one in the hotel trash bin. I had joked with Robin that my concession speech was far better than my victory speech, not dreaming at the time that it would be the one I would deliver. As I faced my tired and teary-eyed audience, I first thanked them for waiting out the long evening.

I have just called Mr. Talent and conceded this race.

I want to congratulate him for his effective and victorious campaign.

But I also want to thank my staff.

There is none more devoted then they.

None more deserving of praise then they.

I also want to thank the working men and women who have united so forcefully in this common cause.

You fought courageously against overwhelming odds and gave yourself tirelessly to an effort in which you firmly believed.

We are all the better for the battle.

We proclaimed our hopes and our vision for the future and we did it with energy born of conviction and of compassion.

Ours is a cause that has not been lessened by defeat or by the heartache we feel this night.

As always, others will come to lift the fallen torch.

The fire will not go out.

This evening let me thank you for the deep honor of allowing me to serve the two years of my husband's term. It was a momentous time in our nation's history.

It is my hope that those who write of such things in years to come will say: Missouri's first woman to serve in the United States Senate—though she did not serve us long—she served us well.

Yes, I was proud of what my staff and I had accomplished in so brief a time. Knowing we didn't have six years to prove ourselves, we had jumped in wholeheartedly to build a legislative record. Ironically, polling data showed that voters found it hard to believe I could have achieved anything in two years. When presented with a list of the things I had done, one member of a focus group shook her head and said, "I just don't believe she could do that much in such a short time." When I heard that, I had to laugh. I told my pollster, "I agree. I can't believe I worked that hard either."

The first piece of legislation I had offered was the Quality Classrooms Act—the bill that Mel had intended to introduce during his first months as a senator. Knowing that made us work all the harder for its passage. The bill provided $50 billion directly to school districts to fund reductions in class size, school construction, alternative discipline programs, teaching specialists in math and reading, and year-round schedules. Several of the provisions passed as an amendment and were included in the president's education package. My staff was ecstatic over the success of our first efforts, a feat they celebrated in my office with a big cake and much satisfaction.

Most of my legislative proposals were in behalf of children, seniors, or our military personnel. I authored a law extending health benefits to reservists returning from active duty and one requiring that all active duty personnel be provided chemical and biological protective gear. Another bill created rapid response units (EMEDS) within the Air National Guard to meet terrorist attacks or natural disasters.

On a related security issue, I proposed creating a federal website on bioterrorism and offered legislation to enhance the safety of nuclear and radiological materials and facilities worldwide. Both measures passed and were incorporated into the larger defense bill and homeland security bill.

Closer to home, I authored legislation to establish a new facility at Fort Leonard Wood to train responders to terrorist attacks. Thanks to the efforts of my staff, the fort was also the site of the first science and technology conference attended by six hundred representatives of Missouri businesses and universities seeking federal funding opportunities.

However, a Republican filibuster blocked my attempt to get unemployment, training, and health care benefits for airline workers following the 9/11 attacks. While well over a majority of senators (56–44) voted for the bill, it lacked the sixty votes needed to break a filibuster.

On the agriculture side, the Carnahan Amendment to the Farm Bill extended farmers' eligibility for bankruptcy protection, and another proposal helped bring relief to those whose crops were hit by armyworms. I was also pleased to get substantial new funding for the fight against methamphetamine production and trafficking in rural Missouri.

Appalled by the many stories I heard from seniors and small business owners about the escalating cost of health care, I conducted a field hearing in Jefferson City to highlight skyrocketing prescription drug prices. One of my greatest disappointments was the failure of the Senate to agree on a meaningful benefit in the face of such apparent need. However, the funding I secured for the Naturally Occurring Retirement Community program (NORC) will assist seniors wanting to stay in their own communities as they age.

As a member of the Governmental Affairs Committee, I initiated and chaired a hearing that explored shortages of childhood vaccines and authored the successful extension of onsite child care for low-income federal employees.

In the wake of the Enron scandal, I introduced the Fully Informed Investors Act. The bill requiring corporate executives to make electronic disclosure of insider stock sales became part of the larger reform package that passed Congress.

But it was responding to individual requests that brought me the most satisfaction. We helped a group of adoptive parents work through the red tape preventing them from getting their Cambodian children to the United States. We worked nights and through the weekend with the Thai government to expedite the recovery and return of the body of a St. Louis man who disappeared while scuba diving. And we worked for needed funding for children's day care and health care.

Yes, the intervention of a U.S. senator can make a big difference for people with perplexing problems. No one understands that better than Sister Berta does. For years, she and two other nuns have run Operation Breakthrough in Kansas City, the largest day care center in the state.

She called my office one day.

"We need at least a million dollars to get started on expansion," she said, citing the necessity for more health and dental services in a community that serves some of the poorest of families. I had visited the children at the center, and her appeal for help was understandable. Without giving any assurances, my office agreed to see what might be available.

In the months ahead, my staff nurtured the request through the appropriations process. We were all excited when approval finally came. I picked up the phone and called the day care center.

"Sister Berta," I said, "I have some good news for you today!"

There was a pause on the other end of the line. When she spoke, it was with deep sadness.

"I have a four-year-old child on my lap whose mother was killed by gunfire in the street last night. In the next room, I have a mother with five children whose home burned yesterday. So you see, Senator Carnahan, I needed some good news today."

Public service, whether it's performed in Congress or in a day care center, is always about improving people's lives.

In the weeks that followed my election loss, I played the all too familiar game of What If?

What if I had run one more commercial?

. . . raised one more dollar,

. . . traveled one more mile,

. . . given one more speech, or

. . . made one different decision?

In my heart, I knew how futile it was to engage in such torment. I recognized, too, that Missouri had become a highly conservative state, not having elected a Democrat to a full term in the U.S. Senate since Thomas Eagleton served between 1968 and 1986. Still, I hoped that the voice of moderation that characterized Senators Eagleton, Symington, and Truman might have some appeal in today's strident political atmosphere.

Those who shared my hopes for strong families, thriving schools and neighborhoods, and a secure nation were counting on me. "Don't let the fire go out!" I heard repeatedly. In my early campaign speeches I often ended by framing a scenario that I hoped would not occur. I said something along these lines:

> *I don't want it to be said when the history of these times is written that Mel Carnahan and his son and aide died on a wooded hillside.*
>
> *... The people of Missouri, wanting something to survive that crash, did what no state had done before—they elected him anyhow.*
>
> *... His wife went to the Senate in his place, taking Harry Truman's seat, served two years ... and lost.*
>
> *That's not the way I want the story to end. And I don't believe you do either.*

It was always an emotional moment that brought a moving response from audiences, most of whom shared my aspirations and beliefs.

How do we rationalize those times when life doesn't give us a storybook ending, no matter how hard we try?

As a writer, I am used to composing the ending that I want. But as most of us know by now, we don't always get to write the closing lines in real life. We do get to "play many parts," as Shakespeare acknowledged, some that come naturally, others of our own choosing, and some that we could do without.

The secret is moving through our various roles with faith and good humor—the most cherished of traveling companions.

Camus said that in every winter of his life he found an invincible summer. I have found within each of my roles—not all of my choosing—the strength for the next. While we don't always get to write the ending, we can determine how we will play the role in which we are cast.

During the weeks that followed my election loss, I found solace in old friends and old books. I uncovered my copy of the writings of George MacDonald, the nineteenth-century Scottish minister, poet, and novelist who expressed his thoughts in such quaint imagery. The much underlined book, its pages charred and water stained from my house fire, still contained timeless wisdom.

"Fold the arms of your faith," MacDonald advised, "and wait in quietness until the light goes up in your darkness. Fold the arms of your faith, I say, but not of your action. Think of something you ought to do and go do it. . . . Heed not your feeling, do your work." For the moment my work was the tedious and uncertain task of transitioning—moving to a new location in St. Louis, opening an office, rebuilding my Rolla home, and redirecting my energy toward some new purpose.

I also reread Adèle Starbird's *Many Strings to My Lute,* which I first enjoyed twenty years earlier. My first copy, given to me by a friend, was lost in my house fire. Knowing how much I loved the book, John Beakley had found a copy on eBay.

In one of Starbird's essays, the Missouri journalist looked at the changing tides in her own life, and her mother's life, as they each adapted to the mother being in a nursing home.

> Mother: Well, things are going well for me . . . I am on an entirely new track. I'm just trying to be pleasant all the time.
> Adèle: Is it a great effort?
> Mother: Did you ever try it?
> Adèle: No, I'm going to wait until I'm your age before trying anything so drastic.
> We both laughed and then she grew serious.
> Mother: It's the only thing that's left now that I can do for anybody. I can't read or write, but I can at least be pleasant and not add to the troubles of others. You know I think that every human being is already carrying about as much as he can bear, and I don't want to make it harder.
> Adèle continues: "Pleasant. She was more than pleasant—she was GALLANT!"

Gallant is not a word we use often, unless we're referring to a Revolutionary War hero. It describes those who are self-sacrificing, yet spirited. What a great combination!

I am told the Japanese language has a similar word: "gaman." It means enduring something difficult, and it is an esteemed quality.

In the political realm, I think of Jimmy Carter in those terms.

I recall reading an interview of President Carter shortly after he lost his bid for reelection. It must have been especially devastating to this good and godly man to undergo such public rejection.

A news reporter, hoping to get some visceral reaction, quizzed him along these lines:

> Reporter: "Do you believe that God loves you?"
> Carter: "I most certainly do."
> Reporter: "Do you believe that He cares for you and wants the best for you?"
> Carter: "Yes, I do."

And then the zinger . . .

> Reporter: "Why did you lose the presidency?"

I am recalling this from memory, so I don't have Carter's exact response, but he ended with the words of Saint Paul, who found himself in prison during much of his career as a servant of God.

Carter quoted from the letter that Paul wrote to the Romans declaring that nothing could separate him from the love of God.

Nothing.

"Neither death, nor life, nor angels, nor principalities, nor powers, nor things present, nor things to come, nor height, nor depth, nor any other creature can separate us from the love of God."

Interestingly, Paul, on the heels of that wonderful affirmation, writes in the next verse, "I have great heaviness and continued sorrow in my heart."

He is trying to tell us that hurt and faith can exist side by side. Faith does not dispel the hurt; it does make it bearable.

The hurt is overcome.

Overruled.

It is no longer dominant.

Carter emerged from his defeat (no, I should say that he emerged from the loss of what he wanted at the time) to do the work of Habitat for Humanity and to win the Nobel Peace Prize, perhaps the greatest of world distinctions.

How we react makes the difference. We get to choose our response to every event, to every hurt, to every life situation, and to every person we meet.

In that spirit, a Depression-era farmer hung a sign from his barbed-wire fence that read:

> Burned out by droughts,
> Drowned out by flood waters,
> Et out by jack rabbits,
> Sold out by sheriff,
> Still here!

I am amazed by the number of people "still here"—still in the arena leading victorious lives despite overwhelming domestic, financial, and physical problems. I meet them on the streets, in the malls, and at airports all over the country. Strangers still recognize me—the byproduct of millions of dollars spent on political advertising—and take time to thank me for serving or to ask what I'm currently doing. They speak of endurance and strength, often wanting me to autograph an item or to meet a child or grandchild. I treasure their warm and caring words. The writer John Dos Passos says there is nothing "on earth more wonderful than those wistful incomplete friendships that one makes now and then. . . . You never see the people again, but the lingering sense of their presence in the world is like the glow of an unseen city at night."

One such incident occurred as Robin and I were returning to St. Louis from the farm. I felt that we both looked too scruffy to stop in town for dinner. We decided to take our chances on a small diner along the highway where neither of us had ever eaten. Was I ever surprised! When I walked in the door, everyone in the place stood up and applauded! Such reactions still surprise me, for I know that I have never done anything but what appeared, at the time, to be my duty.

Nonetheless, to some I will always be a tragic figure, like a character in some ancient Greek drama. Fortunately, I do not feel that way about myself. If I can be a messenger of hope and healing, there is purpose in what I say, and write, and do each day. If people look at me and say, "Hey, if she can do it, so can I," then I am pleased by that reaction.

Letters and cards from across the country still arrive, some with no more address than "Senator Carnahan, Missouri." Two were especially meaningful. The comments written by my former legislative director, David Schanzer, were sent to me by one of his relatives. It was David's contribution to a family newsletter following the election. Because we had worked together daily in the "pressure cooker" of Washington politics, I was deeply moved by his gracious sentiments. He wrote:

> It has now been five days since the terrible disappointing election in Missouri and while it is still very raw and emotional for me, the wounds are beginning to heal and I am able to be a bit more reflective about what has occurred.
>
> I was incredibly fortunate two years ago to be invited to join the Carnahan team . . . which as I learned is really an extended family. And I had the incredible experience of building a relationship with Senator Carnahan who is the most extraordinary person I have ever met. She accepted a huge responsibility at a time of enormous personal anguish and took on the daunting challenge of running for re-election a mere twenty-two months after taking office.
>
> She had to learn the difficult job of being a senator from scratch, with very little policy background and a bare minimum of experience dealing with the media, constituents, lobbyists, etc. Yet, she did it all. She went to the Senate floor and offered amendments, debated the issues, tangled with witnesses at hearings, read her briefing books until the wee hours every night, dealt with every imaginable question from her constituents and the media, and then, at the end acquitted herself very well in two televised debates against her polished opponent.
>
> And while trying to learn to be a senator and get up to speed on a huge volume of issues, she had to spend a tremendous amount to time raising money for the campaign. . . . She is sixty-eight years old, but for two years she worked six to seven days a week, twelve to sixteen hours a day. Although to the very end, she was gracious, inspirational, stoic, and a source of strength of all who came into contact with her.

So I am sad for Missouri and the country that they will not have the benefit of Senator Carnahan's leadership. Sad for the senator herself, because she worked so hard and deserved the status and prestige that would have accompanied a victory. And sad myself for losing the opportunity to continue to serve with her and my colleagues for four more years in a job that I loved. Upon reflection though, I had the opportunity to participate in a special period in Missouri and United States history and to fight hard for something worth fighting for. Having had that experience was well worth the sorrow attached to not having the end result come out quite the way we all had hope it would.

David is typical of the many bright, idealistic young people with whom I worked during my two years in the Senate. They had a great sense of what was important and committed themselves wholeheartedly to serving their country in the public arena.

Another letter that meant a lot to me came from a thirteen-year-old girl who had volunteered in my campaign. She wrote in response to my thank-you note:

Dear Senator Carnahan:

I wanted to thank you for the letter I received a few days ago about the campaign. I also want to thank you for the opportunity of working on the campaign in the first place. I'd never felt like I could make a difference before.

Yet, while screaming and cheering at the opening of the St. Louis campaign headquarters, when I usually can't read loud enough in class, I could.

While asking over one hundred people for their votes on Election Day when I'm usually too afraid to ask questions, I could.

Like your letter said, one voice can make a difference. Thank you for all your work for the people of Missouri in the past two years. I made a promise on the morning of October 17, 2000 [the morning after the plane crash] to do everything I could for the Democratic Party in honor of Governor Carnahan.

In the days following that terrible day, you showed more courage than I think I have ever seen in one person. I have been able to fulfill my commitment and feel like I really made a difference. Obviously, the results of the election weren't what I wanted, but I still believe 100% in the Democratic cause and will always continue to fight for it.

Thank you again, Senator Carnahan for everything you have done for Missouri and for your courage to be a true leader.

Sincerely, Lauren, age 13

When I read these letters and recall my husband's unfinished work carried by me to the U.S. Senate, I know that striving and serving give meaning to life. Yes, ordinary, fear-stricken, hurting people can do extraordinary things, surprising even themselves.

So many Laurens, of all ages and backgrounds, were fired up by a common cause during the 2000 election. But we need not wait for some catastrophic event to call us to action. Our enthusiasm can brighten and strengthen lives and communities everyday. Small deeds, like pebbles cast into the water, have a rippling effect that reaches far beyond our imagination, fostering courage in countless others.

A half century ago, an Ozark teenager, stirred by his father's example, set out to make life better for everyday Missouri families. Mel Carnahan, like a modern-day Don Quixote, saw possibilities rather than problems. Despite the hazards, he never doubted that public service was a high calling worthy of his best. He firmly believed that the bold experiment we call "self-government" could work if we each did our part. Mel's daring inspired me, and others, to join in his venture. Like Lauren, I did something I never dreamed I could do—and when I did, I found strength beyond measure.

You would think that my kids, living in the aftermath of a tragedy that permanently marred our family, would want no part of the political arena. Yet they have plunged into the fray, knowing well the many risks and uncertainties. My son Russ has announced for the congressional seat being vacated by Rep. Richard Gephardt, and my daughter, Robin, is running for Missouri's secretary of state.

Did I encourage them? Not really. But I could not bring myself to discourage them either, for within them I see the fervor of a young Mel Carnahan blazing brightly.

But I also recognize that life does not give a "fairy-tale ending" to each of our endeavors no matter how hard we try or how much courage we expend. Too often, our best efforts go unacknowledged and unrecorded, but that should not deter us in the least. Our fulfillment, our joy, must come in the striving. The good news is that exhausting ourselves for a worthy purpose has both value and virtue. That, of course, is the essence of the strenuous life, but it is also the story of America.

Acts of personal courage not only enrich our lives, acts of moral and political courage craft our national character. We are defined as a people by the scope of our tasks and the vigor of our undertaking.

Did the 2000 election have meaning? Did my abbreviated time in the Senate make a difference?

You bet it did!

Each of us has the power to change whatever we touch, if only for a moment in time . . . and perhaps forever.

Farewell to the U.S. Senate

FLOOR STATEMENT
November 18, 2002

Two years ago when I came to the U.S. Senate, it was with a heavy heart.

Life had not turned out the way it was supposed to.

My husband, not I, was supposed to have been sworn into the U.S. Senate.

And I was to be seated in the gallery, beaming with delight at the joint victory we had won.

But as someone once pointed out,

"Life is not the way it's supposed to be . . . it's the way it is. The way you cope with it is what makes the difference."

Well, I had some difficult lessons to learn on that front.

It was not by chance that, as I stepped from the dais after being sworn in, the first to welcome me was Sen. Joe Biden.

He had come to this chamber many years ago after a tragic loss in his own life.

He told me the story of having been greeted by Senator McClelland of Arkansas, who looked him in the eye and said, "Work . . . hard work. It's the sure path to healing."

Senator Biden said, "I thought at the time, 'How calloused that advice was. He just doesn't understand how deeply I hurt.'"

But he later found out that McClellan spoke from having experienced a family tragedy of overwhelming proportion.

Joe took the advice to heart, and passed it on to me.

239

You were right, Joe, and I thank you for that wisdom.

There has been much work to throw ourselves into during the 107th Congress.

It has been a monumental period in our nation's history.

A time marred by

. . . deep political divisions,

. . . economic upheavals,

. . . corporate corruption,

. . . threats to our national security, and

. . . the gathering clouds of war.

Through all these disasters, we have seen a triumph of the American spirit.

Yes, Americans have taken to heart the advice that Louis Pasteur once gave to a group of young people.

He said: "Do not let yourselves be discouraged by the sadness of certain hours which pass over nations."

Thankfully, the Congress has refused to be discouraged.

We have endured anthrax attacks,

. . . dismantled offices,

. . . tightened security measures,

. . . major alterations to the Capitol complex,

. . . not to mention three shifts in legislative leadership.

Through it all we have managed to address a number of important issues.

. . . We passed a historic tax cut,

. . . reformed education,

. . . overhauled campaign finance laws,

. . . called corporate America to a higher standard, and

. . . prepared our nation to respond to global terrorism.

We have found that being the guardian of freedom is a relentless and consuming work.

The immensity of our task would cripple a lesser people.

Rather than be cowered by events, America and her institutions have always been emboldened during times of crisis.

I am convinced that the Author of Liberty, who has blessed and protected our nation in the past, will enable us to meet the stern responsibilities of the present.

As you take on this new burden, I will not be among you, but my prayers will be with you.

I leave realizing that to have served in the U.S. Senate—for even a short while—is an honor afforded very few.

I am forever grateful to the people of Missouri who have allowed me and my family to serve them for three generations.

Reporters often ask me to reflect upon those years.

Most recently I was asked, "What impressed you most during your time in the Senate?"

I replied that it was the "diligence beyond duty" shown by all who are a part of this Senate chamber—Democrats, Republicans, Independents, staff, parliamentarians, clerks, pages, security officers, maintenance workers, elevator operators.

All spend long hours serving America.

For the most part, their names and their selfless deeds will go unrecorded, but their lives and work demonstrate a deep devotion to duty.

Mr. President, in recognition of the loyalty and exemplary work of my own staff, I would like permission to insert their names in the record.

[Presiding Officer: Without objection.]

Reflecting on this legislative body, I recognize, sadly, that two great towers of strength will be missed.

My friend and colleague Max Cleland from his wheelchair stands taller than most men ever will.

The U.S. Senate will be greatly diminished by his absence.

That we will no longer hear the spirited voice of Paul Wellstone summoning us to "stand up and fight" will likewise diminish the fervor of this body.

Our nation and party have been further blessed by the courageous leadership of Sen. Tom Daschle and Sen. Harry Reid.

They have shown the "grace under pressure" that marks true greatness.

I would be remiss in not mentioning the "women of the Senate" whose friendships have blessed and brightened my life.

I am grateful, too, for the wholehearted and unwavering support of my Democratic colleagues in my every endeavor.

I especially appreciate those from the other side of the aisle—though far fewer in number—who graciously encouraged me as well.

Tradition affords those who leave the Senate, either by their own will or the will of the electorate, the opportunity to reflect on their time in this historic chamber—to perhaps even engage in some unsolicited advice.

My advice comes, not as a seasoned insider, but as one who came for a season to serve among you.

Mine are simple maxims that spring from a heart filled with love for the U.S. Senate and for my country.

When you think on the role of government, seek a balance between one that does everything and one that does nothing.

Where there is talk of war, let there be the free and open debate that becomes our great nation.

When there are judges to appoint, let them be selected for their temperament and jurisprudence, not for a political ideology that satisfies a special interest group.

When you lay out an energy and environment policy, let it not be for short-term gain, but for the well-being of our grandchildren and the survival of our planet.

When you speak of "leaving no child behind," let that not be a mantra, but a mission, fervent and funded.

When you think on the health care needs of children, families, and seniors—and I hope that will be often—I urge you to lay partisanship aside . . . and heed the plight of the hurting and helpless in our society.

I will vote for the homeland security bill, as I have each step of the way. For we must make certain that the information disconnect that allowed a 9/11 to occur never happens again.

During an earlier global conflict, President Franklin Roosevelt called for "stout hearts and strong arms with which to strike mighty blows for freedom and truth."

That is what I am hoping this consolidation and coordination of effort will help us to accomplish.

But as I vote for this bill, I do so with a caution.

The pursuit of terrorists and the protection of basic freedoms is our greatest challenge in the years ahead.

But in the quest to uproot terrorism, let us take care to preserve those precious liberties upon which our nation is founded and upon which democracy depends.

I have no doubt that, in this good and godly work, we will ultimately succeed.

Let me conclude by saying that this farewell to the U.S. Senate is a bittersweet moment for me, one that churns up a mixture of memories and emotions.

Earlier this year I took time out to visit the Corcoran Gallery to see the Jackie Kennedy exhibit.

One of the displays featured a handwritten letter that Mrs. Kennedy sent to a friend after completing an extensive project at the White House.

She wrote, "How sad it is when a work we love doing is finally finished."

I know how she felt.

But I still believe—as did my husband—that public service is a good and noble work, worthy of our lives.

Perhaps a former member of this chamber said it best. He was not of my party, but he was certainly of my principles.

Sen. Lowell Weicker wrote, "For all the licks anyone takes by choosing public service, there is the elation of having achieved for good purpose what none thought possible. And such feelings far exceed . . . whatever the hurt for having tasted the battle."

Mr. President, I yield the floor.

Epilogue

In 2004, after a two-month trial, a Jackson County, Missouri, jury found that the plane crash that took the lives of Gov. Mel Carnahan, Randy Carnahan, and Chris Sifford was caused by the failure of the vacuum pumps produced by airplane parts manufacturer Parker Hannifin Corporation.

After hundreds of known failures and at least forty-eight deaths, the company finally ceased making the part after the crash of the Carnahan plane.

Acknowledgments

The moment we cease to hold each other, the moment we break faith with one another, the sea engulfs us and the light goes out.

—James Baldwin, *Nothing Personal*

It was impossible to weave into a narrative a mention of all those who touched my life and continue to do so in such amazing ways. Knowing that I am a computer junkie, former employees stay in contact with me, often by email or instant messenger. They send me photos and small gifts. They keep me informed of their new jobs and addresses and include me in birthday celebrations, showers, and weddings, as they get on with their own lives. Some still address me as "Senator," observing the political custom of calling anyone by the highest rank ever attained.

When I'm in Kansas City, Amy Jordan Wooden still sets my schedule, meets my plane, and lodges me overnight just as she has done for Carnahan family members for years. Rachel Storch, John Beakley, and Tim Ogle still say to me, "Call whenever I can be of help." And I do. In my post-Senate role, I share an office with Steven Stogel in Clayton and with it the splendid assistance of Cyndy Crider, who has determinedly kept me organized.

Not wanting to be a boastful grandmother, I realize I made little mention of my grandsons, Austin, fourteen, and Andrew, ten. I delight in teaching them the meaning of some new word, showing them how to ride a horse, retelling some bit of family lore that they currently find boring, or sharing computer news. In return, they review the latest movies or television shows that I never intend to see, coach me in VCR programming, tell me what's "cool" and what's not, and patiently answer my questions about their school, sports, and scouting activities.

I am thankful, too, for my "extended family." While in Washington our office celebrated birthdays, farewells, and legislative achievements with cake, pizza, or some homemade recipe. On the anniversary of Mel's death, there were always fresh flowers on my desk. My staff didn't know it at the time, but they were a big part of my recovery and, for that, I will always be grateful.

The quality and depth of my staff made it possible for my office to be active in the legislative process from the beginning. Roy Temple served as chief of staff, assisted by deputy chief Rachel Storch and earlier Susan Harris. David Schanzer, my legislative director, led a team composed of Amy Barber, Sandy Fried, Stephen Neuman, Neal Orringer, Larry Smar, and Stephen Sugg. Assisting them were our legislative fellows, Susan Barnidge, Jim Clapsaddle, Lisa Jaworski, and Sarah Lennon.

Our communications director, Tony Wyche, was assisted by Dan Liestikow and Alex Formuzis. John Beakley directed scheduling, along with his assistants Ryan Rhodes and Stacy Henry, who would later become our campaign scheduler.

With the introduction of anthrax into our building, working the mail was a hazardous assignment for director Garon Robinett and his legislative correspondents: Isaiah Akin, Justin Hamilton, Margaret Hsiang, Bryan Mitchell, Skip Schrock, Vance Serchuk, and Courtney Weiner.

Rounding out the staff were office manager Michael Carrasco; my executive assistant, Lucia Sanchez; and staff assistants Chad Chitwood, Sarah Elmore, Allison Paul, Jonathan Pearl, and Pam Townsend.

Back in Missouri, constituents were well served by my five regional offices. The St. Louis office was headed by Todd Britt assisted by Rogerique Wilson, Caroline Pelot, Ann Price, Sonja Cureton, Carlos Perez, and Julie Egermayer. Their counterparts in Kansas City, working under the direction of Amy Jordan Wooden, were Jan Singelman, Qiana Combs, Rosie Haertling, Michele Ludeman, Darren Smith, Angie Kennedy, and Joe Frey.

My Jefferson City Senate office was staffed by Jason Ramsey, Ann Bickel, and Brad Epperson; the Springfield office by Kris Stock; and the Cape Girardeau office by Rich Lamb and later Tom Neumeyer.

I was fortunate to have Rebecca Lambe, a seasoned and devoted staffer who took on the task of campaign manager for a race that got underway sooner than normal for a new senator. She was ably assisted by political director Maggie Thurman, along with Patrick Campbell, Anne Huppert, Caleb Weaver, Christine Glunz, Theresa Hassler, Yedidah Raskas, Rachel Smith, Jim Kottmeyer, Meredith Smith, Laura Katzif, Lisa Linsdey, and Stefany Brot.

My fund-raising team included, at one time or another, Dave Unanue, Yael Ouzillou, Emily Elbert, Kelly Dietrich, Melissa Schwartz, Deborah Jansen, Matt Felan, Steve Redlinger, Ben Hovland, and Alicia Johnson. In the course of raising $20 million, needless to say, I came to know the members of my fund-raising team better than any others on staff.

Scott Sorrell, our long-serving and highly talented information systems manager, was assisted by Roberta Wallace and Bradley Johnson, while my friend of many years Peggy Pyron cared for the bookkeeping.

No modern-day campaign runs without political consultants to bring perspective to a multi-million-dollar operation. Campaigns must be able to grow quickly and adapt to ever-changing situations, with little margin for error. Mel and I were served by what I jokingly called the "A-team," a core group that would drop everything for a political cause in which they believed. They included media consultant Saul Shorr, Marc Farinella, Roy Temple, Matt McCorkel, Christopher Klose, and Mike Muir, along with pollsters Goeff Garin and Fred Yang. Working in advertising preparation and website development were Howard Coffin, Andi Johnson, Russell Williams, Rich Davis, Syed Doha, Paul Summitt, and Ben Green.

In addition to his other duties, John Beakley ran our intern program in Washington, acquiring an enormous array of talented and enthusiastic young people including Megan Brengarth, McClaine Bryant, Kate Christensen, Morgan Cook, Ben DeClure, Paul Dobbins, Marcella Donkin, Chris Elders, Melissa Fallah, Karen Greenwood, Sarah Hamilton, Adam Harris, Doug Henry, Natalie Hunter, Sinead Kenny, Jason Krigel, Kristin McDougall, Meghan McPherson, Kevan Morshed, Brian Myers, Kate Noland, Lexi Norris, Lauren Palmer, Stan Pearson

II, Diane Peters, Heather Price, Adam Smith, Rachel Stanley, Pam Townsend, Emily Wade, and Catharine Zurbrugg. First-term members do not normally have the opportunity to appoint a U.S. Senate page. However, we were allowed the summer appointment of Caitlin Sapp.

I would be remiss if I failed to mention all those who served during Mel's two terms as governor, particularly his excellent chiefs of staff: Marc Farinella, Roy Temple, Brad Ketcher, Chris Sifford, and Mike Hartmann. If there is an award for unsung hero, it would go to Joe Bednar, whose judgment Mel valued so greatly. In his capacity as chief legal counsel for the governor's office, he had to deal with the gruesome details at the crash site. Days later, he brought me a small box containing Mel's wedding band and Masonic ring.

Alice O'Neal, having worked as Mel's assistant since the sixties, deserves special recognition for her many years of dedicated and continuous service, as does Phyllis Allsbury, another assistant who began working for Mel when he was a Rolla attorney.

Others serving on the governor's staff and security detail, not already mentioned, were: Isaiah Akin, Shirley Anders, Linward Appling, Edward Aylward, Pamela Brauner, Chris Brown, Dru Buntin, Robyn Burnett, Patricia Churchill, Michelle Coleman, Arie Crawford, Tony Credit, Rob Crouse, Paula Cunningham, Terry Davis, Dixie Dickerson, David Dillon, Brad Douglas, Rosie Eppennaur, Susan Esvelt, Jeanne Fitzler, Jill Friedman Wilson, Tracie Gully, Susan Harris, Ginger Hatfield, Dawn Heidbreder, John Hilker, D. K. Hirner, James Hoagland, Tamilynn Holder, Joy Holliday, Tami Holliday, Gary Hurt, Sandra Hurtado, Ilayn Irwin, Eric Jaffe, Lori James, Donald Johnson, Shirley Johnson, Greg Johnston, Scott Jungert, Eric Kayira, Kim Kempker, David Kessel, Deborah Kincade, Julia Kitsmiller, Tracy Knutson, Chris Kuban, David Lackman, Susie Lamb, Danine Lard, Ewell Lawson, Barry Lindsey, Brian Long, Patrick Lynn, Elbert Marshall, Rich Mason, Kristin Matisziw, Chris Mertens, Barb Meyer, Mike Meyer, Jeffrey Milke, Mark Mlynarczyk, Gary Moore, Scott Murphy, Jerry Nachtigal, Karen Nelson, Rachel Fayman Nelson, Marilyn Nobbman, John O'Connell, Carla Owens, Marilyn Parrish, Margie Peters, Darrell Prenger, Rebecca Reeds, Anthony Roberts, Juanita Robinson, Angie Heffner Robyn, Kelly Roussin, Andrea Routh, Stacy Rummel, Mike

Rutherford, Jerel Schomer, Sharon Schreiber, Mary Schwartz, Liz Sharp, Patty Shelton, Victor Sholar, Ken Sieve, Cheryl Simmons, Kelvin Simmons, Julia Sommer, Sunny Dickerson Spence, Reyna Spencer, Brad Spicer, Diane Springs, Susan Stearns, Kelli Stiles, Leah Tillman, Laura Thompson Unanue, Bonnie VanHook, Teddie Verreri, Alan Walton, Jimmie Walz, Mark Ward, Beth Wheeler, Quentin Wilson, Diann Wingrath, Mike Wolff, David Woodruff, and Vicki Zimmerman.

Mel had outstanding cabinet directors over the course of his two terms in office and spoke highly of them at every opportunity. They included Jay Angoff, Bob Bartman, Jerry Conley, Maureen Dempsey, Joe Driskill, Henry Hungerbeeler, Gary Kemper, Kent King, Coleen Kivlahan, Terry Knowles, Catherine Leapheart, Janette Lohman, Steve Mahfood, Charles McClain, Jeanette McCrary, Karla McLucas, Joe Mickes, Sandra Moore, Wayne Muri, Jerry Presley, Steve Renne, John Saunders, C. Keith Schafer, Dora Schriro, David Shorr, Gary Stangler, Kala Stroup, Keith Wenzel, Quentin Wilson, Roy Wilson, and director of administration Richard Hanson, a long-time state employee whom Mel greatly admired for his commitment to making government work. Missouri National Guard generals Raymond Pendergrass and John Haven provided extraordinary leadership during some of the most difficult of times for our state.

At the Governor's Mansion, I had an impressive group of workers including my first mansion manager and friend of many years, Joyce Bunch, and, later, Jill Erickson. Paula Earls took on the ever-expanding task of mansion manager, growing to be a fine executive.

The Governor's Mansion greatly benefited from the care of Mary Pat Abele, director of Missouri Mansion Preservation, and her creative assistants Jill Bednar, Chris Carr, and D. J. Nash. At Christmas they were joined by volunteers Cindy Singer, Bob Fennewald, and Mary Jo Hilker in transforming the mansion into a Victorian showcase. The mansion was further enhanced by architect Ted Wofford, interior design consultants Richard Baumann and Ed Rohlfing, and a cadre of docents.

Accolades are due those who worked behind the scenes at the mansion, especially Norma Jean Davidson, our housekeeper, chefs Jerry Walsh and, before him, Sheri Wolf, and a corps of dedicated Missouri Highway Patrol troopers, Capitol police, prison guards, as well as inmate help.

So many people stepped up to help in the final days of the 2000 campaign. Among them were the singers Sheryl Crow and Don Henley and actor Kevin Kline, who came to Missouri to put on a benefit performance that rallied our supporters and gave new life to the campaign. I am grateful, also, to former U.S. senator Tom Eagleton and his wife, Barbara, who graciously took time to brief me on life in Washington. I am blessed with good friends and supporters like Jim Nutter Sr., Tom Green, and Gary and Anita Robb. They stand for high ideals in public life and have been an inspiration to my family, as well as their communities.

Many thanks to my children, Russ and his wife, Debra, Robin, and Tom, my grandsons Austin and Andrew, my brother-in-law, Bob Carnahan, and his wife, Oma, as well as my friends of many years Ethel and Sam Burton, Wilma Turner, Lucy Sutcliffe, Jamie Anderson, and Ruthanne Phillips. I am especially grateful to Bob and Oma, the Burton family, and Joel Winn for housing and feeding our family on numerous weekends when we were in Rolla after the house fire and to Steve and Kim Harrison for letting Robin use their landing strip near the farm. I deeply appreciate Mike Bauman and Randy Gehres for coming to my rescue repeatedly when I was in Washington by troubleshooting electronic problems that befuddled me. Many thanks to Wendy Werner for her wonderful photography and heart-lifting humor. On my birthday last year, she comforted me with these words: "Not to worry," she said, "seventy is the new fifty."

I am pleased that those who knew and worked with Chris Sifford still get together each spring for a bass fishing tournament in Puxico. Each year, they gather for the Sifford Scramble, a tournament for golfers, and nongolfers, held in August around the time of his birthday. Both events raise money for the Chris Sifford Memorial Scholarship Fund. It's a wonderful remembrance of a young man whose ingratiating smile and caring spirit still warm our lives.

I am delighted, too, when former staffers or supporters tell me they are running for elective office, working for a presidential aspirant, or helping some local candidate—as a number of them are doing in 2004. Their enthusiasm and idealism fire my hope for the future. Working together, we once made a difference. And we can do it again, any time we try.